Praise for *What Type of Leader Ar*

"Ginger's newest book is a practical tool for executives interested in real evolution as leaders. The information in *What Type of Leader Are You?* is pragmatic and results focused, and it doesn't shortchange the underlying depth of the Enneagram as a tool for transformation. In this book, Ginger offers a unique combination of business savvy, organization development, and in-depth self-development perspectives. Her solid understanding of today's business environment makes the book a tool that leaders can use repeatedly to enrich and expand their capabilities, turning already effective leaders into truly influential ones."

—**Colleen Gentry**, senior vice president
for Executive Development,
Wachovia Corporation

"*What Type of Leader Are You?* creates a crucial bridge between big business and the Enneagram. Ginger's latest book is designed for the true professional: she applies the Enneagram to mainstream business applications through competencies such as Leadership Self-Mastery, Know the Business: Think and Act Strategically, and Make Optimal Business Decisions. Not only do readers learn about their leadership characteristics, but they're also provided with self-assessment exercises and Enneagram style–specific development recommendations for each competency area. As the managing director of one of the nation's leading hearing health care manufacturers, I recommend *What Type of Leader Are You?* and can't wait until Ginger creates training classes for this material. I will be filling her courses with enthusiastic employees."

—**Chad Jorgensen**, managing director,
NU-EAR Electronics, Inc.

"No other approach to leadership growth is as accessible, relevant, and powerful as the path-breaking framework provided in *What Type of Leader Are You?* I have shared this approach with my leadership team, and I've observed breakthroughs by dozens of leaders. Ginger Lapid-Bogda's integration of the Enneagram with the seven critical leadership competencies is brilliant. Her methods enable you to increase self-awareness while also acquiring the concrete tools and emotional energy you need to become the leader you really want to be. I have seen this book change lives—it certainly has changed mine."

—**Todd Pierce**, vice president,
Corporate Information Technology,
Genentech, Inc.

"If you are a leader and think you've seen your share of books on this subject, don't stop until you've added this to your collection. Clearly, Ginger Lapid-Bogda has deep experience in coaching and consulting to a wide variety of leaders and their teams. Her sound advice is based on years of practice and strong theory, and this book is chock-full of excellent suggestions and astute examples that amplify her points and provide readers with a multitude of teachable moments."

—**Beverly Kaye, Ph.D.**, founder/CEO of
Career Systems International and
coauthor of *Love 'Em or Lose 'Em:
Getting Good People to Stay*

"I have been reading this book with complete interest and amazement. *What Type of Leader Are You?* contains a unique combination of both Eastern and Western perspectives on leadership essence and development. Ginger Lapid-Bogda has contributed a culturally relevant view of what constitutes leadership success—self-awareness, interpersonal relationships, and business savvy. She illustrates her ideas in a practical, compelling, and straightforward way. The nine Enneagram styles and related leadership competencies identify strengths and opportunities that are specific, achievable, and relevant to the business of leadership development. I strongly recommend the book to anyone on the leadership journey."

—**Cresencio Torres, Ph.D.**,
senior enterprise associate,
Center for Creative Leadership

"An excellent book that focuses the Enneagram's powerful insights on understanding and improving the reader's natural style of leadership. Filled with boots-on-the-ground examples, *What Type of Leader Are You?* is not just for leaders but for anyone who wants to grow and excel. It will help you identify and stretch your core competencies and natural talents, both on the job and off."

—**Thomas Condon**, author of
The Enneagram Movie and Video Guide

"Ginger Lapid-Bogda has once again come up with an outstanding work. *What Type of Leader Are You?* is practical, insightful, thoughtful, and specific. Ginger covers all aspects of leadership, from business practices to leadership skills and people skills, and she offers a rich array of vignettes, examples, and exercises. Each chapter is virtually a book in itself. What Ginger achieves in this book is an integration of Enneagram understandings and business practices, which alone would make the book well worth reading."

—**David Daniels, M.D.**, coauthor of
The Essential Enneagram,
cofounder of the Enneagram Professional
Training Program, and clinical professor,
Department of Psychiatry,
Stanford Medical School

"Dr. Lapid-Bogda adroitly describes how different types of people fulfill the core competencies of leadership in their own ways. Through the lens of the Enneagram, she directs our attention back to ourselves, and in a remarkably evenhanded and constructive way creates nine professional development programs, each anchored in self-observation and mindfulness of our own internal patterns."

—**Helen Palmer**, author of *The Enneagram*
and *The Enneagram in Love and Work*

"We recommend this book for anyone in leadership wishing to use the superbly insightful tool of the Enneagram to access their innate gifts, identify their biases, and become truly great leaders."

—**Don Richard Riso and Russ Hudson**,
The Enneagram Institute,
authors of *Personality Types*
and *The Wisdom of the Enneagram*

"Ginger has waved her creative wand over what is known about effective leadership skills and what the Enneagram says about nine personality styles, and out has popped this very readable brew of both. If you want to be a *conscious* leader, this book will wake you up."

—**Jerry Wagner, Ph.D.**, author of
The Enneagram Spectrum of Personality

"Ginger Lapid-Bogda's new book makes a vital contribution to the area of developing successful leadership skills. *What Type of Leader*

Are You? is an essential book for people in leadership positions who wish to develop and raise the level of their true capabilities. The huge pressures and global challenges facing today's leaders make excellence in leadership critical to the success of any enterprise. This book is a superb tool for working with people of different cultures with intelligence and understanding."

—**Nuala Ahern**, former member of the European Parliament (Ireland)

"To be a great leader is a desire of all executives, but it is a challenge for many. This book is like a treasure map that shows the nine different ways to reach excellence in leadership. Enjoy this journey!"

—**Sara Isabel Behmer**, human resources executive director, AVON Cosmetics, Ltd.

"*What Type of Leader Are You?* is different from other Enneagram books in that it describes real life leadership lessons and provides practical and concrete guidelines, diagrams, and examples, all of which are very useful and apply to business life. I highly recommend that leaders at all levels of management read this book if they want to create winning teams in their organizations."

—**Pravit Chitnarapong**, president and CEO, Black Canyon Coffee Co. (Thailand), Ltd.

WHAT TYPE OF LEADER ARE YOU?

WHAT TYPE OF LEADER ARE YOU?

USING THE ENNEAGRAM SYSTEM TO IDENTIFY AND
GROW YOUR LEADERSHIP STRENGTHS AND ACHIEVE
MAXIMUM SUCCESS

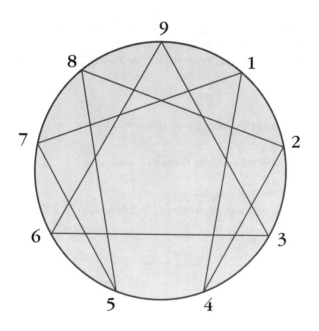

Ginger Lapid-Bogda, Ph.D.

McGraw-Hill
New York   Chicago   San Francisco   Lisbon
London   Madrid   Mexico City   Milan   New Delhi
San Juan   Seoul   Singapore   Sydney   Toronto

The McGraw·Hill Companies

1 2 3 4 5 6 7 8 9 10 11 12   FGR/FGR   0 9 8 7

ISBN-13: 978-0-07-147719-2
ISBN-10: 0-07-147719-5

McGraw-Hill books are available at special quantity discounts to use as premiums and sales promotions, or for use in corporate training programs. For more information, please write to the Director of Special Sales, Professional Publishing, McGraw-Hill, Two Penn Plaza, New York, NY 10121-2298. Or contact your local bookstore.

Library of Congress Cataloging-in-Publication Data

Lapid-Bogda, Ginger.
  What type of leader are you? / by Ginger Lapid-Bogda.
    p. cm.
  ISBN 0-07-147719-5 (alk. paper)
  1. Enneagram. 2. Typology (Psychology) 3. Leadership. I. Title.

BF698.35.E54L373 2007
155.2'6—dc22   2006036455

To Todd Pierce

Contents

Acknowledgments xiii

Introduction xv

CHAPTER 1 What Type Are You? 1

CHAPTER 2 Drive for Results 35

CHAPTER 3 Strive for Self-Mastery 65

CHAPTER 4 Know the Business: Think and Act Strategically 99

CHAPTER 5 Become an Excellent Communicator 137

CHAPTER 6 Lead High-Performing Teams 183

CHAPTER 7 Make Optimal Decisions 215

CHAPTER 8 Take Charge of Change 253

CHAPTER 9 Stretch Your Leadership Paradigms 289

Resources   295

Index   301

Acknowledgments

a book is never the result of one person's efforts alone, and I would like to acknowledge a number of people and groups who have influenced what you are about to read. First, Mary Nadler eloquently edited the initial manuscript, and Lon Davis used intelligence and skill in designing the graphics.

The organizational models you'll see are, with one exception, mine. However, all of them have their roots in the field of organization development. In my work as an OD consultant, I have been influenced by two organizations: the National Training Laboratories (NTL) and the Organization Development Network (ODN). The organizational model used in the chapter "Take Charge of Change" is an adaptation of earlier work by Dick Beckhard, an OD consultant who created both theory and practice that have stood the test of time and enabled us to better serve our clients.

The idea of a book linking the Enneagram system with core leadership competencies came from a conversation with my client and colleague Todd Pierce. Without Todd as a thought partner and an inspiration, I would not have written this book.

Many clients have given me ideas for this book. They include Sally Baehni, Hal Barron, Amanda Battle, Brad Davirro, Hilarie DeGroot, Joe Delateur, Diane Fry, Rob Garnick, Tom Hill, Kenneth

Hillian, Chris Jones, Terry Kendall, Catherine Lee, Robyn Melzer, Margaret Pometta, Bob Quinn, Mark Rogers, Marsha Underhill, Ken Wilcox, Mary Wujek, Richard Wyatt, and Rama Yunus.

A number of my colleagues have influenced this book's direction, including Pat Bidol-Padva, Jennifer Joss Bradley, Michael Caress, Bea Chestnut, Carole Henmi, Andrea Isaacs, Beverly Kaye, Hwan Young Kim, Wajasit Losereewanich, Uranio Paes, Susan Resnick-West, Martin Salzwedel, Jeff Weakley, and Jeff Young.

I am indebted to several individuals for my knowledge of the Enneagram system. None of us would know the Enneagram system of personality as we currently do without the seminal work of Claudio Naranjo, who brought the Enneagram to northern California in the 1970s after having worked with Oscar Ichazo in South America. I am further indebted to Claudio for his full-hearted support of my work in using the Enneagram in organizations. My first Enneagram teachers, Helen Palmer and David Daniels, provided me with an excellent foundation. In addition, I have been influenced by the work of Don Riso and Russ Hudson, Kathy Hurley and Theodorre Donson, Tom Condon, and Jerry Wagner.

My personal thanks to my brother, Martin Snapp, who has always believed in me; to my assistant and friend, Natalie Toy; and especially to my 15-year-old son, Tres Bogda, who asks me daily, "How's the writing going?"

Finally, my appreciation to Jane Roberts and Muriel Nellis, my literary agents at Creative and Literary Artists, Inc., for their excellent guidance, and to Donya Dickerson, my insightful editor at McGraw-Hill.

Introduction

This book is about leadership success—extreme success. It's about growing by pushing your limits, personally, professionally, and organizationally. Along the leadership path, you will encounter numerous successes, but you may also face detours and challenges. Occasionally, you may have to forge your own trail through seemingly impassable places. It helps to take a cue from the sport of extreme mountain biking, where riders look on such challenges as invigorating opportunities to discover their true capabilities. I encourage you to keep that approach in mind as you work your way through the core leadership competencies in this book, challenging yourself to become the best leader you are capable of being.

Leadership excellence is one of the most critical challenges facing organizations today. Most top leaders leave their positions in three years or less under duress, even when they have had highly successful track records in previous jobs. Companies across the globe are in leadership succession crises, trying to find and/or develop sufficient leadership talent.

Why is it so difficult to find great leaders? One reason is that an individual's prior leadership skills may not transfer to a new leadership position, company, or industry. Another factor involves the demands placed on today's leaders. With a constantly changing business environment, a global marketplace, and the need both to get products to market quickly and to create sustainable organizations for the long run, today's leaders are faced with confounding ambiguities and competing priorities. However, perhaps the biggest reason for the leadership shortage today is that we are not even sure what truly great leadership is, much less how to develop it.

The most helpful clue about what makes an excellent leader comes from the field of Emotional Intelligence (EQ). An individual's EQ is the strongest predictor of that person's leadership success, consistently outranking both traditional IQ and on-the-job experience. Of course, if you have all three—a high EQ, a high IQ, and relevant on-the-job experience from which you have learned and grown—your chances for success are even greater.

EQ is made up of two factors: *intrapersonal intelligence*, or the ability to know and accept oneself and to become self-managing and self-motivating, and *interpersonal intelligence*, or the ability to interact effectively with other people. The Enneagram—an ancient psychological and spiritual development system—is the most powerful and insightful tool available to help you develop your EQ.

The leaders with whom I have worked say that the Enneagram helps them to understand and accept themselves at a very deep level, and that it is a profound tool for developing their leadership capabilities. They find the Enneagram freeing; as one leader commented, "I used to feel I was in a box. The Enneagram doesn't put me in a box; instead, it shows me the box I've been in and provides a development path out of these constraints."

To that end, this book focuses on today's most important leadership competencies and integrates them with the wisdom and insights of the Enneagram. Excellent leaders need to be skilled in the following seven core competency areas (see Figure I.1):

1. Drive for Results
2. Strive for Self-Mastery

FIGURE I.1 Core Leadership Competencies

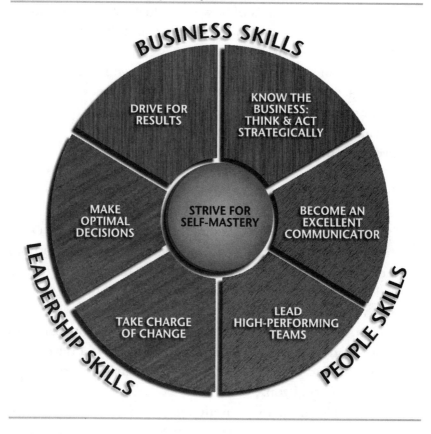

3. Know the Business: Think and Act Strategically
4. Become an Excellent Communicator
5. Lead High-Performing Teams
6. Make Optimal Decisions
7. Take Charge of Change

In the first chapter, you will learn the Enneagram system and identify your Enneagram style. Each of the chapters that follow focuses on one leadership competency and includes the following information:

- Definition of the competency
- Description and analysis of how individuals of each Enneagram style demonstrate both excellence and developmental needs with respect to that competency
- Development stretches for individuals of each Enneagram style to accelerate their growth in that competency area
- Additional tips to assist everyone, regardless of his or her Enneagram style, in both personal and professional development

The final chapter provides additional tools for working on your personal and professional growth.

If your organization is to continue growing, so must you. Organizational growth requires a commitment to growth from both leaders and those whom they lead. Your challenge is to decide which leadership path you will take: no growth, moderate growth, or extreme growth (see Figure I.2).

You can, of course, take the route of no growth. If you make this decision—and be aware that making no decision *is* a decision— you will soon find that your organization and many of your peers have moved beyond you.

You can take the path of moderate growth, making yourself comfortable and going at your own pace. If you do, your teams and your organization will follow this rate of growth for a while, but then the organization, your peers, and your followers will begin to outpace you.

Or, you can follow the path of extreme growth. If you choose this path, you will be amazed at your capacity and at the vitality that a commitment to growth brings. You will also find that your rate of personal development and the growth rate of the organization are aligned and synchronized. There is no greater experience.

This book is intended for multiple audiences. Current and future leaders at all organizational levels can use it for their own personal and professional development. Executive coaches will find it a valuable aid in helping their clients. Training and devel-

FIGURE I.2 **Choices**

opment, organization development, and human resource professionals can utilize the information in this book to help them
develop leadership capability within their organizations.

This book is ideally suited for companies competing in the
global marketplace. The Enneagram describes people of every culture accurately. However, there can be subtle cultural nuances to
the actions of individuals who come from different countries but
have the same Enneagram style; thus, this book offers organizations the opportunity to create a global cadre of highly skilled leaders who share a common frame of reference and a commitment to
self-development and leadership excellence.

As an organization development consultant, training professional, and executive coach for more than 30 years with clients in

Fortune 500 companies, service organizations, nonprofits, and law firms, I have observed that every excellent company has excellent leadership. It is equally true that every organizational problem that I have helped to solve has required that a leader change his or her behavior. This is not to say that leadership issues are the cause of all organizational problems, but simply that effective leadership is required to solve all organizational problems.

There is, therefore, a great deal of pressure on today's leaders, many of whom are already carrying an overwhelming amount of weight on their shoulders. Leadership is not easy. I have been a leader myself, in both for-profit and nonprofit organizations, so I understand leadership's challenges and rewards. There were times as a leader when I never felt more fulfilled and inspired, and other times when my fatigue and frustration led me to wonder whether I even wanted to be in a leadership role.

To be a great leader requires talent, commitment, effort, and guidance. It is my hope that this book will provide that guidance to both current and future leaders and to those who support them.

Chapter 1

What Type Are You?

he Enneagram, which dates from at least 2,000 years ago and has its roots in Asia and the Middle East, derives its name from the Greek words *ennea* ("nine") and *gram* ("something written or drawn"). The term refers to the nine points, or numbers, of the Enneagram system seen in the Enneagram symbol (Figure 1.1). This ancient system offers profound insights into the different ways in which people think, feel, and behave, since the nine different Enneagram styles represent distinct worldviews, with related patterns of thinking, feeling, and taking action. Even more important, each Enneagram style is connected to a specific high-impact development path. Thus, the accurate identification of your Enneagram style is important if you want to grow and develop as a leader and as a person.

Although each of us has only one position or number on the Enneagram and our style remains the same throughout our lifetime, our Enneagram style–based characteristics may soften or become more pro-

FIGURE 1.1 Enneagram Symbol

nounced as we grow and develop. In addition, there are four other Enneagram styles that may also contribute traits to our personality. These four additional Enneagram styles, explained later in this chapter, do not change our core style; they merely add to our complexity as a person and can provide us with useful development opportunities.

How to Determine Your Enneagram Style

Although there are several helpful Enneagram tests currently available, none of them will determine your Enneagram style with absolute certainty. Ultimately, you must rely on your own self-assessment to identify your Enneagram style. While you know yourself best, including what motivates you and drives your actions, you may be so used to thinking, feeling, or behaving in certain ways that you may not even notice some of your customary patterns. As a result, the process of determining your Enneagram style can take you on a self-reflective journey that can be invaluable to your growth as a leader. Having to identify your Enneagram style yourself will not only help you in learning the Enneagram system, but also help you become more introspective and objective about yourself.

In this chapter, you will first gain information about each Enneagram style that includes the following:

- A graphic image and style description
- The core focus associated with the style
- The common labels used for the style
- The style's four basic issues
- Leadership paradigms for each style, along with related strengths and areas for development
- Questions to ask yourself to assess whether this is your style

After you understand the nine Enneagram styles in more depth and begin to identify your Enneagram style, additional information about the Enneagram system will be provided.

The Nine Enneagram Styles

As you read through the nine Enneagram style descriptions that follow, keep this question in the back of your mind: *Which of the Enneagram styles most accurately describes me?*

Ones

Ones seek a perfect world and work diligently to improve both themselves and everyone and everything around them.

Core focus: What is right or wrong, correct or incorrect?

Common labels: Perfectionist, reformer, crusader, moralist

Enneagram Style 1
DILIGENCE

Basic Issues for Ones

PERFECTIONISM Ones continuously compare what is to what should be. They appreciate something that is exceptionally well done—for example, a play, a symphony, a book, a project, or anything else that exemplifies quality to them. Ones hold both themselves and others accountable for acting responsibly and for measuring up to their high standards.

A RIGHT WAY Ones believe that every problem has a correct solution; they are quick to react to a situation by offering what they believe is the right approach or the right answer. Even when Ones do understand that the correct answer is rarely black and white, they will still assert that there is one "right" way by saying, "Nothing is ever black and white. It is almost always gray."

RESENTMENT Because being responsible is an overarching value for Ones, they usually approach their work with diligence, demonstrating qualities such as follow-through, timeliness, and attention to detail. When others do not display these same characteristics, Ones often feel resentful and think, *Why do I work so hard, when others seem to get away with a less than stellar performance?* Resentment can build up in Ones, and they tend to express it through flares of anger that often take others by surprise. Most Ones need to feel righteous or justified in their outrage in order to express the deep-seated anger that frequently lies below the surface.

JUDGMENT AND SELF-IMPROVEMENT Ones have a highly active inner critic that can be relentless, telling them what they have done wrong, what they should have said, and how they ought to have behaved. The self-recriminating inner voice, which is usually "on" 85 percent or more of the time, has a purpose: to keep Ones from making mistakes. This internal judge also assesses what has gone well and what can be done for self-improvement.

Ones also tend to be judgmental of others, expressing this through explicit verbal criticism and body language. Even Ones who do not appear to be critical may, in fact, simply be keeping their thoughts to themselves. For example, when a One was asked why she did not seem to be overtly critical of others, she responded, "Oh, but you should hear what's going on inside my head!" The One's judgment of others may also be positive—for example, Ones can be thrilled when they observe excellence in someone's thinking process, behavior, or work product.

Ones: Leadership Paradigm and Related Characteristics

PARADIGM: A leader's job is to set clear goals and inspire others to achieve the highest quality.

Place a check next to the leadership characteristics that describe you well.

Areas of Strength	Areas for Development
☐ Leads by example	☐ Reactive
☐ Strives for quality	☐ Overly critical
☐ Pursues perfection	☐ Defensive when criticized
☐ Organized	☐ Often unaware of deep anger
☐ Consistent	☐ Detail-focused
☐ Perceptive	☐ Controlling
☐ Honest	☐ Opinionated
☐ Practical	☐ Impatient

QUESTIONS TO ASK YOURSELF TO DETERMINE
WHETHER YOU MIGHT BE AN ENNEAGRAM STYLE ONE

1. Do I have a voice or message in my head, like a tape recorder, that continually judges me and other people in terms of what has been done wrong, what has been done well, and what needs to be improved?
2. Do the four basic issues—perfectionism, a right way, resentment, and judgment and self-improvement—apply to me?
3. Does the Style One leadership paradigm fit my view of leadership?
4. Did I check 10 or more items in "Areas of Strength" and "Areas for Development"?

Twos

Twos want to be liked, try to meet the needs of others, and attempt to orchestrate the people and events in their lives.

Enneagram Style ②
GIVING

Core focus: Am I needed? Will others like me?

Common labels: Giver, helper, caretaker, enabler

Basic Issues for Twos

RELATIONSHIP ORIENTATION Most Twos believe that personal relationships are the most important part of their lives. It is quite common for Twos to have many close friendships, with the Twos providing support, advice, or whatever they believe another person needs. Although Twos often feel that others are dependent on them, they themselves become dependent on their relationships for personal affirmation and a sense of self-worth.

FOCUS ON OTHER PEOPLE Twos usually display an intuitive ability to understand what others need and a willingness to provide what is needed. Their capacity to reach out to other people can be either generalized (for example, anyone who appears in need) or highly selective (specific individuals who the Two believes have high status). In the latter case, Twos will alter their image and behavior to meet the other person's perception of desirability. Generally, Twos instinctively know how to present themselves so that others will like them.

DENIAL OF OWN NEEDS Because Twos focus so intently on others, they often pay little attention to themselves. When asked what they themselves need, most Twos either become confused or say, "I need to be needed." Since they are out of touch with their needs, Twos often have difficulty getting those needs met directly. Instead, they give to others, often unaware that they want something in return.

PRIDE Twos typically take great pride in their self-image as a "good" person and in their ability to know what people need or situations require better than most other people do. Although they may be quite competent at orchestrating situations and managing people (often behind the scenes), there is a downside to this quality: while Twos become quite elated when things go well, they can become deflated and angry when events do not turn out as planned.

Twos: Leadership Paradigm and Related Characteristics

PARADIGM: A leader's job is to assess the strengths and weaknesses of team members and to motivate and facilitate people toward the achievement of organizational goals.

Place a check next to the leadership characteristics that describe you well.

Areas of Strength

- ☐ Develops excellent relationships
- ☐ Empathic
- ☐ Supportive and generous
- ☐ Optimistic
- ☐ Likable
- ☐ Responsible and hardworking
- ☐ Has insight into others' needs
- ☐ Able to motivate others

Areas for Development

- ☐ Enraged when others are mistreated
- ☐ Has difficulty saying no
- ☐ Angry when unappreciated
- ☐ Unaware of own needs
- ☐ Overemphasizes relationships
- ☐ Indirect
- ☐ Overextends in doing for others
- ☐ Unaware of giving to get something in return

QUESTIONS TO ASK YOURSELF TO DETERMINE WHETHER YOU MIGHT BE AN ENNEAGRAM STYLE TWO

1. Do I focus on others rather than on myself, and do I intuitively know what someone else needs, but have a hard time articulating my own needs, even to myself?
2. Do the four basic issues—relationship orientation, focus on other people, denial of own needs, and pride—apply to me?
3. Does the Style Two leadership paradigm fit my view of leadership?
4. Did I check 10 or more items in "Areas of Strength" and "Areas for Development"?

Threes

③ Enneagram Style
PERFORM

Threes organize their lives to achieve specific goals and to appear successful in order to gain the respect and admiration of others.

Core focus: How can I gain the respect and esteem of others?

Common labels: Performer, achiever, succeeder, initiator

Basic Issues for Threes

IMAGE Threes are known as the chameleons of the Enneagram, because they can change their image to match a particular situation. They do this not to blend in or fit in, but rather to create a positive impression—usually one of self-confidence, optimism, and success. This shape shifting is more intuitive than conscious; for instance, a Three might say, "I'm just able to read my audience well."

GOAL ORIENTATION Threes focus on achieving results, which tends to make them highly productive. However, their productivity can come at the expense of their and others' feelings. Threes usually perceive emotions, especially those of sadness or fear, as having the potential to derail their accomplishments, and they can become quite agitated when obstacles appear in their paths.

SUCCESS Because their sense of self-worth depends on their doing a job successfully, Threes tend to focus on "doing" rather than "being." They believe they are valued for what they accomplish rather than for who they are. Ever active, most Threes are likely to respond with confusion if it is suggested that they might spend less time doing and more time simply being. "Being?" they might ask. "What is that?"

FAILURE AVOIDANCE   In order to avoid failing, Threes often pursue activities in which they are competent and are therefore likely to be successful. If and when they fail—as everyone does at some point—Threes may still say, "I've never really failed," or they may reframe the failure as a learning experience.

Threes: Leadership Paradigm and Related Characteristics

PARADIGM: A leader's job is to create environments that achieve results because people understand the organization's goals and structure.

Place a check next to the leadership characteristics that describe you well.

Areas of Strength
- ☐ Success-oriented
- ☐ High energy
- ☐ Reads an audience well
- ☐ Overcomes problems
- ☐ Optimistic
- ☐ Entrepreneurial
- ☐ Confident
- ☐ Achieves results

Areas for Development
- ☐ Overly competitive
- ☐ Not always forthcoming
- ☐ Abrupt or rushed
- ☐ Hides deep-level feelings
- ☐ Becomes overextended
- ☐ Impatient with others' feelings
- ☐ Believes that my image is my true self
- ☐ Limited time for personal relationships

QUESTIONS TO ASK YOURSELF TO DETERMINE WHETHER YOU MIGHT BE AN ENNEAGRAM STYLE THREE

1. Do I do all the things I do so that others will value and respect me?
2. Do the four basic issues—image, goal orientation, success, and failure avoidance—apply to me?
3. Does the Style Three leadership paradigm fit my view of leadership?

4. Did I check 10 or more items in "Areas of Strength" and "Areas for Development"?

Fours

Enneagram Style
MOOD

Fours desire deep connections both with their own interior worlds and with other people, and they feel most alive when they authentically express their personal experiences and feelings.

Core focus: Will I be rejected or not feel good enough? Can I express myself?

Common labels: *Tragic-romantic, artist, aesthete, individualist*

Basic Issues for Fours

EXTREMES OF EMOTIONAL LIFE   Fours tend to live at the extremes of the emotional spectrum, with depression at one end and hyperactivity at the other. Some may swing between the two. Fours believe that their intensity of experiencing life's highs and lows far surpasses the ordinary happiness for which others settle. Many Fours give the impression that they believe the statement: "I am my feelings."

LONGING   Fours idealize that which they believe is beyond their grasp, romanticizing it and/or yearning for it. As a result, the commonplace can seem boring and ordinary by comparison. Most Fours think of melancholy as a positive, or at least not a negative, emotion that makes them feel both in touch with their deepest self and very much alive.

AUTHENTICITY   Fours are on a continuous quest for the true, the real, and the authentic. Their primary focus is on the authenticity of their own self-expression (usually through the arts or interpersonal communication) and the genuine connections they feel with other people. Searching for meaning through emotional expression, Fours tend to express themselves through personal stories and often believe that the world of personal experience and feelings is what is real.

COMPARISONS   Blatantly or subtly, consciously or unconsciously, Fours compare themselves to others on a regular basis. As a result of these constant comparisons, Fours conclude that they are defective, superior, or both. When Fours assess that they fall short in comparison to another, they experience envy. Envy refers to the sense that "Others have something that I am missing. Why not me?" as opposed to jealousy, which refers to "They have it, and I want it!"

Fours: Leadership Paradigm and Related Characteristics

PARADIGM: A leader's job is to create organizations that give people meaning and purpose so that they are inspired to do excellent work.

Place a check next to the leadership characteristics that describe you well.

Areas of Strength
- ☐ Inspiring
- ☐ Creative
- ☐ Introspective
- ☐ Expressive
- ☐ Intuitive
- ☐ Compassionate
- ☐ Searches for excellence
- ☐ Seeks meaning through interpersonal connections

Areas for Development
- ☐ Intense
- ☐ Self-conscious
- ☐ Moody
- ☐ Easily bored
- ☐ Guilt-ridden
- ☐ Difficulty accepting criticism
- ☐ Aloof
- ☐ Deeply critical of others

**QUESTIONS TO ASK YOURSELF TO DETERMINE
WHETHER YOU MIGHT BE AN ENNEAGRAM STYLE FOUR**

1. When I feel something very strongly, do I hold on to my emotions intensely for long periods of time, often replaying my thoughts, feelings, and sensations?
2. Do the four basic issues—extremes of emotional life, longing, authenticity, and comparisons—apply to me?
3. Does the Style Four leadership paradigm fit my view of leadership?
4. Did I check 10 or more items in "Areas of Strength" and "Areas for Development"?

Fives

Enneagram Style
5
KNOWLEDGE

Fives thirst for knowledge and use emotional detachment as a way of keeping involvement with others to a minimum.

Core focus: Will demands for my time, energy, and resources be made on me?

Common labels: Observer, recluse, thinker, investigator

Basic Issues for Fives

THIRST FOR KNOWLEDGE   Fact-focused, objective, and analytical, Fives are fascinated by information, especially in their areas of interest. It is not unusual for Fives to have an extensive personal library in a room that is entirely their own. This library, which may contain books, CDs, DVDs, or magazines, is not just a storehouse of knowledge, but a personal retreat—the place where the Five can be alone and free of external demands.

PRIVACY   Fives usually crave privacy, as it allows them to recharge and ready themselves for interactions with others. At one extreme, a Five can be a hermit, leading a reclusive life of the mind. On the other hand, a Five can assume public roles, as long as these roles are clear and circumscribed and allow the Five to keep emotions to a minimum. Fives may confide in a trusted few but expect them to zealously protect their confidences.

EMOTIONAL DETACHMENT   Fives automatically detach from their emotions and then reexperience their feelings later, when they are alone and feel safe. Fives often note that their emotions are more available and accessible to them when no one else is around to observe them, saying that they need this time alone to sort out their feelings and thoughts.

COMPARTMENTALIZATION   Fives often separate or compartmentalize the different parts of their lives. They often have different friends for work, recreation, or community service. Fives also compartmentalize knowledge, placing information in separated "slots" or mental categories.

Fives: Leadership Paradigm and Related Characteristics

PARADIGM: A leader's job is to develop an effective organization through research, deliberation, and planning so that all systems fit together and people are working on a common mission.

Place a check next to the leadership characteristics that describe you well.

Areas of Strength	Areas for Development
☐ Analytic	☐ Detached
☐ Insightful	☐ Aloof
☐ Objective	☐ Overly independent
☐ Systematic	☐ Unassertive
☐ Plans thoroughly	☐ Underemphasizes relationships
☐ Excellent in crises	☐ Doesn't share information
☐ Persistent	☐ Stubborn
☐ Expert	☐ Critical of others

**QUESTIONS TO ASK YOURSELF TO DETERMINE
WHETHER YOU MIGHT BE AN ENNEAGRAM STYLE FIVE**

1. When a situation gets emotional or intense, do I automatically disconnect from my feelings of the moment and then reconnect with these emotions later at a time and place of my choice?
2. Do the four basic issues—thirst for knowledge, privacy, emotional detachment, and compartmentalization—apply to me?
3. Does the Style Five leadership paradigm fit my view of leadership?
4. Did I check 10 or more items in "Areas of Strength" and "Areas for Development"?

Sixes

Enneagram Style
(6)
DOUBT

Sixes have insightful minds and create anticipatory or worst-case scenarios to help themselves feel prepared in case something goes wrong.

Core focus: What could go wrong here? Whom can I trust? Am I making the best decisions?

Common labels: Devil's advocate, loyalist, questioner, skeptic

Basic Issues for Sixes

ANTICIPATORY PLANNING AND WORST-CASE SCENARIOS   Sixes usually have active and vivid imaginations that continually generate worst-case scenarios. In fact, Sixes can be quite insightful, anticipating and averting potential problems, but they also can miss the mark, projecting their own thoughts and feelings onto others and causing themselves anxiety in the process. Some Sixes—called phobic Sixes—are aware that they tend to create worst-case scenarios, while other Sixes are counterphobic, engaging in high-risk activities to prove both to themselves and to others that they are not fearful. Most Sixes, however, fall somewhere between these two extremes and may display phobic and counterphobic behavior under different circumstances.

PROCRASTINATION The Six's tendency to worry about what could happen often results in procrastination. It is not that Sixes forget to do something; they simply become uncertain about which alternative is the best course of action. When their anxiety intersects with self-doubt, Sixes can become immobilized by "analysis paralysis."

LOYALTY Sixes value loyalty to the team and the organization, believing that those in authority will recognize and reward them for their dedication and that their peers will support them if something goes awry. The Sixes' focus on loyalty to the group does not mean that all Sixes want to be an integral part of a group, however. Some prefer to stay on the periphery, with the freedom to move in and out of the group setting as they please.

FOCUS ON AUTHORITY Sixes tend to focus on those in authority, believing that authority figures have the ability either to keep them safe or to hurt them. They hope for the former and, at the same time, are wary of having the latter occur at any moment. The more phobic Sixes tend to be compliant toward authority figures, whereas the more counterphobic Sixes tend to challenge authority. Most Sixes exhibit both reactions.

Sixes: Leadership Paradigm and Related Characteristics

PARADIGM: A leader's job is to solve organizational problems by developing a creative problem-solving environment in which each person feels that he or she is part of the solution.

Place a check next to the leadership characteristics that describe you well.

Areas of Strength
- ☐ Responsible
- ☐ Practical
- ☐ Collaborative
- ☐ Strategic
- ☐ Sharp intellect
- ☐ Persevering
- ☐ Anticipates issues or problems
- ☐ Loyal to company and employees

Areas for Development
- ☐ Worrying
- ☐ Dislikes ambiguity
- ☐ "Analysis paralysis"
- ☐ Reactive
- ☐ Self-sacrificing
- ☐ Overly cautious or overly risk taking
- ☐ Overly compliant or overly defiant
- ☐ Projects own thoughts onto others

QUESTIONS TO ASK YOURSELF TO DETERMINE WHETHER YOU MIGHT BE AN ENNEAGRAM STYLE SIX

1. Do I constantly worry or engage in anticipatory planning in order to avoid negative possibilities? Do I enjoy facing risky situations and overcoming them?
2. Do the four basic issues—anticipatory planning and worst-case scenarios, procrastination, loyalty, and focus on authority—apply to me?
3. Does the Style Six leadership paradigm fit my view of leadership?
4. Did I check 10 or more items in "Areas of Strength" and "Areas for Development"?

Sevens

Sevens crave the stimulation of new ideas, new people, and new experiences; avoid pain; and create elaborate plans that will allow them to keep all of their options open.

Enneagram Style 7
OPTIONS

Core focus: What is exciting? Do I feel constrained? Can I avoid pain and discomfort?

Common labels: Epicure, generalist, visionary, connoisseur

Basic Issues for Sevens

CRAVING OPTIONS   Sevens are buoyed by their belief that life's possibilities are unlimited, and they want to make sure that they retain all of their options. When Sevens feel that their alternatives have been limited, they tend to feel trapped and anxious. Although Sevens do make commitments, they also make sure they have backup plans, just as a precaution.

OPTIMISM   Seven is the most optimistic style on the Enneagram. Effervescent and enthusiastic, Sevens remain upbeat because, even in times of duress, they believe that if things do not work out today, they will work out tomorrow. In challenging times, their energy is sustained by their fascination with interesting things and people, as well as by their ability to reframe negative experiences. For example, a Seven who is criticized for missing a meeting might say, "Yes, but I was reviewing a document and found a way we could dramatically improve this project."

PAIN AVOIDANCE   Seeking positive experiences and reframing negative ones provides Sevens with a way to avoid pain, discomfort, and difficult situations. Sevens can be deeply moved and available to help someone else who is in pain, but the typical Seven motto is, "Don't worry, be happy!"

A SYNTHESIZING MIND   The Seven's mind is called the "monkey mind" because it moves rapidly from one idea to the next. Consequently, Sevens are often creative, being adept at synthesizing seemingly unrelated thoughts and developing innovative ideas. However, this method of mental processing also causes most Sevens to become unfocused, as their attention directed toward completing one idea or task becomes derailed by their focus on another stimulating thought, endeavor, or person.

Sevens: Leadership Paradigm and Related Characteristics

PARADIGM: A leader's job is to get people excited and to create new ventures so that the organization can take advantage of important business opportunities.

Place a check next to the leadership characteristics that describe you well.

Areas of Strength	Areas for Development
☐ Imaginative and creative	☐ Impulsive
☐ Enthusiastic	☐ Unfocused
☐ Curious	☐ Rebellious
☐ Engaging	☐ Avoids painful situations
☐ Multitasking	☐ Inconsistent empathy for others
☐ Upbeat	☐ Reactive to negative feedback
☐ Quick thinker	☐ Dislikes routine
☐ Able to connect disparate data	☐ Rationalizes negative experiences

QUESTIONS TO ASK YOURSELF TO DETERMINE WHETHER YOU MIGHT BE AN ENNEAGRAM STYLE SEVEN

1. Do I continually seek new and stimulating people, ideas, or events to keep life exciting and moving forward?

2. Do the four basic issues—craving options, optimism, pain avoidance, and a synthesizing mind—apply to me?
3. Does the Style Seven leadership paradigm fit my view of leadership?
4. Did I check 10 or more items in "Areas of Strength" and "Areas for Development"?

Eights

Eights pursue the truth, like to keep situations under control, want to make important things happen, and try to hide their vulnerability.

Core focus: Is everything under control in an effective and just way?

Enneagram Style
CHALLENGE (8)

Common labels: Boss, leader, challenger, protector

Basic Issues for Eights

CONTROL Eights like to exert direct influence over the people and events that affect their lives. They are also acutely sensitive to the power-oriented or controlling behavior of others. While Eights usually respect someone who uses power and influence effectively, the reverse is also true, with Eights having an instinctive negative reaction to someone whom they feel is abusing authority or exerting control in an ineffective manner. Eights are quick to sense chaos and lack of control and will step in quickly to make sure things are moving in the right direction.

JUSTICE Eights seek the truth and appreciate honesty, expect people to take responsibility for their own behavior, and demand that authority figures take charge in a just and nonmanipulative way. When they sense injustice, Eights will charge forth with great passion to assert their own beliefs and values, redress the situation, and protect those whom they perceive to be innocent victims.

VULNERABILITY Most Eights believe that the world can be divided into two groups of people: the tough and the weak. Given this worldview, Eights opt to be among the tough and strong. However, Eights have a hidden, childlike vulnerability that they usually prefer not to reveal. While some Eights even conceal their vulnerability from themselves, others are willing to share their softer side with those whom they trust and respect.

REVENGE Many Eights do not view their behavior as vengeful. Instead, Eights see it as rebalancing the score, pursuing justice, standing their ground, or avenging a wrongdoing, even when others might see the same behavior as retaliatory. The challenge for many Eights is to understand that even other confident and assertive people can, at times, feel intimidated by the Eight's boldness and tendency to dominate situations.

Eights: Leadership Paradigm and Related Characteristics

PARADIGM: A leader's job is to move the organization forward by leading decisively, getting capable and reliable people in the right jobs, and empowering competent people to take action.

Place a check next to the leadership characteristics that describe you well.

Areas of Strength	Areas for Development
☐ Direct	☐ Controlling
☐ Highly strategic	☐ Demanding
☐ Overcomes obstacles	☐ Impatient
☐ Energetic	☐ Agitated with a slow pace
☐ Protective of others	☐ Disdains weakness
☐ Moves projects forward	☐ High expectations of self and others
☐ Supports others' success	
☐ Self-confident and authoritative	☐ Feels used when others do not perform to expectations

**QUESTIONS TO ASK YOURSELF TO DETERMINE
WHETHER YOU MIGHT BE AN ENNEAGRAM STYLE EIGHT**

1. Do I have an extremely strong exterior, one that is sometimes intimidating to others (intentionally or unintentionally), that hides a less visible but vulnerable interior?
2. Do the four basic issues—control, justice, vulnerability, and revenge—apply to me?
3. Does the Style Eight leadership paradigm fit my view of leadership?
4. Did I check 10 or more items in "Areas of Strength" and "Areas for Development"?

Nines

Nines seek peace, harmony, and positive mutual regard and dislike conflict, tension, and ill will.

Core focus: Is everyone being heard, including me?

Enneagram Style ⑨
HARMONY

Common labels: Mediator, peacemaker, connector, harmonizer

Basic Issues for Nines

HARMONY Nines tend to be relaxed, easygoing, and nonjudgmental, and they feel most content when they sense unity and rapport both between themselves and other people and within groups that are important to them. Most Nines appreciate the natural harmony in nature, and they are also prone to merge or blend with other people whom they enjoy.

CONFLICT AVOIDANCE Because Nines desire harmony so ardently, they shun direct conflict whenever possible. Consequently, Nines tend to avoid taking actions that could generate controversy—for example, saying no, challenging someone else, and making tough decisions. Desirous of restoring harmony, Nines are also adept at mediating disagreements, as long as they themselves are not principal parties in the conflict situation.

TAKING A POSITION Nines tend to discount and lose track of their own thoughts, feelings, and needs, and they allow others to be the more active and assertive parties in their relationships. It can be extremely difficult for Nines to take a strong position in a number of situations—for example, when discussing what movie to see, deciding what family car to buy, or stating a direct opinion in a discussion about a contentious issue. Saying no can be particularly troublesome for Nines, because doing so potentially creates tension and conflict with other people. Nines more typically say yes and go along with the agendas of others, even if they really mean no. In this regard, the Nine's behavior can be passive-aggressive, when the Nine gives a yes answer in response to a request that he or she has no intention of actually fulfilling.

DIFFUSION OF ATTENTION When tasks are pressing or important decisions are pending, Nines tend to lose focus and divert their energy to secondary tasks and activities—for example, doing nonessential paperwork, watching TV, or adhering to a time-consuming routine.

Nines: Leadership Paradigm and Related Characteristics

PARADIGM: A leader's job is to help achieve the collective mission by creating a clearly structured and harmonious work environment.

Place a check next to the leadership characteristics that describe you well.

Areas of Strength	Areas of Development
☐ Diplomatic	☐ Avoids conflict
☐ Easygoing	☐ Unassertive
☐ Consistent	☐ Forgets priorities
☐ Inclusive and collaborative	☐ Procrastinates
☐ Develops lasting relationships	☐ Indecisive
☐ Patient	☐ Uncertain
☐ Supportive of others	☐ Low energy
☐ Assimilates the big picture by way of operational details	☐ Passive-aggressive when pressured

QUESTIONS TO ASK YOURSELF TO DETERMINE WHETHER YOU MIGHT BE AN ENNEAGRAM STYLE NINE

1. Do I automatically blend with other people's positive energy, but get quite distressed when I am around negativity, anger, and conflict?
2. Do the four basic issues—harmony, conflict avoidance, taking a position, and diffusion of attention—apply to me?
3. Does the Style Nine leadership paradigm fit my view of leadership?
4. Did I check 10 or more items in "Areas of Strength" and "Areas for Development"?

Which of the nine styles did you feel most accurately described you? Take a piece of paper and list your top four choices in rank order, starting with the style that most described you. Please keep these four choices in mind as you read the remainder of this chapter.

More Information to Help You Determine Your Enneagram Style

Enneagram Centers of Intelligence

Each Enneagram style is rooted in one of three Centers of Intelligence: the Head Center, the Heart Center, or the Body Center. The idea of these centers, which stems from a long Eastern philosophical tradition, refers to the ways in which we typically react to events and process information. While we all have heads, hearts, and bodies, our personality is organized around one of these three centers or modalities. Each center contains three of the nine Enneagram styles, with one of the three styles being the core style of that center and the other two styles being variations on the core style.

HEAD CENTER STYLES: THREE PERSONALITY STYLES ORGANIZED AROUND REACTIONS TO FEAR   The Head Center contains Enneagram Styles Five, Six, and Seven (see Figure 1.2). These three mental styles share a tendency to engage first in elaborate analysis as a reaction to their common emotion, fear. Fives respond to fear by withdrawing, retreating into their minds in order to understand. Sixes react by anticipating worst-case scenarios and devising plans to prevent what could go wrong. Counterphobic Sixes may not be aware of feeling fearful because they run headlong into risky situations as a way of assuring themselves that they are not afraid. Sevens take a different route, quickly moving from fear into pleasurable possibilities. Although most Sevens do not appear to be fearful, they are actually running from fear and pain—an avoidance reaction. Enneagram Style Six is the core style of the three Head Center styles, with Styles Five and Seven being variations of Enneagram Style Six.

FIGURE 1.2 **Head Center**

HEART CENTER STYLES: THREE PERSONALITY STYLES ORGANIZED AROUND CREATING AN IMAGE Your Enneagram style may be in the Heart Center—Styles Two, Three, and Four (see Figure 1.3). Individuals with Heart (Emotional) Center styles work hard to project a particular image, and they use their emotions to perceive how others are responding to them.

Twos try to create an image of being likable, and they look to others for affirmation of their self-worth. Threes work to project an image of success, and they seek the respect and admiration of others for what they accomplish. As the most inwardly focused of the three Heart Center styles, Fours try to

FIGURE 1.3 **Heart Center**

create an image of being unique or different, and they use their emotional sensitivity to defend against rejection. Enneagram Style Three is the core style of the three Heart Center styles, with Styles Two and Four being variations of Enneagram Style Three.

BODY CENTER STYLES: THREE PERSONALITY STYLES ORGANIZED AROUND ANGER Your Enneagram style may be in the Body Center, also called the Gut Center or the Instinctual Center—Styles Eight, Nine, and One (see Figure 1.4). There is anger in the emotional substructure of these three styles. Eights tend to express their anger frequently and directly. Their anger, which begins in the gut and moves rapidly upward and outward, can be stimulated by an injustice done to someone, weakness in others, someone taking ineffective control of a situa-

FIGURE 1.4 **Body Center**

tion, and someone lying. Nines tend to avoid direct anger and conflict, preferring a feeling of rapport and comfort with others. Their anger, which is so deeply buried that it has been called the "anger that went to sleep," surfaces when they feel either ignored or forced to do something, in which case their anger may turn into passive-aggressive behavior. Ones' anger is often manifested as frequent irritations followed by flares of resentment. Ones also tend toward self-criticism, which is anger turned inward. Enneagram Style Nine is the core style of the three Body Center styles, with Styles Eight and One being variations of Enneagram Style Nine.

Which center of intelligence and which style within it most describes you? As mentioned earlier, there are four Enneagram styles—in addition to your core style—that can influence your personality. Your *wings* are the styles (numbers) on either side of your core style, and your *stress* and *security points* are the numbers or styles that have lines with arrows pointing either away from or toward your core style. A wing number and/or a stress or security point number may have been among the top four styles you listed. The information about wings and stress and security points that follows may further illuminate your core style and clarify the dynamics of the Enneagram system.

Enneagram Style Wings

As noted earlier, wings are the Enneagram styles on each side of your actual Enneagram style. These are secondary styles of your core personality style, which means that you may also display some of the characteristics of these Enneagram styles. Wings do not fundamentally change your Enneagram style; they merely add additional qualities to your core personal-

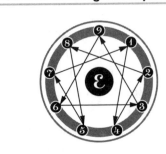

FIGURE 1.5 **Enneagram Style Wings**

ity. As can be seen on the Enneagram symbol, Nine and Two are wings for Ones, One and Three are wings for Twos, Two and Four are wings for Threes, and so forth (Figure 1.5).

You may have one wing, two wings, or no wings at all. It is also common to have had one wing be more active when you were younger, and to have had another appear as you matured. People of the same Enneagram style and identical wings may use their wing qualities differently. However, the general wing descriptions for all nine Enneagram styles given here may serve as guidelines to help you explore this aspect of the Enneagram and also help you to identify your wing or wings.

CHART 1.1   Wing Descriptions for All Nine Enneagram Styles

9 1 2 Wings for Ones	Ones with a Nine wing still seek perfection, but they may also be more relaxed, react less quickly, and enjoy nature's perfection. Ones with a Two wing still seek perfection, but they may also be more generous and gregarious and focus their work on helping other people.
1 2 3 Wings for Twos	Twos with a One wing still focus on helping other people, but they may also be more serious, critical, and dedicated to their work. Twos with a Three wing still focus on helping other people, but they may also be more comfortable being in the spotlight and more focused on being successful.
2 3 4 Wings for Threes	Threes with a Two wing still focus on success, but they may also be more empathic and pursue activities and work that help others. Threes with a Four wing still focus on success, but they may also be more emotional and have stronger aesthetic interests.
3 4 5 Wings for Fours	Fours with a Three wing still focus on deep experiences, feelings, and meaning, but they may also be more energetic and sophisticated and may pursue higher-profile work. Fours with a Five wing still focus on deep experiences, feelings, and meaning, but they may also be more subdued, private, and analytical.

(Continued)

CHART 1.1 (Continued)   Wing Descriptions for All Nine Enneagram Styles

4 **5** 6 Wings for Fives	Fives with a Four wing still seek knowledge and tend to be emotionally detached, but they may also experience more emotions internally and be more artistic. Fives with a Six wing still seek knowledge and tend to be emotionally detached, but they may also be more skeptical and cautious.
5 **6** 7 Wings for Sixes	Sixes with a Five wing still engage in anticipatory planning, but they may also be more internally focused and passionate about information gathering. Sixes with a Seven wing still engage in anticipatory planning, but they may also be more upbeat and take more risks.
6 **7** 8 Wings for Sevens	Sevens with a Six wing still engage in optimistic scenario building and future planning, but they may also be more overtly fearful and deliberate. Sevens with an Eight wing still engage in optimistic scenario building and future planning, but they may also be more direct and assertive.
7 **8** 9 Wings for Eights	Eights with a Seven wing still take charge, assert themselves, and hide their vulnerabilities, but they may also be more high-spirited, independent, and adventurous. Eights with a Nine wing still take charge, assert themselves, and hide their vulnerabilities, but they may also be warmer, calmer, and more oriented toward consensus.
8 **9** 1 Wings for Nines	Nines with an Eight wing still seek harmony and avoid conflict, but they may also exhibit more personal power and take more control of situations. Nines with a One wing still seek harmony and avoid conflict, but they may also be more punctual, discerning, and judgmental.

Do any of these combinations of Enneagram styles and wings sound like you?

Enneagram Stress and Security Points

In selecting the four top possibilities for your Enneagram style, you may have actually selected either your stress point or your security point as well as your core style and one or both of your wings. The arrow lines on the Enneagram symbol are important, as the interconnections of the arrow lines indicate two other Enneagram styles that may augment the characteristics of a person's core Enneagram style.

In situations of stress, an individual's behavior typically becomes an accentuated version of the negative aspects of that person's Enneagram style. When a person is feeling secure or relaxed, the strengths of his or her style often become more apparent.

The Enneagram symbol also shows a dynamic pattern of how each Enneagram style might move across the Enneagram under conditions of stress or security, called the person's stress point and security point, respectively. The stress point is the place on the Enneagram to which you move when you are feeling under pressure; the arrow points *away* from your core Enneagram style. The security point is the place on the Enneagram to which you move when you are feeling relaxed; the arrow points *toward* your core Enneagram style. When they are feeling stressed or secure, *individuals do not change their core style*; they simply start showing some traits of their stress or security point.

Stress may not be altogether negative for some people; they may demonstrate the positive characteristics of their stress point when they are under pressure. For other people, stress is undesirable, bringing out their stress point's negative qualities. Similarly, security may not be altogether beneficial for some people, who may, when relaxed, demonstrate the negative characteristics of their security point. For other people, security and relaxation are desirable, accentuating their security point's favorable qualities. The most useful way to think about your stress and security points is to view them as two additional places on the Enneagram that will give you insight into your thoughts, feelings, and behaviors.

Stress Points

If you look at the Enneagram, you will see a counterclockwise movement of the arrows under conditions of stress. The Enneagram style that your style's arrow is pointed toward is your stress point.

THE INNER TRIANGLE: STRESS
Under stress, Nines move to Six, Sixes move to Three, and Threes move to Nine (see Figure 1.6). Stress refers to any kind of pressure, ranging from mild demands (such as moderate deadlines) to circumstances of extreme duress (such as being passed over for a promotion).

FIGURE 1.6 **Inner Triangle**

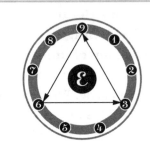

FIGURE 1.7 **The Hexad**

THE HEXAD: STRESS Now look at the interior lines of the Enneagram, with the inner triangle removed (Figure 1.7). This configuration, called a *hexad*, shows the six other Enneagram styles and their interconnections under stress. Ones move to Four, Fours move to Two, Twos move to Eight, Eights move to Five, Fives move to Seven, and Sevens move to One.

Security Points

Under conditions of security, also called relaxation, the Enneagram arrows flow clockwise. The Enneagram style whose arrow points toward your style is your security point.

FIGURE 1.8 **Inner Triangle**

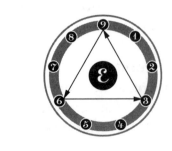

THE INNER TRIANGLE: SECURITY
When secure, Nines move to Three, Threes move to Six, and

Sixes move to Nine (Figure 1.8). Security or relaxation refers to lack of pressure, worry, or demands.

THE HEXAD: SECURITY Looking at the six Enneagram patterns in the hexad of the Enneagram diagram, you can see that Ones move to Seven, Sevens move to Five, Fives move to Eight, Eights move to Two, Twos move to Four, and Fours move to One (Figure 1.9).

FIGURE 1.9 The Hexad

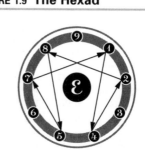

You may have strong links to one arrow number, both arrow numbers, or neither arrow number. People of the same Enneagram style who have strong links to their arrow numbers may use these arrow qualities quite differently. However, the general descriptions given here for all nine Enneagram styles can help you to understand your own connections to your stress and security points.

CHART 1.2   Stress and Security Points for All Nine Enneagram Styles

4 **1** 7

Stress and Security for Ones

Ones with a strong link to Four still seek perfection, but they may also be more emotional, more original in their creativity, and more introspective.

Ones with a strong link to Seven still seek perfection, but they may also be less concerned about social rules and more inventive and fun-loving, particularly when on vacation or away from work and home.

8 **2** 4

Stress and Security for Twos

Twos with a strong link to Eight still focus on helping other people, but they may feel a deeper sense of personal power and be bolder and more aggressive.

Twos with a strong link to Four still focus on helping other people, but they may also be more in touch with their own deeper experiences and feelings and more original in their creativity.

(Continued)

CHART 1.2 *(Continued)*   Stress and Security Points for All Nine Enneagram Styles

9 3 6

Stress and Security for Threes

Threes with a strong link to Nine still focus on success, but they may also be more easygoing and more resistant to pressure, and they may engage in unstructured activities to relax.

Threes with a strong link to Six still focus on success, but they may also be more analytical, more insightful, and more aware of their own anxiety.

2 4 1

Stress and Security for Fours

Fours with a strong link to Two still focus on deep experiences, feelings, and meaning, but they may also be more highly attuned to others and more accommodating.

Fours with a strong link to One still focus on deep experiences, feelings, and meaning, but they may also be more objective and judgmental.

7 5 8

Stress and Security for Fives

Fives with a strong link to Seven still seek knowledge and tend to be emotionally detached, but they may also be more playful and more comfortable being visible.

Fives with a strong link to Eight still seek knowledge and tend to be emotionally detached, but they may also be more assertive and personally powerful.

3 6 9

Stress and Security for Sixes

Sixes with a strong link to Three still engage in anticipatory planning, but they may also become more goal-driven under slight to moderate amounts of pressure.

Sixes with a strong link to Nine still engage in anticipatory planning, but they may also be more relaxed and feel particularly at ease in nature.

1 7 5

Stress and Security for Sevens

Sevens with a strong link to One still engage in optimistic scenario building and future planning, but they may also be more detail-focused and precise.

Sevens with a strong link to Five still engage in optimistic scenario building and future planning, but they may also enjoy more moments of solitude.

5 8 2

Stress and Security for Eights

Eights with a strong link to Five still take charge, assert themselves, and hide their vulnerabilities, but they may also be quieter and more reflective.

Eights with a strong link to Two still take charge, assert themselves, and hide their vulnerabilities, but they may also be warmer, more empathic, and more generous.

6 9 3

Stress and Security for Nines

Nines with a strong link to Six still seek harmony and avoid conflict, but they may be more willing to express their insights and concerns.

Nines with a strong link to Three still seek harmony and avoid conflict, but they may also procrastinate less by focusing on goals and results.

Do any of these patterns of movement under stress or security describe your behavior?

Putting It All Together

Now that you have learned about the nine styles and their associated wings and stress and security points, take some time to determine which Enneagram style you believe most accurately describes you. Examine the nine configurations of Enneagram styles and their related wings and stress and security points given in the following chart, and study the motivations and drives inherent in each style. Closely analyze your patterns of thought, feeling, and behavior over your lifetime, not just in recent years. Please refer to the top four Enneagram styles you selected earlier in this chapter. Among them may be your core style, your wings, and/or your stress and security points.

CHART 1.3   Wings and Stress and Security Points for All Nine Enneagram Styles

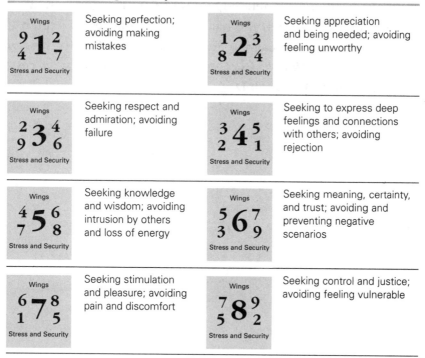

Wings / Stress and Security	Description
9 1 2 (Wings); **4 ... 7** (Stress and Security)	Seeking perfection; avoiding making mistakes
1 2 3 (Wings); **8 ... 4** (Stress and Security)	Seeking appreciation and being needed; avoiding feeling unworthy
2 3 4 (Wings); **9 ... 6** (Stress and Security)	Seeking respect and admiration; avoiding failure
3 4 5 (Wings); **2 ... 1** (Stress and Security)	Seeking to express deep feelings and connections with others; avoiding rejection
4 5 6 (Wings); **7 ... 8** (Stress and Security)	Seeking knowledge and wisdom; avoiding intrusion by others and loss of energy
5 6 7 (Wings); **3 ... 9** (Stress and Security)	Seeking meaning, certainty, and trust; avoiding and preventing negative scenarios
6 7 8 (Wings); **1 ... 5** (Stress and Security)	Seeking stimulation and pleasure; avoiding pain and discomfort
7 8 9 (Wings); **5 ... 2** (Stress and Security)	Seeking control and justice; avoiding feeling vulnerable

(Continued)

CHART 1.3 *(Continued)* **Wings and Stress and Security Points for All Nine Enneagram Styles**

Wings	Seeking harmony and comfort; avoiding conflict
8 **9** 1 6 3 Stress and Security	

As you read the following chapters, each one focused on a critical leadership competency, you will learn how leaders of each Enneagram style both excel and have areas for development in each competency area. If you are still uncertain of your Enneagram style or have narrowed it down to two or three choices, these examples of real leaders in action will help you clarify your own Enneagram style.

To Learn More . . .
Read one of the recommended books under "The Enneagram" in the Resources section at the back of this book; read Chapter 1, "Discovering Your Enneagram Style," in *Bringing Out the Best in Yourself at Work: How to Use the Enneagram System for Success*, by Ginger Lapid-Bogda, Ph.D.

Chapter 2

Drive for Results

*I*t is important for you to build credibility with customers by delivering sustained, high-quality results. Your customers depend on you to deliver timely and effective products, processes, and systems. By continually driving for results and taking the promise of your own potential to greater heights, you can continue to make gains in productivity, push the envelope of new product development, excel in your financial goals, and support your organization as a leader in its field.

Having the ability to Drive for Results means that you are skilled in the following six competency components:

1. Setting overall direction and establishing common goals
2. Creating workable plans
3. Assigning tasks effectively
4. Expecting, measuring, and rewarding high performance
5. Providing ongoing stewardship
6. Evaluating results and utilizing what you learn from the evaluation

As you read further and reflect on the six competency components of Drive for Results, rate yourself in each area on a scale of

FIGURE 2.1 **Drive for Results**

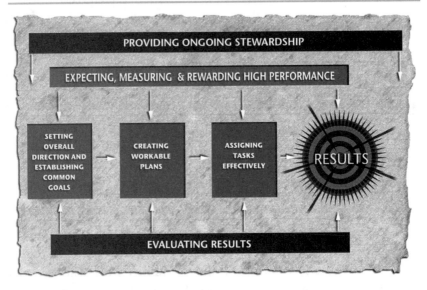

1 to 5. This will help you determine your areas of strength, and also the areas needing development.

The Six Competency Components of Drive for Results

Component 1: Setting Overall Direction and Establishing Common Goals

This component involves placing a top priority on setting challenging goals, while astutely scoping out the project's end results; setting explicit performance standards and clear, unambiguous roles and responsibilities; accurately defining the length and difficulty of the tasks, the projects involved, and the resources required; and aligning all work with the vision and strategy of the project, team, and organization.

Low				High
1	2	3	4	5

Component 2: Creating Workable Plans

This component involves developing realistic and well-organized schedules and timelines; making and communicating decisions in a clear and timely manner; defining achievable and high-quality deliverables; and demonstrating flexibility in all of these areas so that changes can be made as needed.

Low				High
1	2	3	4	5

Component 3: Assigning Tasks Effectively

This component involves delegating tasks and decisions appropriately to those who know the work best and who possess the required skill sets; distributing the workload evenly and equitably; and empowering others by trusting them to perform and complete their jobs.

Low				High
1	2	3	4	5

Component 4: Expecting, Measuring, and Rewarding High Performance

This involves creating an environment of accountability by communicating clear expectations (e.g., expectations regarding participation, performance, and teamwork); providing ongoing coaching, feedback, and support for meeting performance goals; regularly monitoring team and individual performance and providing rewards, recognition, and sanctions accordingly; personally modeling the behavior you desire in others, such as demonstrating initiative and high personal standards of performance as measured against performance expectations; and looking inward for reasons when things go wrong.

Low				High
1	2	3	4	5

Component 5: Providing Ongoing Stewardship

This involves monitoring work processes, progress, and results on a continuous basis; ensuring that feedback loops are designed into the process and that corrective action is taken as needed; meeting timeline commitments and anticipating and adjusting for problems; keeping others informed as necessary; addressing obstacles in a problem-solving manner rather than in an avoidant or blaming one; and providing ideas, insights, coaching, and resources to others as needed.

Low				High
1	2	3	4	5

Component 6: Evaluating Results and Utilizing What You Learn from the Evaluation

This involves assessing results on an ongoing basis and at the end of the project by employing input from multiple sources (e.g., customers, project team members, bosses, and others); evaluating results using multiple measures of success; and conducting post-project debriefing meetings to assess project successes and failures so that insights gained in these meetings can be carried forward into future projects.

Low				High
1	2	3	4	5

Enneagram Dimensions of Drive for Results

Enneagram Style Ones

Enneagram Style
① DILIGENCE

Enneagram Style One leaders are typically adept at setting goals for both themselves and others, getting a task done quickly and efficiently, and then driving the work to completion. Timelines, schedules, and deliverables usually come naturally to the systematic mind of the Style One leader, as do moving a project along, holding people accountable, and achieving closure on specific tasks and overall project outcomes. As masterful organizers, Ones can delineate tasks clearly, make effective job assignments, address questions and concerns, and dedicate themselves to making sure that everything is complete and on schedule, even if that means working long hours themselves.

Because they set high standards for themselves and diligently try to live up to these ideals, Ones often lead by example, setting a standard for others to emulate. With a keen nose for talent, Ones can spot excellence in others and inspire them to achieve outstanding results.

Here is some feedback from a person who worked for an exemplary One leader:

> "I adored working for John. He was clear and completely organized, and the team had never functioned better. No stone was left unturned or work left undone under John's watch (even if he was here until midnight). The organization is lucky to have had him."

At the same time, the One leader's strength in focusing on getting tasks done perfectly can also be a derailer (a quality that can lead to problems, or even failure, on the job). One leaders can drive to accomplish concrete tasks at the expense of taking time at the beginning of a project to create a compelling, shared vision or to make certain that everyone is aligned with the project's strategy.

Because they sometimes focus more on the details of the work at hand than on the motivation of the people involved, Ones may appear to their project team members, peers, or bosses to be demanding, critical, micromanaging, not sensitive enough to others, and too reactive. For example, Ones can respond defensively to challenges or to perceived criticisms of their work responsibilities. These can include customer complaints and/or new ideas that appear to the One as last minute or as contradicting what the One perceives to be the right way to do things.

The following example illustrates how Ryan, a One leader, unintentionally appeared too critical and demotivated an employee named Leslie.

> Leslie, the coordinator of a project, sent an e-mail to Ryan, the project manager, saying that registrations for a special program being offered were slow and suggesting that he send out a reminder e-mail. Ryan sent Leslie this e-mail in response:
>
> "I received an e-mail from a colleague who couldn't get through on the listed phone number. I am not certain if this person was calling the right number, but if other people are having this experience, it's no wonder that registrations have dropped off.
>
> Please look into it, and respond to this person by e-mail. Here's the e-mail address."

Development Stretches for Ones

CREATE COMPELLING VISIONS   Create a vision for each project you lead, and be certain that all team members are aligned with it before you develop the project planning tasks and timelines. Although there are different ways to create compelling visions, the following process is a practical way to get started. Convene a team meeting for the purpose of creating a vision. Ask each team member to list his or her three most important goals and/or values for the project. Next, write all these items on a chart pad, and give each member four removable red dots. Instruct each member to place a red dot next to the four items on the list that he or she believes are the most important to the success of the project. After this task is complete, select the five items from the list with the most dots and, taking each item in turn, brainstorm answers to the following question: *If this value or goal were to become part of our daily way of working, how would we work on this project?*

PAY ATTENTION TO PEOPLE   Pay as much attention to people's feelings and motivation as you do to tasks, particularly at the beginning of a project, at key milestones, and when potential obstacles to the project's success arise. Ask others about their well-being, and see what you can do to help them. Try to enjoy the people as much as you do the task.

FOCUS MORE ON SUCCESSES THAN ON MISTAKES   Pay particular attention to your use of right/wrong thinking, critical language, and a focus on mistakes when you're interacting with people connected to your project. The idea is to force yourself to think first about what is positive rather than about what is missing the mark. In addition, when you send an e-mail to someone about anything other than a direct compliment, reread it several times and even have someone else (with a different Enneagram style) review it for tone and content before you send it.

Enneagram Style Twos

Enneagram Style
GIVING

Enneagram Style Two leaders are usually skilled at helping every employee stay focused and aligned at the place where the organizational, team, and individual goals intersect. Insightful and intuitive, Enneagram Twos tend to be accurate assessors of an individual's strengths and development areas, and they are adept at helping others find the right fit for their skills and talents. Because they are conscientious and careful, Twos also work very hard, organizing work and people so that projects can succeed, with quality deliverables provided on schedule.

Since they are sensitive to customer requirements and requests, Twos typically respond to customers quickly, listen carefully to their requests, and make adjustments if they can. As leaders, Twos are also gifted at helping everyone involved focus their work on service to others.

Here is a quote from a 360° feedback assessment about Kelly:

"Kelly, our project leader, is an amazing person, always making time for people, no matter what time of day it is or what the work demands may be. Part coach and part confidant, Kelly always has some useful perspective or on-target advice for each of us. This approach always seems to bring out the best in us, and it also gets the work done."

The Two leader's strength in attending to people's needs can also become a derailer, however. Enneagram Two leaders can spend so much time and energy focusing on the needs of their employees, peers, bosses, and customers that they feel caught between the competing wishes of different individuals or, more likely, exhaust themselves in the process of trying to accommodate everyone's desires. Although Twos focus on both tasks and people, Two leaders run the risk of placing too much emphasis on the latter.

Twos may also have trouble giving direct feedback to individuals who they know are already under duress. In addition, Two leaders can become angry when others do not act in a responsive, appreciative manner or in a way that the Two thinks is appropriate. They become even more agitated when they are overextended and near the point of exhaustion, and they are often unaware that this is occurring or that they are taking insufficient time for themselves and their personal lives.

Here is an e-mail from James, a Two, regarding a recommendation for someone who used to work for him. Although the e-mail is gracious, in it you can read the implied slap on the wrist and the writer's undertone of annoyance for perceived inappropriate behavior:

Rod Samuels called yesterday re: a reference for you for a part-time teaching position at the university. I, of course, gave you an excellent one. In the future, however, I would

appreciate a heads-up when you are using me as a reference so that I can tailor what I say to what you need/want.
James

Development Stretches for Twos

FOCUS AS MUCH ON THE WORK OBJECTIVES AS YOU DO ON PEOPLE
Because you will always be sensitive to people's personal needs, it is important that you shift your emphasis and focus equally on work objectives. This will enable people to work more independently of you, and it will allow you to feel less obliged to make everything okay for everyone else.

HAVE THE COURAGE TO DELIVER TOUGH NEWS People need to know where they stand, even at times when they are under duress, whether for personal or work-related reasons. Be kind, clear, and compassionate, but make sure you do not withhold negative information from people. Give constructive feedback.

DON'T OVEREXTEND YOURSELF Do you know when you are overextending yourself to the point of exhaustion? When you're exhausted, you will not be performing at your best, and you may also react in ways that create barriers between you and others. Make sure you consider yourself as well as other people, acknowledging that you have needs for rest and support, and that you expect—and accept—that others can and will step up to tasks.

Enneagram Style Threes

Enneagram Style Three leaders often feel precisely in their element when they drive for results. The ability to maintain a laserlike focus and to achieve outstanding goals and results is at the core of the Enneagram Three's personality architecture. Three

Enneagram Style
PERFORM ③

leaders know how to select the most important targets and then to organize both their work and that of others in the most efficient and effective way, and other people often respect them for the ease with which they appear to accomplish these tasks. In addition, Threes are usually highly responsive to client feedback and have the ability to earn long-term client trust.

Because Three leaders avoid work-related failure, they often have multiple strategies for overcoming obstacles to success; for the Three, not getting work done well and on time is simply not an option. Threes can also be excellent team leaders, particularly when their teams are composed of highly competent people on whom they can depend.

Here is the positive feedback that Lana, a Three leader, received:

- A great engineer, but also knows the business side well
- Sees the whole organizational picture
- Good at customer relations
- Credible
- Bright
- Excellent financial skills
- Highly skilled in operations
- Well organized
- Wide management experience
- Gives excellent constructive feedback
- Knows when to manage closely and when not to

At the same time, the Three leader's intense drive for results, combined with his or her singular, unrelenting focus, can lead to potential problems. This is a good example of how a strength, when overused, can become a derailer. For example, Threes can become so focused on completing tasks and getting the job done that they forget their generally well-honed interpersonal skills. As a result, they may come across to coworkers, bosses, and subordinates (although only rarely to clients) as cold or abrupt. This same overfocus on goals can cause Threes to do the following:

(1) become dismissive of others in the organization whom they do not perceive to be both competent and confident; (2) become overly competitive, especially with peers; (3) expect subordinates to have the same focus on goals as they do, but without giving them enough concrete direction on how best to accomplish these goals; and (4) work themselves to exhaustion.

Here is the negative feedback that Mike, a Three leader, received:

- Doesn't sufficiently organize the work of the group
- Needs to provide more direction and set clearer expectations
- Needs to delegate more
- Under stress, becomes irritated or angry, which makes us lose respect for him
- Should be more collaborative with his direct reports and peers
- Needs to balance work and personal life better; can't sustain 60-hour weeks

Development Stretches for Threes

PROVIDE MORE EXPLICIT DIRECTIONS While some of those who work for you may need only minimal supervision beyond a simple understanding of the goals and objectives, others may require greater clarity and definition of tasks, and even some guidance in developing an effective work plan. Having this latter work style does not mean that these individuals are any less competent or confident than you are; it simply means that they need a greater level of detail in order to proceed.

TREAT YOUR SUBORDINATES, PEERS, AND BOSSES AS IF THEY WERE CLIENTS If you think of those with whom you work as clients, you will respond to them quickly, listen closely to them, and pay attention to their needs. Your graciousness and social skills will be at their best, and your tendency to focus primarily on tasks will be supplemented by an equal focus on people. This will also reduce the tendency you may have to be abrupt or to give the impression that you don't have enough time for others.

REGULARLY ASK YOURSELF HOW YOU ARE FEELING   Threes often suspend their feelings when they are working hard, believing that these will get in the way of achieving results. Because your focus on work may come at the expense of paying attention to your own needs and feelings, give yourself time each day to ask yourself these questions: *How am I feeling right at this very moment? Am I concerned about anything? Am I angry about something? What am I feeling happy about?* Paying attention to your feelings will help you be more genuine in your interactions with others, let you appear more human to your employees, and enable you to feel more empathy when others approach you to discuss important issues.

Enneagram Style Fours

Enneagram Style
④   MOOD

Enneagram Style Four leaders often operate from an inner core of passion and values, as well as a compelling vision. Once these elements become activated in the Four, he or she easily enlists others in the effort and supports them in the achievement of high levels of performance. Creative, original, and empathic, Four leaders are willing to work hard themselves and to coach, counsel, and cajole others to be responsive to customers, come up with new solutions, ask the right questions, and put in the extra hours needed to get the job done. Working from the deliverable backward, Four leaders typically set up key interim milestones and check in with subordinates at these points. More than anything, Four leaders inspire others to find meaning in their work and to produce excellent results. They can also be extremely sensitive to the needs and feelings of those who work for them.

The positive feedback for Robert, an engineering manager, given here paints a portrait of a Four leader.

- Tells personal stories
- Really knows the industry
- Is popular
- Sees the big picture
- Is bright
- Works very hard
- Is aware of other people's feelings
- Is creative
- Is an excellent engineer
- Has good organizational skills
- Is the best technical boss ever
- Instills loyalty in employees
- Asks the right questions

The Four leader's intense attraction to vision and meaning can also have a downside. For example, if the Four finds the work to be pedestrian and routine, he or she may lose interest. In addition, many employees are not as compelled by vision as the Four and prefer more concrete goals and tasks.

The Four leader's sensitivity, while a strength, can also be an Achilles' heel (and thus become a derailer) if the Four focuses more on personal experiences and feelings—both his or her own and those of others—than on work. This can also create a dilemma for Fours when they need to deliver negative performance feedback: on the one hand, they want to give truthful feedback in an authentic and empathic way; on the other, they may put themselves in the other person's shoes (actually, the Four's own shoes, projecting his or her own feelings and experiences onto the other person) and become reluctant to deliver bad news lest they demoralize the other person. In addition, Fours can have a tendency to overpersonalize work and working relationships.

Besides his positive feedback, Robert also received the following negative feedback:

- Stories, though interesting, often go on too long at meetings
- Makes another manager the butt of some of his jokes
- Takes oppositional ideas personally
- Keeps his group too insular
- Communication with those outside his group needs to increase
- Needs to solicit more input on engineering designs
- Needs to manage poor performers better; doesn't want to hurt these people's feelings
- Needs to plan and schedule more systematically

Development Stretches for Fours

FOLLOW YOUR MIND AS WELL AS YOUR HEART Most Fours tend to look at their own inner experience and feelings first and then use their analytical function to make sense of their reactions. They also have a tendency to overemphasize the feelings of others—for example, structuring work or job responsibilities around someone's preferences rather than around what's best for the organization. The key is not to ignore your own and others' personal experiences, but rather to use your objective reasoning in conjunction with your sensitivity.

GIVE PEOPLE WHAT THEY NEED, NOT WHAT YOU THINK THEY NEED While being empathic and sensitive to others is a strength, it is important to differentiate how you might react in a given situation from how the other person actually feels. The best way to do this is either to ask others directly how they feel or what they want, or to tell them what you imagine they want and then solicit their confirmation or disconfirmation. In addition, don't withhold negative feedback from people for fear that they may be hurt by it or get angry at you. If you frame the feedback in objective terms, at the same time maintaining your positive regard for the individual, the person is likely to respond in a constructive way.

MAKE THE FINER DETAILS OF PROJECT PLANS MORE EXPLICIT
Although some people can work easily from a common vision, shared goals, and key milestones, others may need more explicit direction and oversight. Thus, laying out plans in more detail can be extremely helpful.

Enneagram Style Fives

Enneagram Style Five leaders excel at many aspects of Drive for Results. Five leaders do their background research and tend to be analytical, planning-oriented, and organized. As a result, they typically create systematic, specific, and practical work plans and monitor the results to ensure that the final deliverable meets the designated specifications. In addition, Five leaders often have a good sense for resource allocation, rarely overspending and being realistic about the amount of time required for each step of the project.

In a crisis, Five leaders tend to be cool, calm, and collected, taking an analytical, problem-solving approach to removing obstacles, reconfiguring the work, and doing whatever is needed to get the job done well and on time. They also understand the importance of having a clear purpose and well-defined roles and tasks; this understanding, combined with their ability to focus and organize well, helps Fives achieve excellent results. Because Fives like research and analysis, they frequently analyze and evaluate projects upon completion so that they can channel their insights into future successes.

Here's an example of a Five leader in action:

Chad, a Five project manager, created an exemplary internship program that eventually became a state-of-the-art,
benchmarked program. After he conceived the idea, Chad
thoroughly researched similar programs in other companies.
Finding very little useful information, he designed the entire
program himself, systematically gained organizational
support for the concept, and became the internship program
director for three years—all this in addition to performing his
regular job beyond expectations. His goal, which he realized
within the first year, was to recruit and develop people for
his division so that he could pass along the knowledge that
he had accumulated over the years.

Five leaders' strengths can also become their shortcomings and
cause them to derail as leaders. For example, with their emphasis
on analysis, research, and planning, Five leaders can sometimes stop
short of execution because they want to make sure that they have
all the facts, have thought through all contingencies, and have analyzed all the information correctly before they act—in other words,
they may spend so much time saying *Ready, aim/ready, aim* . . . that
they never get to *fire*. For some Five leaders, the extensive focus on
the development of strategies and plans is another strength that,
when overused, can become a weakness. For example, the Five
leader may confuse a specific strategy or tactic with the larger vision
and mission. In addition, while Five leaders are usually adept at
planning, monitoring, and evaluating projects, they must continually remind themselves that they need to enlist the support of other
people on both a cerebral and an emotional level, as Fives tend to
overemphasize the former. Finally, Fives must also be attentive to
the necessity of engaging in two-way communication with team
members, customers, and peers throughout the project.

Chad also experienced the downside of the Five's characteristics:

After three years, the senior manager position in Chad's
work group became available. Although Chad was more

competent, knowledgeable, and conscientious than his competitor for the position, he was passed over for the following reasons: his competitor had developed more relationships in the organization that would be an asset in the new position, and she also took action more quickly than Chad did.

Development Stretches for Fives

THINK BEFORE YOU ACT, BUT ACT, ACT, ACT   Thinking, researching, and planning are essential for achieving excellent results. Just remember that taking action is equally important. Take action twice as quickly as you do now. Review your past three projects and answer this question: *What could I (or others under my supervision) have done to move each project along more quickly?* Think about someone at work whom you admire and who takes effective action quickly. Observe what this person does, or, better yet, ask how he or she moves to action so readily.

ASK THE BIG QUESTIONS   At all points in the project, ask yourself these questions: *Why are we doing this project? How does this project align with the organization's vision and strategy and the business unit's vision and strategy? Do the people I work with also understand this bigger framework? If they do not, what actions can I take to communicate it to them?*

COMMUNICATE CONTINUOUSLY   Because Fives tend to keep their thought processes and ideas to themselves, you can stretch and grow by constantly sharing ideas with those with whom you work. Even if you increase the frequency of your communication fivefold, it might still be too little. You need to communicate vision, strategy, plans, progress, thoughts, feelings, and information to other people on an ongoing basis, and you also need to make sure that the communication is reciprocal.

Enneagram Style Sixes

6 Enneagram Style
DOUBT

Industrious, responsible, and analytical, Six leaders usually prepare excellent project plans, know exactly what they are doing and why, and find a way to include all relevant people in the planning process. Because Sixes have an eye for detail and a nose for potential pitfalls, the planning and execution of results come easily to most Six leaders. For example, Sixes can usually anticipate the most likely problem scenarios and develop effective contingency plans. Further, given their focus on team cohesion and loyalty, Sixes are able to enlist the support of team members and motivate them to achieve high levels of performance. Team members frequently feel driven to support the Six leader, not wanting to let down the person who is watching out for their well-being in so many different ways. Always concerned that projects go well and are not derailed for some preventable reason, Six leaders can be counted on to monitor individual, team, and overall performance on a regular basis, reminding people of their deliverables and providing assistance when possible.

Here's an example of an excellent Six team leader:

Jan's group was overworked, but its members had all become used to the idea that sometimes the reward for excellent work is more work. The team members knew that the organization counted on them to do the most difficult assignments because their group had a reputation for excellent work quality and timely delivery. When asked the secret of her success as a leader, Jan would say, "It's the great team I have." The team members responded to the same question by saying that Jan creates the most cohesive teams in the company: "She asks our opinions, helps us out when needed, appreciates our individual and collective contributions, and sticks up for us no matter what."

The Six leader's strengths also mirror his or her potential shortcomings or derailers. Sixes usually start with anticipatory or worst-case planning—i.e., what could go wrong. While this approach has great value, it also has downsides. The first is that Six leaders may overfocus (often unintentionally) on the concerns of their teams or projects at the expense of the strategic priorities of the organization, division, or other work units. This is referred to as suboptimization, where a subunit maximizes its interests in a way that is not optimal for other parts of the organization. Second, while worst-case planning is an important part of planning and management, so is best-case scenario planning. Focusing on the negative too early or placing more emphasis on the negative than on the positive can demotivate a team and lead to overanalysis and "analysis paralysis." Finally, when problems do arise, it's possible that the Six will be extremely calm, but it's also possible that he or she will react strongly, becoming overly concerned and taking action that may not be as considered and deliberate as it could be.

Here is a story about a Six leader who was competent in many respects but was also failing with his staff:

Although Charles was technically capable and his staff always commented that they thought he was a good human being, they had difficulty working for him. The staff's biggest complaint was that Charles managed their work too closely, wanting to know the most minute details of their plans and progress. Not only did they believe that this wasted their time, but they also felt micromanaged and disempowered. Because they could not understand why the boss would want to be so closely involved in the work of staff members with their high level of capability, they interpreted his behavior to mean that he was anxious and lacked confidence. This perceived lack of confidence undermined Charles's authority as a leader, and the staff doubted whether he would be able to come to their aid, if needed, on important issues (e.g., garnering resources for the group, fending off new work that was not in their line of business, or dealing with any intrastaff conflict).

Development Stretches for Sixes

EACH TIME YOU THINK OF A WORST-CASE SCENARIO, THINK OF A BEST-CASE SCENARIO AS WELL It will be almost impossible for you to not anticipate problems, but, at the same time, you should also use your scenario-planning skills to create positive scenarios. Discipline yourself to create a viable positive scenario in addition to (not instead of) a negative scenario. When you do this as a regular part of the planning process, eventually both positive and negative alternatives will come easily to you.

USE BEST-CASE SCENARIO PLANNING WITH YOUR TEAM BEFORE INTRODUCING WORST-CASE SCENARIOS It is best to begin planning with best-case scenarios rather than worst-case ones, as the former motivate people to move forward, while the latter can deplete their energy and focus. After the positive possibilities have been discussed, consideration of the worst-case scenarios will be very helpful for grounding the decisions and plans in reality.

STAY CALM IN A CRISIS When things go awry, and they will, people will look to you for ideas, plans, alternatives, and calmness. There is nothing wrong with conveying a sense of urgency about resolving problems. However, it is best to do so in a calm and deliberate manner. Sometimes it helps to take a walk before responding or to say some calming words to yourself—e.g., "It's worked out before, and so it will this time," or "I know that I'm going into my Six worrying, and I can choose either to continue to do that or to stop it if I want to."

Enneagram Style Sevens

Enneagram Style Seven leaders tend to be visionary, flexible, innovative, and strategic. The Seven
leader includes others and encourages their participation in most steps of a project, from the ini-
tial thinking and planning phase to the assessment
of final results. Once Seven leaders grasp what is required for the
success of a project—which usually occurs in a nanosecond—they
are ready to move quickly. Whereas Five leaders can be described
as *Ready, aim/ready, aim*, Seven leaders can best be described as
Ready, aim, fire, fire, fire.

Although Sevens are rarely at a loss for ideas, Seven leaders like
input from others and become energized by brainstorming various
ideas and possibilities. They like to motivate others (and to be motivated themselves), and they enjoy problem solving, as long as the
obstacles do not seem insurmountable and they feel that they have
enough authority to get things done. As many hours as they work,
Sevens do their best to keep the work environment lively and stimulating, both for themselves and for everyone around them.

Here's an example of how an exemplary Seven leader provides
the necessary support as his team drives for results:

> Terry never thought of himself as the incredible leader that
> he in fact was. His greatness came from his belief that
> everyone could achieve remarkable results, and he had an
> endless capacity for self-development. He understood the
> relationship between excellent results and the need for
> leaders to continually work on themselves so that they can
> serve as conduits for organizational excellence. To this end,
> Terry provided a clear vision, a deliberate but flexible
> strategy, well-formulated goals, and an array of training and
> development opportunities for those who understood the
> importance of developing themselves both as leaders and as
> human beings.

For Sevens, as for all Enneagram styles, a person's greatest strengths, if overused, can also become his or her derailers. For example, the Seven's way of mental processing—generating new ideas on a continual basis and becoming excited about most of them—can create too many projects for employees and coworkers to handle, as well as confusion about which project to do first and how thoroughly to do it. Because Sevens are usually adept at multitasking, they assume that others are as well. While most people can handle two or three projects at a time, and some people work best with only a single focus, Sevens can usually deal with eight or more projects simultaneously. Thus, Seven leaders can unwittingly create havoc and commotion for those who are following them.

In addition, because Sevens enjoy working on simultaneous tasks, they may leave certain tasks to the last minute, knowing full well that they will do whatever it takes to get these tasks completed on time. They may also be averse to the level of detailed planning that others may need in order to understand the workflow and execute the work on time. Detailed planning often makes Sevens feel boxed in, restricting their ability to act spontaneously. However, a lack of specific plans or instructions can cause others to become stressed and frustrated and thus possibly produce lesser-quality work.

The downside of a Seven leader under duress can be seen in the following story:

Dan was a Ph.D. who was well respected in the industry. When he was hired as a senior manager, those who were about to work with him and for him had high expectations. Their hopes, however, never materialized. Although Dan had been successful in his previous jobs, the new position required him to produce multiple projects in an incredibly fast-paced environment. His tendency to take on too many projects without having enough time to complete them, combined with his reliance on staff members to produce

high-quality finished products before they had been sufficiently trained to do so (Dan was too busy with his own work
to train his staff), created a chaotic situation. The staff felt
overworked, confused, and angry. Dan's approach was to
micromanage the staff and to work inhumanly hard himself
for months on end. Ultimately, his staff rebelled, and Dan
was demoted to a staff position.

Development Stretches for Sevens

STAY FOCUSED   When you move quickly from idea to idea and
activity to activity, this can create an upsetting frenzy for those
around you, even if they find the ideas and activities stimulating.
Practice staying focused three times as long as you currently do,
and learn to tame your mind when it jumps around, bringing it
back to the original thought.

CREATE THE WORK PLAN AT THE RIGHT LEVEL OF DETAIL   Sevens tend
to be good planners, but their plans tend to be at the big idea and
execution level, with many of the steps in between getting less
attention. In developing a collaborative work plan, make sure that
you describe all tasks, milestones, and deliverables along the way
in sufficient detail, and hold yourself and others accountable for
following through.

GET THINGS DONE IN ADVANCE   Although Sevens will get most, if not
all, of their work done either on time or only a little late, they may
have to work long hours at the last minute (and require their
coworkers to do the same) in order to meet their commitments.
Remember that you tend to overcommit to interesting work, that
unexpected demands that need your attention will always arise, and
that not everyone (including you) can do his or her best work at the
zero hour. Make a commitment to get every piece of work for which
you are responsible completed three days before the deadline.

Enneagram Style Eights

Enneagram Style
CHALLENGE

While some people say that Enneagram Style Eights are natural-born leaders, it is more accurate to say that Eights like to make important things happen, want everything to be under control, and will take charge when things are in disarray (they have a unique sensitivity to this and can sense it at the earliest stages). They also have less ambivalence than most other people about being direct and directive. They like results to be as big and to have as much impact as possible, and their authoritative leadership style often inspires confidence in and support from those they lead.

Eights also have an eye for vision and a nose for strategy, making them easy for people to follow without the Eight's having to micromanage; Eight leaders give competent employees a great deal of autonomy with which to excel.

The following story demonstrates how Eights rise to leadership in even the most difficult situations:

Marianne had started her consulting firm all on her own, providing technical consulting services to a variety of clients, but particularly to those whose values she supported—for example, organizations that provided goods and services that improved people's lives or protected the environment. Because Marianne was excellent at what she did, her firm grew by 30 percent annually, and she expanded her staff from 3 to 45 over a four-year period. However, a major project ended unexpectedly because of funding issues. This project had accounted for half of the firm's revenue, and Marianne was left with an overhead that she could not afford and a staff that was counting on her. Rather than laying off even one person, she rose to the occasion, focusing everyone on results, marketing, and quality service to existing clients. With sheer drive and will, Marianne brought the firm from the brink of bankruptcy to a position where it was attractive enough to be bought out by a bigger firm.

Eights can be a force to be reckoned with, but their leadership strengths of being bold and assertive can become possible derailers. Although they are sensitive, Eights don't always show this externally. Their certitude, combined with their gut sense that they have made the best decision, may make it difficult for others to feel fully comfortable expressing a contrary opinion. In addition, while Eights give employees whom they believe to be competent and reliable a great deal of autonomy, they do not do the same with people who they believe have an attitude problem or competence issues. Eight leaders may feel a need to micromanage these individuals (while feeling resentful that they must do so), may act dismissively toward them (not because they want to cause them harm, but simply because the Eight leader just doesn't want to be bothered), or may ignore them altogether.

In contrast to the previous story, the following story shows how a focus on results, but inattention to important details, can cause an Eight to derail:

Anthony had risen from a staff position to the role of manager within three years, and he was pleased with the competence and motivation of his eight-person staff. Because he believed in his staff's capabilities, when a major organizational crisis required his attention, he diverted his focus from operations and staff needs and lent his support to his own boss during this time of organizational turmoil.

Within a year, Anthony was on the verge of losing his entire staff and was at a loss to explain why. Although he employed two different consultants to help him understand and resolve the issues, a year later, he still could not understand his staff's concerns, and things were steadily getting worse. Finally, a third consultant enabled Anthony and his team to identify the core issue: Anthony's strength as a leader was so central to his staff's performance that when he was no longer available to them, even though they did not literally need him, the result was a leadership vacuum in his group that made its members so anxious that it destabilized them. Although this surprised Anthony because his staff was so able, he learned that even mature staff members become dysfunctional when the person they consider their "rock" seems to disappear.

Development Stretches for Eights

EMPOWER OTHERS TO TAKE ACTION   Because you move to action quickly and others are used to following your lead, the more you do, the less others are inclined to take action on their own. If you want to empower others to take the initiative, you need to act less often and less quickly. When you use this approach on an ongoing basis, others will eventually rise to the occasion. For example, don't always be the first to express an opinion. This will reduce people's reliance on you as a thought leader. When someone else suggests a good idea, affirm the person and ask him or her to explain it in more detail.

PUT YOURSELF IN CHARGE OF WORKING WELL WITH EVERYONE   It has been said that Eights do not suffer fools gladly, nor do they like being around people whom they perceive as incompetent or as not taking responsibility for their own behavior. However, since we can all be "fools" sometimes and very few people always take full responsibility for their own behavior, it is important that you learn to be more accepting or, at the least, not to give people the impression that you don't want to make time for them. Try to find something you appreciate in people whom you find troubling; this will help you to respond to them in a warmer way.

HAVE MORE FUN   This may be the biggest challenge of all for Eights, who tend to be serious at work, especially when the work demands are high (and this always seems to be the case when

Eights are involved). However, because Eights can be so demanding and intense, it is even more important that they and those following them also relax and enjoy themselves. Others will usually follow your lead, both because they admire you and because they don't want to get on your bad side. If you are extremely serious, your employees will be too; if you can relax more, others will also be more relaxed, and this will improve their productivity.

Enneagram Style Nines

Enneagram Style
HARMONY (9)

Enneagram Style Nine leaders coalesce their teams around common missions and develop well-organized, well-structured work plans. Because Nines project a sense of calmness and predictability in their work, their projects often move along smoothly, with attention being given simultaneously to both the larger project purpose and the details of the work. In addition, the desire of Nine leaders for harmony among people and unity within the team contributes to their ability to create high-performing work teams whose members have a common sense of direction. With their affable demeanor, Nines get along with just about everyone—coworkers, subordinates, bosses, customers, and vendors. In addition, their ability to solicit and integrate multiple opinions enables Nine leaders to make decisions that are thoughtful and purposeful.

The following story demonstrates what happens when Nine leaders excel:

All the members of Aaron's team knew that they could talk to him about anything and that he would make time for them. Even more important, they respected Aaron's ability to develop and manage the process of any project assigned to their group, and they trusted him to make sure that everyone on the team followed the agreed-upon process. They enjoyed coming to work and felt respected by their coworkers. With the easygoing and comfortable work environment that Aaron established, the members of his team knew that they would be high performing even when the inevitable crises, changes, and unexpected events came their way.

However, the Nine leader's strength in creating cohesion can also become a derailer. Because Nine leaders value harmony so highly, they may be reluctant to take strong positions on project-related issues or to assert themselves fully when teams need clear guidance. Because Nines tend to avoid conflict for the sake of keeping the peace, others often do not know just where the Nine leader stands on an issue.

Nine leaders also need to pay attention to their tendency to pro-crastinate. Their attention can easily become diffused, switching focus from a high-priority work item to something else that is much less important. This forgetting about the task at hand and moving away from it can result in multiple items piling up on their desks, creating bottlenecks in projects. Nines need to learn to move things off their desks soon after these items arrive and to pay less attention to small details that, while needing to be dealt with at some point, are not worth creating project delays for.

There's another side to Nine leaders when they drive for results, as shown in the following story:

Although Marissa was well liked and was perceived as competent by the members of her staff, they did not perceive her to be the decisive leader they needed when times got tough. When projects were running smoothly, Marissa's ability to share insights and bring people together made her much appreciated. However, when conflicts arose between team members, between the team and people in other parts of the organization, or between Marissa and a staff member, Marissa seemed to look the other way or with-draw. Because of this, the team members began avoiding conflict rather than put themselves in a situation where they desperately needed her intervention and she could not or would not help. As a result of this, Marissa's teams often underperformed.

Development Stretches for Nines

KEEP THE WORK MOVING, ESPECIALLY OFF YOUR DESK While you may wish to do your work thoroughly and in a time frame that is comfortable for you, this can create strains, stresses, and bottlenecks for other people. This is especially true when projects are large or complex and when people are depending on you for a response before they can do their own work. It is especially important that you keep the work flowing at a more rapid pace than you might set for yourself alone.

FOCUS ON THE BIG PICTURE Day-to-day operations are important, but when you are in a key role, it is more important that you keep your eye on the big picture. Delegate more to others, and when you do, be specific about what you want others to do. Don't be hesitant to direct their activities; this is part of being a leader.

ASSERT YOURSELF MORE The people who work for and with you really want to know where you stand, even if they disagree with you. If someone has an opinion contrary to yours, having a dialogue about this can bring you and the other person into an even closer work relationship. Don't keep your thoughts and insights to yourself. Make a commitment to say more about what you truly think *early in the discussion* and to ask others directly for what you want and need from them.

Development Stretches for Everyone

* Lead (or co-lead) a complex team or project—for example, manage one of the following types of projects: the integration

of a system, process, or procedure across two teams or business units; a construction, renovation, or major move to new office space; or a high-priority project whose resources are in high demand. Use a mentor, peer, or co-leader with excellent project management skills to review your plan and process at the beginning and end of the project and at key milestones.

- Use the services of a mentor or coach with demonstrated expertise in Drive for Results who can help you create a specific development plan and provide you with ongoing feedback and advice.
- Educate yourself further by reading one of the recommended books under "Drive for Results" in the Resources section at the back of this book; read Chapter 5, "Creating High-Performing Teams," and Chapter 6, "Leveraging Your Leadership," in *Bringing Out the Best in Yourself at Work: How to Use the Enneagram System for Success*, by Ginger Lapid-Bogda, Ph.D.

Chapter 3

Strive for Self-Mastery

E motional Intelligence (EQ) is fast becoming the single greatest predictor of leadership success across the globe, and self-mastery is the key element of Emotional Intelligence. Imagine an organization in which leaders are respected and have integrity, know both what they're good at and the areas in which they need to develop, and take responsibility for selecting the best developmental opportunities for themselves. With leadership succession and scarcity being one of the greatest challenges for all organizations, the need for leaders who Strive for Self-Mastery has never been greater.

Self-mastery refers to your ability to understand, accept, and transform your thoughts, feelings, and behavior, with a full understanding that each day will bring new challenges that are in fact opportunities for your self-development. Self-mastery is not about controlling yourself; it is about becoming an expert on yourself through a commitment to honest self-reflection and the ongoing process of learning and growing from your experiences.

Having the ability to Strive for Self-Mastery means that you are skilled in the following six competency components (see Figure 3.1):

FIGURE 3.1 Strive for Self-Mastery

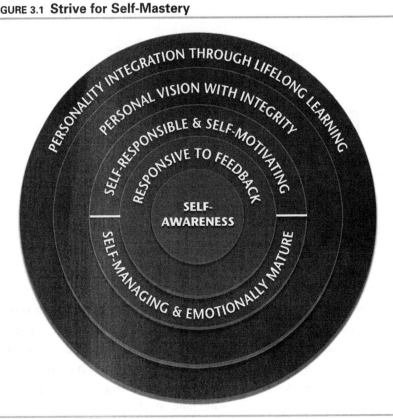

1. Demonstrating a deep level of self-awareness
2. Responding to feedback in meaningful ways
3. Being self-responsible and self-motivating
4. Demonstrating self-management and emotional maturity
5. Possessing integrity that is aligned with your personal vision
6. Being committed to personality integration through lifelong learning

As you read further and reflect on the six competency components of Strive for Self-Mastery, rate yourself in each area on a scale of 1 to 5. This will help you determine both your areas of strength and the areas needing development.

The Six Competency Components of Strive for Self-Mastery

Component 1: Demonstrating a Deep Level of Self-Awareness

This means being aware of your thoughts, feelings, and behaviors when they are occurring, rather than denying them or having a delayed reaction to them; appreciating your strengths and gaining insights from your mistakes; being sensitive to your impact on others; knowing when you are projecting your own thoughts and feelings onto other people, and taking responsibility for this; and having neither an overinflated nor an undervalued sense of self-worth.

Low				High
1	2	3	4	5

Component 2: Responding to Feedback in Meaningful Ways

This involves seeking feedback from multiple sources, intentionally including people who may have something negative to say; being equally receptive to positive and negative feedback; differentiating useful feedback from someone's biased opinion; responding to feedback with a willingness to understand the information and take action when needed; being open to discussion of your shortcomings and to undergoing coaching; and listening to and checking with others before forming final judgments and taking action.

Low				High
1	2	3	4	5

Component 3: Being Self-Responsible and Self-Motivating

This means taking full responsibility for your own thoughts, feelings, behavior, and performance; being forthcoming about your own deeper motivations; being able to realistically differentiate your own areas of personal responsibility from those of others in both positive and negative situations; seeking to solve the problem when things go wrong rather than blaming others; having an internal locus of control rather than being other-directed, so that you do not feel victimized by other people and events; feeling personally powerful enough to make things happen; being energized by tough challenges and able to take constructive action; and being generous with your time and resources, while also taking care of yourself.

Low				High
1	2	3	4	5

Component 4: Demonstrating
Self-Management and Emotional Maturity

This involves displaying thoughtful emotional and behavioral responses, rather than being reactive or acting impulsively; being flexible, being clear, and handling change in productive ways; making wise decisions even when it is not possible to have all the information or the total picture, or when the information is ambiguous, negative, or personally troubling; staying open and receptive when things don't go as you expected; being considered mature by a wide variety of people; maintaining your equilibrium under pressure and helping to keep others calm in a crisis; encouraging honest debate while also being willing to end a discussion and move on; and being sensitive to issues of fairness, due process, and effective pacing when interacting with others and taking action.

Low				High
1	2	3	4	5

Component 5: Possessing Integrity
That Is Aligned with Your Personal Vision

This means having a personal vision that is values-based and includes an understanding of what you want out of life and work; adhering to a set of core values in both normal and challenging situations; showing courage and tenacity, particularly in times of duress; being committed to telling the truth and to transparency of thought, feeling, and action; being able to select the right time and place and the most effective amount of disclosure about both yourself and work situations; keeping confidences and being trusted by a wide variety of people; being looked to by others for direction in times of crisis; not misrepresenting yourself for personal gain; following through on what you say you will do; and being steady and consistent.

Low				High
1	2	3	4	5

Component 6: Being Committed to Personality Integration through Lifelong Learning

This involves using your analytical capacity, emotional intelligence, and ability to take action effectively; staying committed to working on improving yourself by leveraging (but not overusing) your strengths, developing your weaker areas, and compensating for any real limitations by utilizing the talents of other people; taking full responsibility for creating and implementing your development plan; sharing your knowledge willingly and being able to learn from others; continuously reflecting on your experience in order to understand yourself and make self-improvements; and knowing when you need to get help from others and being willing to do so.

Low				High
1	2	3	4	5

We are all at different stages of self-mastery (see Figure 3.2). No matter what your current level, you always have room to grow and to strengthen your capacity. Self-mastery is an ongoing, never-ending process. Along the way, you will experience periods of great insight and personal movement, and you will also encounter times

FIGURE 3.2 **Increase Your Self-Mastery**

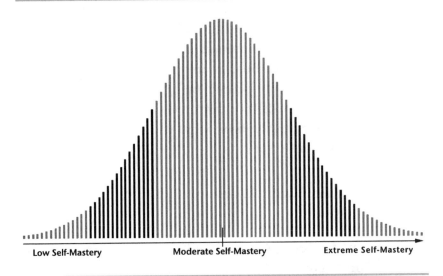

Low Self-Mastery   Moderate Self-Mastery   Extreme Self-Mastery

when you feel frustrated and stuck. During periods of duress, you may even find that your self-mastery level slips. This happens to many people and is not a cause for concern. The insights of the Enneagram and the recommended development activities will help you use difficult times as an opportunity for self-development. Even when it may appear that you are making no progress, if you have patience, you will often find that these periods actually produce the greatest growth of all.

Chart 3.1 shows the three levels of self-mastery[1] (low, moderate, and extreme) and describes how individuals at each stage behave with respect to the competency components of striving for self-mastery. For greater clarity, the six competency components are subdivided into the following categories: self-awareness, responsiveness to feedback, self-responsibility, self-motivation, self-management, emotional maturity, personal vision, integrity, personality integration, and lifelong learning commitment.

---

[1] The Enneagram authors who created and developed the Levels of Development, which can be applied to the issue of self-mastery in leadership, are Don Richard Riso and Russ Hudson in *Personality Types* and *The Wisdom of the Enneagram*. The following material has its genesis in their work, which I am grateful to have their permission to use.

CHART 3.1 Degrees of Self-Mastery

Self-Mastery Component	Low Self-Mastery	Moderate Self-Mastery	Extreme Self-Mastery
General behavior	Exhibits reactive, unproductive behavior most of the time; demonstrates minimal personality integration	May be aware of own inner experience, but responds out of habit more often than not; demonstrates some degree of personality integration	Is highly aware of own inner experience and is able to respond out of choice in productive and highly flexible ways; demonstrates a high degree of personality integration
Self-awareness Self-awareness involves the capacity to be self-observing (being conscious of one's own thoughts, feelings, and behaviors while these are occurring)	Is unaware of own thoughts, feelings, and behaviors and/or is dishonest about true motivations; not self-observing	Can be self-aware, although does not routinely put a high priority on this; has more difficulty being self-aware under duress; is intermittently self-observing	Routinely accesses and is honest about own thoughts, feelings, and behaviors; has a realistic self-image; is able to be self-observing most of the time
Responsiveness to feedback	Defends against, denies, and ignores feedback and/or blames others when criticized	Sometimes responds effectively to feedback, but can also under- or overrespond	Welcomes feedback and uses it constructively; can distinguish between accurate feedback and biased opinion
Self-responsibility	Has distorted perceptions of own motivations; sees others as causing his or her behavior; projects own thoughts and feelings onto others	Can act self-responsibly; under duress, has difficulty differentiating own responsibility from that of others	Takes full responsibility for own actions
Self-motivation	Is either unmotivated or motivated by negative factors such as internal fears or external threats	Is partially self-motivated; often expects others to be the motivating force	Is highly self-motivated and self-determining

(Continued)

71

CHART 3.1 *(Continued)* **Degrees of Self-Mastery**

Self-Mastery Component	Low Self-Mastery	Moderate Self-Mastery	Extreme Self-Mastery
Self-management	Is overcontrolled or out of control; behavior is highly reactive	Sometimes makes conscious choices, but more often acts as if on automatic pilot	Highly self-managing rather than reactive or acting out of habit; is in control without being controlled or controlling; makes conscious and constructive choices
Emotional maturity	Perceives self as victim	Fluctuates between personal reactivity and the ability to have perspective on self, others, and events	Is mature in almost all situations; can rise above personal responses to understand multiple factors and perspectives affecting the situation
Personal vision	Has no personal vision or has a negative vision	Has an unarticulated or oversimplified personal vision	Has a clear, positive personal vision
Integrity	Engages in behaviors and actions inconsistent with values, or has destructive values	Has generally positive values, but behavior is not always consistent with values	Has positive values and "walks the talk"
Personality integration	Behavior reflects a low level of accurate self-knowledge as well as incongruity among thoughts, feelings, and behaviors	Behavior reflects intermittent self-knowledge and/or an overemphasis on thoughts, feelings, or actions; behavior not always congruent with feelings or stated intentions	Behavior demonstrates a high degree of self-knowledge and is congruent and integrated with thoughts and feelings
Lifelong learning commitment	Has no commitment to self-development or lifelong learning	Has a moderate to low commitment to self-development; engages in · self-development when under duress	Has a high commitment to ongoing self-development, demonstrated through continuous action

72

Given the self-mastery descriptions in Chart 3.1, how would you rate your general level of self-mastery on a 1 to 5 scale, with 1 being low and 5 being extreme (high)?

Low		Moderate		High
1	2	3	4	5

We all have variations in our self-mastery behavior. *What is your range of self-mastery? What conditions or factors cause you to operate at your highest and lowest degrees of self-mastery?*

Enneagram Dimensions of Strive for Self-Mastery

The Enneagram dimensions of Strive for Self-Mastery are described on the following pages for each of the nine Enneagram styles, including behaviors at the three different levels of self-mastery (low, moderate, and extreme). For each Enneagram style, the descriptions are followed by three specifically designed self-development activities. As you read the activities in this chapter suggested for your Enneagram style, ask yourself this question: *Which of the activities will be the easiest for me to do?* This activity will give you incremental benefits. Then ask yourself the following question: *Which of the activities will be the greatest stretch for me?* This activity will accelerate your development.

Enneagram Style Ones

Ones seek a perfect world and work diligently to improve both themselves and everyone and everything around them.

Enneagram Style
DILIGENCE ①

CHART 3.2 Ones: Levels of Self-Mastery

	Descriptions
Extreme self-mastery	**The Serene Acceptor**
	Core understanding: Accepting that everything, including imperfection, is as it should be.
	Enneagram Ones who demonstrate extreme self-mastery take their self-development work seriously and understand, befriend, and diminish the influence of their inner critic. While still focused and discerning, they also exhibit dignity, patience, and a peaceful acceptance of the idea that they and everyone else are perfect even with their imperfections. They observe their negative responses before they express them and then make the choice of whether or not to share their reactions. They are light-hearted, and they know how to have fun and let their humor emerge spontaneously.
	Example: In her 20s and 30s, Lillian's reactivity and tendency to be highly critical had caused problems for her in both her personal and professional lives. Because of this, Lillian had pursued multiple avenues in an attempt to understand herself better. Having explored her inner critic and learned to observe rather than to express or repress it, Lillian now feels free to enjoy everything as it is rather than focusing on how she thinks it "should" be.
Moderate self-mastery	**The Teacher**
	Core concern: Making a mistake, being imperfect.
	Ones with moderate self-mastery can be discerning and judgmental, opinionated and reactive, highly organized and methodical, witty and wry, and easily irritated and resentful. Events that suggest mistakes on either the One's part or another's—particularly mistakes that violate the One's values, high standards, or sense of him- or herself as being beyond reproach—cause Ones to react with strong negativity. Although they're often aware of their critical thoughts and feelings and try to hide them from others, they often convey their reactions through body language, or they may erupt angrily at a later time over something that is of little consequence. They can also become so enamored of excellence in others that they overlook otherwise dysfunctional behavior in these individuals.
	Example: At a large conference of which Samuel was the co-chair, a presenter whom he had highly recommended was not being well received. As the presenter exceeded his scheduled time and people were walking out halfway through his talk, Samuel's co-chair whispered in his ear that she was concerned about the time. Samuel retorted loudly, within earshot of others, "Don't you dare interrupt this presentation!"

(Continued)

CHART 3.2 *(Continued)*   **Ones: Levels of Self-Mastery**

	Descriptions
Low self-mastery	**The Judge**
	Core fear: Being bad or malevolent; having something deeply, intrinsically wrong with them.
	Ones with low self-mastery can be intolerant, tightly wound, inflexible, volatile, unstable, and punishing. Judgmental and unforgiving, they become prosecutor, judge, and jury, all rolled into one. These reactions can be aimed either at others or at themselves and can be provoked by even minor perceived infractions.
	Example: Janet was certain (but wrongly) that Ryan had stolen her ideas, so when he came up for a promotion, she nixed his candidacy. While doing this, Janet made up a reason why Ryan was not fit for the position; behind the scenes, however, she made it known that he was a person who lacked moral integrity.

Development Stretches for Ones

PAY ATTENTION TO YOUR PATTERNS OF RIGHT/WRONG THINKING Without trying to change yourself, write down all the ways in which you judge, evaluate, and critique events, objects, other people, and yourself. Include your language patterns (your thoughts, words you have written or spoken) and nonverbal behavior and identify what triggers these responses in you. Paradoxically, the more you become aware of this behavior without trying to change it, the more you will gradually begin to shift your responses.

USE YOUR FEELINGS OF RESENTMENT AS A CLUE TO DISCERN DEEPER-SEATED ANGER Whenever you feel irritation or resentment, ask yourself these questions: *Am I really angry about something else that has little to do with this person or situation? Is there some core value that I hold that I believe has been violated? Is there something in how I see myself or how I want to see myself that has been threatened?*

LEARN TO APPRECIATE WHAT IS POSITIVE IN EVERYTHING—EVENTS, INANIMATE OBJECTS, YOURSELF, AND THE BEHAVIOR OF OTHER PEOPLE

Whenever you have negative reactions, add an equal number of positive ones. If you try to erase or submerge your negative feelings or thoughts, they are likely to become stronger or else go underground temporarily, only to reappear more strongly at a later date. However, if you add positive reactions to the mix, you will begin to neutralize some of the negativity and build up your ability to see the positive.

Enneagram Style Twos

Twos want to be liked, try to meet the needs of others, and attempt to orchestrate the people and events in their lives.

Enneagram Style
② GIVING

CHART 3.3 **Twos: Levels of Self-Mastery**

	Descriptions
Extreme self-mastery	**The Humble One**
	Core understanding: There is a profound purpose to everything that occurs that is independent of one's own efforts.
	Enneagram Twos with extreme self-mastery do not give to get, and they do not feel a need to reinforce their self-worth by getting others to like them and orchestrating other people's lives. Gentle, generous, humble, inclusive, and deeply compassionate, they give simply to give and express their own deeper needs directly. Their sense of well-being and warmth draw others to them.
	Example: Before the age of 35, Maurice would have avoided or felt hostile toward people who criticized him or made excessive demands on him. However, after doing a great deal of self-development work, Maurice found that when these situations occurred, he was able just to listen to the kernel of wisdom in a criticism, say no nicely to demands that he could not meet, and carry no lingering resentments when others did not follow his advice.
Moderate self-mastery	**The Friend**
	Core concern: Feeling valuable, liked, needed, appreciated, and worthy.

(Continued)

CHART 3.3 *(Continued)*   **Twos: Levels of Self-Mastery**

	Descriptions
	Twos with moderate self-mastery often have many friends and/or are at the center of social groups or institutions. They read people well and tend to engage others through flattery, giving attention, doing favors, and other forms of interpersonal behavior—such as showing warmth—that are sometimes sincere, but sometimes not. They may also be emotional, aggressive, and hovering. Having difficulty saying no, they often orchestrate interpersonal dynamics behind the scenes. They can be compassionate and helpful, often offering useful advice that they expect others to take.
	Example: If Jill had a negative feeling about someone, that person wouldn't know it unless he or she was part of Jill's inner circle. With this group of friends, Jill shared what she really thought about everyone, and these comments were often far more negative than any comments she expressed directly to the individuals involved.
Low self-mastery	**The Manipulator**
	Core fear: Being unwanted, discarded, and deemed intrinsically unworthy.
	Twos with low self-mastery can be master manipulators, using guilt, blame, or shame to control others. These Twos fall into psychological despair, then try to make the other person feel responsible. When their efforts are thwarted, these Twos will use full force to get what they want, but will take no responsibility for their unproductive behavior.
	Example: Although Vince had been a well-respected executive coach, he felt threatened when the organizations with which he worked began to use other coaches as well. He not only became more prescriptive and controlling with his clients, but also began to systematically undermine his competitors with people he knew in the client organizations.

Development Stretches for Twos

SPEND TIME ALONE   Engage in solo activities that allow you either to reflect or to do nice things for yourself (self-nurturing). When alone, Twos have a tendency to maintain contact with others through e-mails, phone calls, or even just thinking about someone else. Time spent truly alone will give you the chance to pay more attention to your inner experience instead of continually diverting your focus to others.

ASK YOURSELF: *WHAT DO I REALLY NEED?* Becoming more aware of your feelings can lead to greater clarity about your true needs. Repeatedly ask yourself what you need until your answers become deeper. Or, ask yourself the simple question *What am I feeling right now?* and explore these feelings in depth. This question is important because Twos tend to repress their feelings—that is, when they have a feeling, they may either not acknowledge it or underestimate its depth and intensity.

EXAMINE THE WAYS IN WHICH YOU GIVE IN ORDER TO GET SOMETHING IN RETURN Make a list of everything you have done for other people in the last week, whether it's bringing someone home from the hospital or listening longer than you may have desired. Next to each item, write down what you wanted in return. Continue this list for several weeks. You may find that your behavior changes simply as a result of your becoming more aware of giving in order to get. If not, then reflect on the price you pay for continuing this behavior.

Enneagram Style Threes

Enneagram Style
③
PERFORM

Threes organize their lives to achieve specific goals and to appear successful in order to gain the respect and admiration of others.

CHART 3.4 **Threes: Levels of Self-Mastery**

	Descriptions
Extreme self-mastery	**The Believer**
	Core understanding: Everyone has intrinsic value, and there is a natural flow and order to everything.
	Threes with extreme self-mastery have looked inside themselves to find out who they really are (apart from what they accomplish) and what they truly feel (instead of masking their emotions). Willing to admit that they don't always feel

(Continued)

CHART 3.4 *(Continued)* **Threes: Levels of Self-Mastery**

Descriptions

on top of things and that they have foibles like everyone else, these Threes possess a contagious enthusiasm, genuineness, and confidence. Moreover, they are deeply spontaneous because they trust that they are not responsible for making everything happen.

Example: After recovering from a critical illness, Pam began a process of intense self-examination. Not only did she learn to examine her own intense drive to succeed, often at the expense of herself, her family, and her colleagues, but she also realized that she could value herself simply for who she was, apart from her accomplishments. As a result, Pam became not only much more relaxed but also more authentic. She became a person that she genuinely liked.

Moderate self-mastery	**The Star**

Core concern: Feeling successful, avoiding failure, and gaining the respect of others.

At the mid-level of self-mastery, Threes focus on goals and work, usually at the expense of their relationships. Driven and competitive, they seek recognition and have a need to outdistance their rivals. Although Threes at this level often appear friendly, they're most often motivated by their desire for success. Many times, what looks like an emotional response from them is more the kind of response that they believe a person in their situation should have, not an authentic reaction. At times, even they wonder who they really are.

Example: To Devon's colleagues, it looked as if nothing ever shook his confidence. He was able to give speeches to 500 people, work with the most challenging clients, and complete tasks under a tremendous amount of pressure. While many people enjoyed and admired Devon, others perceived him as superficial.

Low self-mastery	**The Calculator**

Core fear: Extreme fear of failure, since failure would make a Three feel that he or she has no value.

At the lowest level of self-mastery, Threes may be described as phony, self-serving, opportunistic, and a variety of other adjectives that are often used to depict people who go after whatever they want (usually, the external trappings of success—e.g., money, status, and fame), with little regard for whoever or whatever stands in their way. Although they become extremely isolated, these Threes hide their inner emptiness by believing that they actually are the image or façade they have created. However, that image is only a shell masking a hollow interior.

(Continued)

CHART 3.4 *(Continued)*   **Threes: Levels of Self-Mastery**

Descriptions
Example: In her fund-raising job for a nonprofit organization, Heather constantly interrupted people or demanded attention by using an extremely loud voice. When she did this while trying to solicit funds, her attempts were unsuccessful. Most people thought she was obnoxious, and others felt used by her, perceiving her as being interested in interacting with them only as a means of getting money and making herself look good.

Development Stretches for Threes

TAKE THE TIME TO GET TO KNOW YOURSELF   Make a commitment to spend at least 30 minutes each day just *being*. This means not working or engaging in any activities in which you focus on something external (such as watching a film or going shopping). If you don't quite understand the idea of "being," ask three people who are very different from you what this concept means to them, and how they go about simply being. Experiment with some of the ideas they suggest.

LEARN TO AVOID OVERIDENTIFYING WITH YOUR WORK   Make a list of answers to this question: *Who am I?* Now place a check mark next to all the items that reflect roles you play, such as spouse, worker, and family member. How many of the items on your list are not roles? Now answer this question: *If I am not the roles I play, then who am I?* Keep adding to this list on a daily basis, and commit to appreciating that who you are is far more than just the roles you play.

ACKNOWLEDGE YOUR WEAKNESSES   When you are feeling concerned, anxious, or sad, can you admit this to someone else? Can you admit to and discuss your mistakes or failures? If your answer is yes, then practice doing this even more. If your answer is no, then seriously consider what it is *within you* that keeps you from doing this. Imagine how you would feel if you could allow yourself to acknowledge and share more of your weaknesses. Commit to discussing at least one of your weaknesses or areas of anxiety with one new person each day.

Enneagram Style Fours

Fours desire deep connections both with their own interior worlds and with other people, and they feel most alive when they authentically express their personal experiences and feelings.

Enneagram Style
MOOD ④

CHART 3.5 **Fours: Levels of Self-Mastery**

	Descriptions
Extreme self-mastery	**The Appreciative One**
	Core understanding: Everything has meaning and significance, and everyone is connected at the deepest levels.
	Enneagram Fours with extreme self-mastery emanate centeredness, tranquility, and calm. Their artistic expression is universal because they are open to both the delight and the sadness that life brings. Grateful and graceful, they deeply appreciate what they have rather than lamenting what they lack. These Fours exhibit an inner wholeness and constancy, and their gentle empathy and genuine concern draws others to them. When facing a difficult challenge, they do not go into emotional turmoil because they are able to reflect on their own experience, understand the other person's point of view, and examine the related contextual factors.
	Example: In the past, Andrew would often be so overwhelmed by his feelings that he would become immobilized, then lash out at either himself or others. After experiencing a life-threatening illness, Andrew chose to make the effort to appreciate who he was and what he had rather than focusing on what was missing. He now demonstrates great emotional balance; when a difficulty arises, Andrew is able to handle it with poise and grace.

(Continued)

CHART 3.5 *(Continued)*   **Fours: Levels of Self-Mastery**

	Descriptions
Moderate self-mastery	**The Unique One**

Core concern: Feeling significant, feeling special, and finding meaning.

With a moderate degree of self-mastery, Fours can be either dramatic or reticent as they seek meaningful relationships and authentic conversations. They can also be quite imaginative, transforming their inner experience, anguish, and search for meaning into artistic expression. Their conversations are frequently self-referencing, with excessive use of words such as *I*, *me*, and *mine*; telling of prolonged personal stories, and redirection of conversations to themselves. Constantly comparing themselves with others to determine whether they are superior or deficient, these Fours have difficulty being self-accepting. Yearning, moody, and sometimes melancholic, they can also be reflective, empathic, and gifted.

Example: Nancy was the author of several excellent books on self-development and was considered highly creative. Yet no matter what she created or how much self-reflection she did, Nancy never felt satisfied. She often wondered: *Will I ever be happy?*

Low self-mastery   **The Defective One**

Core fear: Being intrinsically defective and completely disconnected.

Fours with low self-mastery are bitter, depressed, emotionally volatile, hypersensitive, and self-absorbed, and they feel deeply wounded by anything they perceive as a slight or a rejection. Unable to extricate themselves from their negative self-perception, they can become tormented, deeply ashamed, alienated, rageful, withdrawn, or highly aggressive, accusing individuals in particular and life in general of intentionally harming them. While they may express themselves in a variety of artistic forms, their art has a tragic quality from which there seems to be no escape.

Example: Jonas was such an envious person that whenever anyone else was the recipient of an award, was promoted, received attention in a group, or even was spoken of positively, he would become highly agitated and then either do something to draw attention to himself or criticize the other person. Because it was clear that these behaviors annoyed and offended others, Jonas became increasingly sullen, withdrawn, and intermittently aggressive.

Development Stretches for Fours

APPRECIATE THE ORDINARY   Do a task that you find tedious, paying attention to every aspect of it. Stay in the present moment while doing the task, not thinking about anyone or anything else, and find pleasure in it. Select a different mundane task each day and follow these same directions. Learning to appreciate the present will help you focus less on both the past and the future.

FIND ENJOYMENT IN OTHER PEOPLE'S POSITIVE QUALITIES AND ACCOMPLISHMENTS   A counterintuitive way to do this is to first take genuine pleasure in your own positive attributes. Do not use any caveats or "buts," such as "I'm smart, but he's smarter" or "I'm empathic, but I spend too much time thinking about myself." Simply enjoy who you are. Once you can do this, allow yourself to appreciate other people's qualities and achievements. Each day, think positively about yourself, then select another person to think positively about without making any comparisons to yourself.

MINIMIZE YOUR SELF-REFERENCING BEHAVIOR   Self-referencing behavior means that you tend to focus on yourself rather than on other people—even if you are not aware of doing this—through word choice, storytelling, and the sharing of intense experiences and feelings. To challenge yourself every day, practice talking with one person and really listening to him or her, making no verbal references to yourself and not sharing any personal stories.

Enneagram Style Fives

Fives thirst for knowledge and use emotional detachment as a way of keeping involvement with others to a minimum.

Enneagram Style
KNOWLEDGE ⑤

CHART 3.6 **Fives: Levels of Self-Mastery**

	Descriptions
Extreme self-mastery	**The Integrated Wizard** **Core understanding:** True wisdom involves an integration of thoughts, feelings, and action and comes from direct experience. When Fives have done the personal work of learning to fully experience their feelings in the moment and to completely engage in life rather than observing it from afar, they become lively, spontaneous, joyful, and imaginative. Their wisdom comes from the full integration of the head, heart, and body. These Fives have moved beyond a primarily cerebral way of existence into a state of contagious zest for ideas, feelings, and experiences. **Example:** From what everyone can observe directly, Tina is very different from what she was like two years ago. After having engaged in some deep personal development work following marital difficulties, Tina is now animated, interactive, and expressive. She is also an excellent listener, one who listens with her heart as well as her head, and people constantly seek her out for personal advice.
Moderate self-mastery	**The Remote Expert** **Core concern:** Conserving inner resources and energy, maintaining privacy, and accumulating knowledge in order to feel competent. At the mid-level of self-mastery, Fives appear remote and private, guarding their time, energy, and autonomy and disliking surprises. They avoid situations in which they are likely to be the center of attention, as well as circumstances that require them to reveal personal information. Detached from their feelings of the moment, they are able to reconnect with their emotions later, when they are alone and feel comfortable. Hungering for knowledge about anything that interests them, they keep their needs to a minimum and tend to be guarded and controlled, although they can be highly spontaneous with the few people they trust. **Example:** At the self-development training program in which Troy was a participant, he said very little. When he did speak, everyone sat back and listened closely because they were curious about him. During breaks and at lunch, Troy kept to himself, standing alone or coming to the dining room after everyone else was already seated. The only time anyone saw him appear extremely uncomfortable was when another program participant said to him, "Troy, tell us something about yourself. We hardly know you."

(Continued)

CHART 3.6 *(Continued)*   **Fives: Levels of Self-Mastery**

	Descriptions
Low self-mastery	**The Fearful Strategist** **Core fear:** Being helpless, incapable, depleted, and overtaken. At the lowest level of self-mastery, Fives become frightened, withdrawn, and isolated. Hostile and haunted, they come to believe that others are planning to do them harm; as a consequence, they will plot and scheme to harm others as a way of circumventing what they imagine will be done to them. Secretive and implosive, they remove themselves from interaction with others and have extremely limited access to their own feelings. Their minds become so overactive that their mental processes seem out of control, even to them. **Example:** Emily, an attorney, felt extremely threatened when the firm hired Scott, an outgoing lawyer with a long client list, to work in her department. Within three months, he had established more positive relationships with other lawyers in the firm than Emily had established in three years. Concerned that Scott appeared to be a superstar, Emily did everything she could to undermine him. For example, she refused to work with him on cases or allow him to use the department's paralegal staff, and she made derogatory comments about him to clients and to anyone in the firm who would listen to her.

Development Stretches for Fives

ALLOW YOURSELF TO NEED OTHERS   Each week, think of one thing that you can't provide completely for yourself and that you therefore need from others. Then think of someone who might be able to provide this for you, and ask that person if he or she will do so. What matters most is not whether the person says yes, but that you identify a need and then ask for it to be met.

CONNECT WITH AND EXPRESS YOUR FEELINGS   For two or three days, every hour on the hour, ask yourself this question: *What am I feeling right now?* Don't settle for a one-word answer. Then ask this: *And what else am I feeling?* After three days, continue asking yourself both questions, but do so at those times when you are aware that you are becoming extremely analytical. These moments of extreme analysis may be covering over your feelings.

INCREASE YOUR CAPACITY TO ENGAGE RATHER THAN TO WITHDRAW
When you attend any sort of social gathering, force yourself to stand or sit right in the middle of where people are interacting. When you do this, look at other people and smile, which will encourage them to approach you. When they do, engage in interaction by asking a question or telling them something about yourself.

Enneagram Style Sixes

Sixes have insightful minds and create anticipatory and worst-case scenarios to help themselves feel prepared in case something goes wrong.

⑥ Enneagram Style
DOUBT

CHART 3.7   **Sixes: Levels of Self-Mastery**

	Descriptions
Extreme self-mastery	**The Courageous One**
	Core understanding: Meaning and support exist both inside and outside themselves.
	Intellectual and insightful, Sixes with extreme self-mastery have learned to trust their own inner authority rather than look to other people to keep them safe. As a result, they are confident, calm, and resilient, and they connect with others in a deep, steady, and warmhearted way. Because they have learned to trust their own inner authority, Sixes with extreme self-mastery are clear and courageous. They know that they can look after themselves and that there is little in the world from which they truly need to be protected.
	Example: After working with an executive coach for two years, Saul had grown confident, consistent, and courageous. Because of this, he could deliver both good and bad news to others with warmth, support, and excellent timing, picking the best opportunity for delivering information in order to achieve the most constructive outcome.
Moderate self-mastery	**The Loyalist**
	Core concern: Safety, belonging, and being able to trust.
	Sixes with moderate self-mastery can be insightful, clever, overly busy, endearing, and approval-seeking, but they can

(Continued)

CHART 3.7 *(Continued)*   **Sixes: Levels of Self-Master**

Descriptions

also be antiauthority, wavering, short-tempered, and reactive. Alternating between being trusting and being distrusting, they are plagued by doubts and confusion. On the one hand, these Sixes desire the safety that cohesive groups can provide; on the other, they fear groups unless these groups are characterized by a strong sense of like-mindedness. They are thus loyal to friends, groups, and leaders whom they trust, but that trust is tenuous at best and is easily broken if others do not live up to the Six's hopes and expectations.

Example: In a team meeting of 30 people, Jeannie was sitting on the edge of her chair, feeling so frustrated that she finally blurted out, in a very loud voice, that she completely disagreed with the assignment that the division manager had given everyone in the room. While some of the team members silently agreed with her, they were aghast and amazed that Jeannie would have taken such a confrontational approach. From Jeannie's perspective, she was merely giving voice to what needed to be said, and in doing so was, in her view, protecting her team.

Low self-mastery   **The Coward**

Core fear: Having no support or sense of meaning and being unable to survive.

Sixes with low self-mastery display an extreme amount of anxiety and frenzy as they go about trying to make their frightening world less dangerous. They engage in continuous worst-case scenario development and projection, imagining all the bad things that could happen to them and believing that these creations of the imagination are completely true. With a tendency toward paranoia, these Sixes can become clingingly dependent, panicky, and punitive. Looking for solace, they find little, because they reject anyone who disagrees with their worldview or dares to offer an opinion contrary to theirs.

Example: Carlos was brilliant, but when he worked with other people, particularly those who were talented and had strong personalities, he was involved in constant battles with them because of his fears that they would (1) take over his work product, (2) do something to harm its quality, or (3) take advantage of him by claiming credit for what he had done. Ultimately, others found Carlos's continuous accusations about their motivations too much to deal with, and no one wanted to work with him.

Development Stretches for Sixes

SHIFT YOUR FOCUS FROM HALF EMPTY TO HALF FULL   Each morning, start your day with 15 minutes of thinking about everything that is going well and is problem free. You can look at items in your home, objects you see on your way to work, and aspects of yourself. This practice will actually begin to change some of your brain's pathways.

TRUST YOUR OWN AUTHORITY   Make a list of all the times you have followed your own advice and found it to be advice well taken. Next to each item, write down all the benefits that accrued from following your own advice. Think of this self-advice as the wisdom of your own inner authority. Each time you feel confused about what to do, ask yourself this question: *If I were going to follow my own inner authority, what advice would it give me?* Then follow that advice.

DIFFERENTIATE BETWEEN AN INSIGHT AND A PURE PROJECTION   Can you tell the difference between an insight and a pure projection? Do you know when you are really being perceptive (an insight) rather than purely projecting (making something up entirely in your own mind, so that instead of reflecting reality, this view actually reflects what you think, feel, or want to do)? Spend 15 minutes each morning making a list of your uncensored thoughts about what you believe will happen that day. At the end of the day, review your list. For each item on the list, answer this question: *Was this an insight, a pure projection, or a mixture of the two? How can I tell the difference?* After several weeks of this, the question *How can I tell the difference?* will give you useful information.

Enneagram Style Sevens

Sevens crave the stimulation of new ideas, people, and experiences; avoid pain; and create elaborate future plans that will allow them to keep all of their options open.

Enneagram Style
OPTIONS (7)

CHART 3.8 **Sevens: Levels of Self-Mastery**

	Descriptions
Extreme self-mastery	**The Focused Inspirer**
	Core understanding: Genuine happiness and a feeling of wholeness come from integrating negative and positive experiences.
	Enneagram Sevens who have chosen to do the difficult work of self-development have learned how to tame their highly active minds, which is not an easy task. In learning to do this, Sevens increase their capacity to focus—on people, tasks, feelings, and learning something in depth—rather than disperse their energy. They complete their work effortlessly, listen well, and emanate happiness and peaceful joy. Spirited and deep, these Sevens have a true sense of wonder and inspire those around them, not by energizing them, but by their calm, yet vital presence.
	Example: It took Brenda a long time to deal with the loss of both of her parents when she was still quite young. However, in dealing with this issue when she was in her thirties, through a great deal of self-reflection and outside help, Brenda had developed a capacity for compassion and had learned to stop avoiding painful issues. Because of this, she was able to focus and to be available to others for extended conversations about important issues. At the same time, she retained her ability to think outside the box, and her ability to do this had actually increased, as had her ability to inspire others to take action.
Moderate self-mastery	**The Stimulator**
	Core concern: Satisfaction, stimulation, and feeling good.
	At the mid-level of self-mastery, Sevens can be creative and engaging, but also frenzied and impatient. Their minds work so fast that they often have a great many half-thought-through notions, most of which they express. They also tend to overestimate their competence or knowledge, considering themselves quick studies. Addicted to the adrenaline rush of experiences that are new and stimulating, they sometimes

(Continued)

CHART 3.8 *(Continued)* **Sevens: Levels of Self-Mastery**

Descriptions

find it difficult to focus and carry tasks through to completion. Energetic and playful, when confronted about something they have done that is less than stellar, they will reframe the event by portraying it in positive rather than negative terms.

Example: Many people seemed to like and enjoy Charles and to appreciate many of his insights and ideas. However, they also wondered why his response to a serious or difficult issue was usually to make light of the issue or to tell a joke, as if to refocus the conversation on something less intense, thereby minimizing its importance.

Low self-mastery	**The Frenetic Escape Artist**

Core fear: Pain, deprivation, and not feeling whole.

At the lowest level of self-mastery, Sevens are so consumed by anxiety that they alternate between manic behavior (hyperactivity to an extreme) and depression. Joyless and prone to causing scenes, these Sevens are perpetually fleeing from self-reflection and looking around to see whom they can blame for their circumstances. Feeling cornered and trapped, they engage in self-destructive or self-defeating behaviors.

Example: Although Sherri was bright, talented, and full of ideas, she created havoc in the team she managed. She did not provide adequate performance expectations for her team members, was too busy to train them, did not take the time to develop adequate work plans, and ran her team meetings with inadequate guidance. In her mind, everyone was equal, and she should not act like a boss; she felt it was important for everyone, including her, to give voice to criticisms of the organization. After Sherri's boss had received numerous complaints from the team members, her boss gave her straightforward feedback about these issues. Sherri's response was to create a series of confrontations with her boss in the office, to reprimand her team members, and to increase her criticisms of the organization, repeating them to whoever would listen. In the end, Sherri was fired.

Development Stretches for Sevens

LEARN TO LISTEN FULLY TO OTHERS   After you have had a conversation with someone, ask that person these questions: *What percentage of the time were you talking, and what percentage of the* *time was I talking? At any time during the conversation, did you feel that I was interrupting, not listening, or appearing distracted?* Do this at least once a day with different people. Listen fully to the answers, without giving counterarguments or explanations for why you did what you did. Your task is to have someone reflect your behavior back to you, whether you agree with the reflection or not.

LEARN TO GO INWARD The biggest challenge for you will be to focus on your physical sensations and emotional reactions. For an hour each day, practice placing your focus on your emotions and physical sensations. Once you have developed the ability to do this, practice this inner focusing on a regular basis, particularly at times when you feel either highly stimulated or anxious.

DEVELOP YOUR EMOTIONAL REPERTOIRE Using the categories mad, glad, sad, and afraid, make lists of all the events in the past year during which you have felt each of these emotions. Analyze your lists to determine which of these four feelings you tend to experience most and least often. Spend one hour thinking about how you can expand your emotional repertoire by eliciting feelings in the emotional categories that you experience least often. Write down your answers. This activity will help you to relate more deeply both to yourself and to others.

Enneagram Style Eights

Eights pursue the truth, like to keep situations under control, want to make important things happen, and try to hide their vulnerability.

Enneagram Style
CHALLENGE ⑧

CHART 3.9 **Eights: Levels of Self-Mastery**

	Descriptions
Extreme self-mastery	**The Truth Seeker**

Core understanding: Vulnerability and weakness are part of being human, and multiple truths must be assimilated in order to reach the real truth.

The challenge for Eights who seek extreme self-mastery is to learn to manage their vast energy and reservoir of anger by fully acknowledging their long-hidden vulnerability. When they have accomplished this, Eights are generous, strong, openhearted, and open-minded. Although still direct and honest, they speak from the heart and the head as well as from the gut, and they solicit and embrace differing opinions. Their protectiveness of others is gentle rather than controlling, and they are grounded, warm, and deeply confident.

Example: The first time Edward became tearful in public, he was deeply embarrassed and didn't even know what was bothering him. His strong and brave façade was crumbling, and he worried that he was falling apart and losing everyone's respect. This event, however, catapulted Edward into a deep level of introspection, and he emerged as a deeply confident, gentle, and empathic person, one whom others would go to for a sympathetic word, a keen insight, and a feeling of being safe.

Moderate self-mastery	**The Immovable Rock**

Core concern: Self-protection and showing weakness.

Eights who possess moderate self-mastery try hard to manage their frustration and anger. Although they can be sensitive and generous, they can also be controlling, dominating, and aggressive. Quick to respond, they are also quick to take action, and they expect immediate responses from others. They have strong opinions, and their presence is almost always felt, even when they are quiet. As a result, others often look to them for decisions and clarity of direction. Although these Eights can be humble regarding their accomplishments and often become embarrassed when complimented in public, they also like to be appreciated and respected. If given a large challenge, they rise to the occasion. Try to constrain these Eights or force them to contain their vast energy, and they become angry, blaming, and/or sick.

Example: One of Carla's greatest attributes was her ability to create an organization that was extremely successful and well respected, with a work environment that fostered teamwork and high morale. Because of this, she felt confused and demoralized when her human resources

(Continued)

CHART 3.9 *(Continued)*	**Eights: Levels of Self-Mastery**
	Descriptions
	director told her that people were leaving the company because Carla intimidated them. Although she had been told before that people found her intimidating, Carla had never understood the reason. When she asked the human resources director for more information, Carla was told this: "They find you warm and generous one day, and then the next day, for no reason they can understand, they find you irritable and short-tempered. These fluctuations scare people."
Low self-mastery	**The Bully**
	Core fear: Being harmed, controlled, or extremely vulnerable.
	Eights with low self-mastery can be direct to the point of cruelty, unleashing a flood of anger and destructive punitive behavior. Believing that they must overcome their enemies by whatever means necessary, they justify their actions by blaming the other person for what is, in fact, their inability to acknowledge their own intense vulnerability. At worst, they can deteriorate into antisocial and/or violent behavior, because they cannot contain or control their explosive anger.
	Example: Ray was one of the new owners of a newly constructed four-unit condominium complex that was having serious problems with construction defects. He was so certain that the other condominium owners were being naïve and making decisions that were not in his best interests that he secretly contacted the developer directly, relayed confidential information from a meeting of the homeowners' association, and reached a side agreement with the developer. When the other unit owners asked him why he had done this, he responded, "Well, the rest of you are too stupid to know better, and the developer thinks you're all idiots anyway. You're just jealous because you didn't make your own deals."

Development Stretches for Eights

TAKE CARE OF YOURSELF PHYSICALLY   Get enough sleep on a regular basis, eat healthfully and in moderation, and exercise regularly. The more you take care of yourself physically, instead of wearing yourself down to exhaustion, the less emotionally reactive you will be.

SLOW DOWN YOUR IMPULSE TO TAKE ACTION   Each time you feel the impulse to take action—for example, giving an opinion, suggesting or demanding that someone else do something, or in any way mobilizing forward action—stop yourself and think: *What is going on inside me that makes me want to move forward so quickly? What will happen if I don't take action right now?*

SHARE YOUR FEELINGS OF VULNERABILITY. How many times have you allowed yourself to feel sad or cry in the last year? How many times have you become angry? It is likely that you have been angry far more often than you have been sad. Can you identify areas of vulnerability that your anger may be masking? Even if your anger has been the result of another person's being treated poorly or someone's not stepping up to perform a task for which he or she is responsible, can you identify an area of your own vulnerability that this is activating?

Enneagram Style Nines

Nines seek peace, harmony, and positive mutual regard and dislike conflict, tension, and ill will.

⑨ Enneagram Style
HARMONY

CHART 3.10 Nines: Levels of Self-Mastery

	Descriptions
Extreme self-mastery	**The Fully Conscious One**
	Core understanding: Unconditional regard connects everyone and everything.
	Nines who have reached the level of extreme self-mastery no longer have difficulty taking a stand. In fact, they approach life in an active and purposeful way, knowing that they have the right to voice their opinions. They are involved, engaged, and extremely vital. Solid, substantial, and alert, they are also serene, deeply content, and "in flow," all of which come from a firm inner core.
	Example: Heidi had been a whistle-blower when she worked for the federal government procurement office. She had

(Continued)

CHART 3.10 *(Continued)*   **Nines: Levels of Self-Mastery**

	Descriptions
	discovered a major theft ring and, after many sleepless nights, had chosen to file a report. Four years later, Heidi prevailed. From this experience, she had learned that she was capable of facing conflict head-on. Because Heidi had faced her biggest fears and had changed as a result, she was engaged and fully present, and she welcomed conflict as a way of building relationships.
Moderate self-mastery	**The Harmonizer**
	Core concern: Stability, harmony, and being heard.
	Nines at the moderate level of self-mastery want everyone to get along, preferring peace and harmony above all else. Because of this, they become adept at mediating differences but are highly anxious when conflict is directed at them. These Nines lose focus, pursuing activities that distract them rather than attending to the challenges in front of them. Nines at this level have trouble asking for what they want, prefer the predictable pace of routine activities, and act so agreeably that they often have many friends, or at least many people who like being around them. They will rarely take a stand on something they believe in, opting instead to go along with what others want.
	Example: Brad was a capable and conscientious engineering manager, able to steer important projects through to completion. When controversy arose among members of his project team, Brad would listen at length to the individuals involved and then try to mediate. Sometimes the conflicts would gradually fade away, sometimes they would just go underground, and sometimes they would escalate into organizational warfare. When the last occurred, Brad would throw up his hands, as if there was nothing he could do about it.
Low self-mastery	**The Sleeper**
	Core fear: Separation from others, being controlled, and discord.
	Nines with a low degree of self-mastery do not pay attention to themselves, and they have no energy to pay attention to anyone else. They ignore even the most life-threatening problems, refusing to face the most obvious consequences of their desire to pretend that everything is okay. Consistently neglectful and forgetful, Nines with low self-mastery become chronically sluggish and immovable. However, should they feel pressured to do something they don't want to do, they become passive-aggressive, saying yes but meaning no, or they burst forth with unleashed and seemingly bottomless fury.

(Continued)

CHART 3.10 *(Continued)*   **Nines: Levels of Self-Mastery**

Descriptions

Example: The day after Nora's husband underwent abdominal surgery, Nora was scheduled to take their four-year-old son for a hospital visit. Although Nora had agreed to do so, she was actually feeling put upon because she had work to do and the hospital was an hour from their home. Much to the disappointment of both her husband and her son, Nora was five hours late in getting the child to the hospital to visit his father, with no explanation other than that she had had work to do at home. Soon after arriving, Nora left the boy in the hospital room with his father (who was unable to move), saying, "I'm just going out for a walk."

Development Stretches for Nines

EXPRESS YOUR NEEDS DIRECTLY   Each day, express one need, preference, or desire to someone else. Suggest where to go for lunch, indicate how to proceed with a project, or ask for a raise. Express these desires without someone first asking you what you want. Take the initiative.

SET PRIORITIES AND KEEP THEM   Commit to completing two tasks or chores each day. Make sure you complete each task without any interruptions.

TAKE A POSITION   Each morning, think about one opinion that you hold strongly, then share that opinion with two people during the day. Every day, select a new opinion or idea and discuss it with two new people. Continue this activity for two weeks, and then reflect on it by asking yourself these questions: *Has it become easier to say what I really think? Are some topics easier to discuss than others? Are some people easier to share with?* After you've answered these questions, continue the activity for one month, each day selecting new topics and new individuals.

Development Stretches for Everyone

- Keep a daily journal of your personal reactions to events and your progress toward self-mastery. Once a week, review your journal entries to look for patterns of responses and progress, and note these patterns in the journal.
- Use your knowledge of the Enneagram every day to observe yourself in work interactions and practice your self-mastery skills. When you know the Enneagram styles of your coworkers, practice adjusting your behavior to bring out the best in them. The more you practice and refine your interpersonal interactions using the Enneagram, the better you will become at self-mastery.
- Educate yourself further by reading one of the recommended books under "Strive for Self-Mastery" in the Resources section at the back of this book; read Chapter 7, "Transforming Yourself," in *Bringing Out the Best in Yourself at Work: How to Use the Enneagram System for Success*, by Ginger Lapid-Bogda, Ph.D.

Chapter 4

Know the Business: Think and Act Strategically

$\mathcal{E}$ xcellent leadership requires that leaders at all levels understand the actual business of their organizations and be able to think and act strategically in big and small ways. Leaders must be able to think strategically about how they serve customers, design products and delivery systems, and allocate resources to both present and future value-producing activities. This big-picture, systems view of the organization enables leaders and organizations to reach the highest levels of performance, effectiveness, and efficiency.

Knowing the business and thinking and acting strategically go hand in hand. Unless you have an in-depth knowledge of the business, you have no context for acting strategically. When you have this information, you need to be able to use it in a strategic way, leading your team by conveying a compelling and common vision, a customer-focused mission, a smart strategy, and effective goals and tactics that are aligned with that strategy.

Having the ability to Know the Business and Think and Act Strategically means that you are skilled in the following 11 competency components.

Know the Business

FIGURE 4.1 Know the Business: Think and Act Strategically

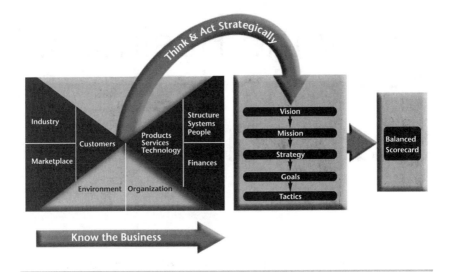

The Business Environment
1. Knowing the industry
2. Knowing the marketplace
3. Knowing the customers

The Organization
4. Knowing the structure, systems, and people
5. Knowing the products, services, and technology
6. Knowing the finances

Think and Act Strategically
7. Creating a compelling vision
8. Defining a viable mission
9. Developing synergistic strategies
10. Creating quantifiable goals
11. Designing successful tactics

When you truly Know the Business and are able to Think and Act Strategically, the result is a Balanced Scorecard for your organization, business unit, or team that measures results not only by financial indicators, but also by other equally important factors— for example, intellectual and other intangible assets, high-quality products and services that are important to valued customers, a motivated and skilled workforce that is able to meet current and future business needs, and a satisfied and loyal customer base.

As you read further and reflect on the 11 competency components of Know the Business and Think and Act Strategically, rate yourself in each area on a scale of 1 to 5. This will help you determine both your areas of strength and the areas that need development.

The 11 Competency Components of Know the Business: Think and Act Strategically

Know the Business: The Business Environment

COMPONENT 1: KNOWING THE INDUSTRY This includes understanding the legal, political, demographic, and other environmental factors affecting the industry; staying current on industry trends; networking with professionals outside your company; speaking and writing as an industry expert; and routinely thinking about and seeking new products and methods to change the way business is done in support of your organization as an industry leader.

Low				High
1	2	3	4	5

COMPONENT 2: KNOWING THE MARKETPLACE This involves knowing how to fully tap into and strengthen your current and potential markets; demonstrating insight into the competition's strengths, weaknesses, and strategies; understanding your own organization's strengths and weaknesses vis-à-vis those of your competitors; and

developing strategies and operational capability to leverage your organization's strengths and address its vulnerabilities.

Low				High
1	2	3	4	5

COMPONENT 3: KNOWING THE CUSTOMERS This involves understanding the expectations and needs of your customers; thinking of customers in terms of classes and segments in order to allocate resources effectively; anticipating the impact of internal and external changes on the customers' business and adapting services or products accordingly; responding proactively to customers' changing business needs; and developing new services or customers in areas that will contribute to the strategic growth of your business.

Low				High
1	2	3	4	5

Know the Business: The Organization

COMPONENT 4: KNOWING THE STRUCTURE, SYSTEMS, AND PEOPLE This requires grasping the organization's values, strategies, structure and flow of work, culture and subcultures, functions of different divisions, and communication and reward systems; knowing how to get things done through both formal and informal channels; developing internal systems and processes that have the greatest positive impact on customer satisfaction and the achievement of financial objectives; creating an organizational infrastructure and developing an employee talent base to support current, medium-term, and long-term growth; understanding and supporting key policies, practices, and procedures, and following these in most instances, using shortcuts when necessary; and recognizing your interdependence with functional areas outside your own work unit.

Low				High
1	2	3	4	5

COMPONENT 5: KNOWING THE PRODUCTS, SERVICES, AND TECHNOL-OGY This means understanding the organization's products, services, and technologies; knowing the requirements for operating in a regulated industry; making decisions and instituting organizational changes that take into consideration the long-term impact on products, processes, and technology rather than focusing on short-term advantages for your unit or the company; and making sure that the products and services you provide for customers support the broader organization's business, rather than just looking at what will benefit your work area.

Low				High
1	2	3	4	5

COMPONENT 6: KNOWING THE FINANCES This involves using budgets, forecasts, and key indicators to measure and manage business performance; understanding the company's basic financial statements (income statement, balance sheet, and financial ratios) and how your unit's goals, processes, and systems affect them; taking an organization-wide view of financial management rather than a view from your business unit only; assuming accountability for the bottom line and demonstrating fiscal responsibility; efficiently and effectively managing ongoing investments (in people, materials, finances, and technologies) in the context of business strategies, organizational priorities, and the deployment of resources to value-producing activities; and demonstrating sound resource and workforce planning to meet anticipated business requirements.

Low				High
1	2	3	4	5

Think and Act Strategically

COMPONENT 7: CREATING A COMPELLING VISION This requires developing a long-term, values-based vision that moves people to action; grounding the vision in a realistic knowledge of the current and future environment and organization and making sure that it is neither too narrow in scope nor too lofty, complex, or imprecise for practical implementation; enlisting and aligning key individuals and groups with the vision; communicating the vision through multiple modalities (written, visual, and auditory) on a continuous basis; and ensuring that the vision is used as a guidepost.

Low				High
1	2	3	4	5

COMPONENT 8: DEFINING A VIABLE MISSION   This involves clearly identifying the business you are in for the medium term; making sure the mission is aligned with the overall vision; accurately identifying your customers and their requirements; providing a unique, value-added contribution to both the customer and the business; understanding your competitors and potential collaborators and how you are positioned in relation to them; and basing the mission on a realistic assessment of the strengths and weaknesses of the organization, business unit, or team.

Low				High
1	2	3	4	5

COMPETENCY 9: DEVELOPING SYNERGISTIC STRATEGIES   This involves creating three to five viable strategies that enable you to achieve both your mission and your vision; clearly defining these strategies so that you can readily determine effective resource allocation and make other critical business decisions; understanding how the different strategies support one another so that all of them can be prioritized, sequenced, and leveraged; analyzing potential conflicts between and among strategies, and either resolving these or accepting the ambiguity; leading from these strategies and making your decisions based on them; and revisiting the strategies at regular intervals to evaluate their success and to adjust goals or tactics as needed.

Low				High
1	2	3	4	5

COMPONENT 10: CREATING QUANTIFIABLE GOALS This involves developing three to five measurable goals for each strategy that represent milestone markers; ensuring that there are enough goals for each strategy to enable its success; effectively communicating goals and measures to all employees and enlisting their support; holding people accountable for achieving the goals for which they are responsible; and leveraging goals and measures so that a single goal can support more than one strategy.

Low				High
1	2	3	4	5

COMPONENT 11: DESIGNING SUCCESSFUL TACTICS This involves developing three to five specific actions and activities for accomplishing each goal; taking thoughtful risks and developing innovative tactics, then monitoring results; designating sufficient resources and the appropriate people for each tactic; assuring that those responsible for executing a tactic understand, commit to, and are held accountable for achieving the goal and strategy for which that tactic is designed; soliciting and utilizing feedback on the progress and success of each tactic; leveraging tactics so that a single tactic can support more than one goal; and making tactical adjustments on a short-term basis, identifying new tactics and implementing them as needed.

Low				High
1	2	3	4	5

Because the Think and Act Strategically components of this competency are complex, Chart 4.1 explains these concepts in more detail, with the example added of Gandhi's progress in leading the people of India to social, political, and economic independence from Great Britain.

As you read the Enneagram dimensions that follow, you will notice that seasoned leaders of all nine Enneagram styles can be highly skilled in the competency Know the Business: Think and

CHART 4.1 Think and Act Strategically

Strategic Element	Definition	Potential Pitfalls	Example: Gandhi
Vision	*A shared, compelling, and enduring picture or understanding of the preferred future* The vision endures for a number of years (three to five or longer) and is the first strategic element to be developed.	Too lofty, too complex, not compelling; not values-based; not grounded in reality; undercommunicated; underutilized	Create a free, independent, and spiritual state of India, with full citizenship and dignity conferred on all its people
Mission	*The concrete business you are in; the value you add to your customers that enables you to achieve your vision* The mission supports the vision and represents your specific contribution to the vision; it remains steady, changing only if the environment changes dramatically.	Too many or too few lines of business; unclear customers; mission not valued by customers; thinking your product is your mission	Have citizens of India in control of the Indian government; integrate Hindus and Muslims into a single country
Strategy	*The approaches you will take in order to accomplish your mission and vision; strategy determines resource allocations and other critical decisions* Strategies contain an action orientation but are not specific activities; they are changed only after altering tactics and/or goals has proved ineffective or when the environment changes significantly.	Confusion of tactics with strategies; no strategy, too many strategies, or too few strategies; strategies that are not comprehensive, linked, or leveraged; strategies that are vague or nonactionable	Peaceful, targeted, and nonviolent large-scale civil disobedience; no economic dependence on outside countries

(Continued)

106

CHART 4.1 *(Continued)*

Strategic Element	Definition	Potential Pitfalls	Example: Gandhi
Goals	*Measurable outcomes that represent key milestones for the strategies* There are usually three to five goals per strategy, although some goals can be leveraged and used for more than one strategy; goals are changed only if alternative tactics prove ineffective.	Too many or too few goals; insufficient commitment to goals; goals that are not linked directly to strategies; goals that are not measurable, clear, or differentiated enough from each other	Independence granted; minimal incidents of violence (prefer no violence whatsoever)
Tactics	*Specific actions to accomplish each goal* There are usually three to five tactics per goal, although some tactics can be leveraged and used for more than one goal; tactics can be readily changed if they are not achieving the goals, strategy, and mission.	Ineffective tactics; insufficient resources for implementation; responsibility not assigned	Vast numbers of people going to jail in protest; salt rebellion (making one's own salt rather than buying it from England); making one's own cloth rather than being dependent on England for textiles

Act Strategically. Similarly, less experienced leaders have more developmental challenges. Competency in this leadership area is particularly dependent on both the leader's experience *and* his or her ability to learn from that experience. However, as you read further, you will find subtle differences in what savvy leaders of each style tend to emphasize, as well as substantial differences in the developmental needs of less experienced leaders.

In addition, while the nine leadership paradigms influence a leader's strengths and development areas in all the competencies included in this book, their influence is particularly apparent in this area. Because of this, the discussion of the Enneagram dimensions for each style begins with the leadership paradigm of that style.

Enneagram Dimensions of Know the Business: Think and Act Strategically

Enneagram Style Ones

Enneagram Style
DILIGENCE

Leadership Paradigm:
Leaders set clear goals and inspire others to achieve the highest quality.

One leaders enjoy taking increasingly complex challenges and organizing them into practical, actionable tasks with concrete goals. Knowing the business—both the environmental and the organizational aspects—is no exception. As Ones grow into high-level leadership roles and acquire responsibility for larger segments of the business, they thrive on the experience and become skilled in analyzing and handling the multiple complexities of industry, marketplace, and customer knowledge. They also absorb in-depth information about the organization—its products, services, and technology, and also its organizational structure, systems, people, and finances. Their excitement about understanding and organizing multipart systems and procedures is matched by their thrill in turning situations that are underorganized into logical and methodical processes that allow people to take action.

One leaders focus on setting clear, precise, and forward-moving goals; selecting a manageable number of well-chosen tactics that are aligned with these goals; and holding themselves and others accountable for the execution of those tactics, with both quality and timeliness in mind. Because follow-through is so important to them, Ones oversee all aspects of execution with diligence and attention to detail.

One of her team members described Anita, a leader with 15 years of management experience, this way:

"Everything works well under Anita's leadership. She understands the complexities of our business, yet everything feels under control. In fact, she thrives on the challenge of taking something big and making it appear manageable. Somehow, there is nothing that eludes her attention."

On the other hand, One leaders—particularly those who are newer to leadership—may find the complexity of knowing the business overwhelming at first. Because they want to know all the details, less experienced One leaders may have difficulty learning all the aspects of the environment and organization to a sufficient extent that they feel comfortable. They may also focus on one component that, in their opinion, is the most important or most pressing—for example, products, services, and technology—without sufficiently grasping the remaining components and how the entire system fits together.

In addition, the One leader's focus on goals and tactics can come at the expense of developing a clear, compelling vision and mission, developing an explicit set of strategies, or communicating these strategies to ensure a high degree of buy-in. Some One leaders may confuse a tactic with a strategy—for example, they may think that providing customers with a customer service hotline is a strategy, when in fact the strategy may be either (1) increasing perceived customer benefits or (2) improving the way in which products and services are utilized. With either strategy, the hotline would be one of several tactics within that strategic area.

Twelve years ago, when Anita was still relatively new to leadership, one of her team members described her this way:

> "I always know what I'm supposed to do, but not always why I am supposed to do it. I know Anita thinks I'm very competent, but I could add much more value to the organization if I just had a larger perspective on both my own work and that of our team."

Development Stretches for Ones

KEEP THE BIG PICTURE IN THE FOREFRONT Your job as a leader is to take the broadest view and to focus on the forest rather than on the trees. You need to let go and leave the detail work to those who work for you. With every project for which you are responsible, ask yourself these questions on a regular basis: *Is the work I am personally doing at the strategic level—i.e., vision, mission, and strategy—and not the tactical level? Have I delegated the tactical work, or am I still involved in the more detailed level of execution?*

LEAD FROM VISION Ask yourself these questions: *What is the greater purpose of the work in front of us? What are we trying to accomplish (not in terms of goals, but rather in terms of the biggest dream or desire) in the next three to five years? What are the values underpinning these efforts that are essential to this vision?* Be sure to gather input from those you work with, and make sure that the final vision is shared with everyone in your work area. When you communicate the vision, have a two-way dialogue and then make adjustments as needed.

LEAD STRATEGICALLY FROM THE HIGHEST LEVEL OF STRATEGY   Ask yourself whether the strategies you have developed are truly strategic or whether they are actually goals or tactics. Sometimes, very important goals and tactics can be strategic in nature (that is, essential to success), but they still may not be strategies, which are essential, overarching approaches to accomplishing the mission and vision.

You may be able to back into the strategies by examining your well-chosen tactics and asking yourself these questions: *As I examine these key tactics, do I find that these activities fall into similar groupings? As I analyze these similar groupings of tactics, what does each grouping have in common?* The answer to the latter question will give you a clue into what is known as *tacit strategy*. Making tacit strategies explicit enables you and others to take action on them more easily.

Enneagram Style Twos

Leadership Paradigm:
Leaders assess the strengths and weaknesses of team members and motivate and facilitate people toward the achievement of organizational goals.

Enneagram Style ②
GIVING

Two leaders use their people orientation as the impetus for knowing the business, focusing on the environment and the organization simultaneously. With a concern for meeting customer needs and being best in class, these leaders emphasize industry trends, marketplace analyses, and knowing their customers.

As a result of their customer focus, Twos usually pay close attention to knowing the organization, particularly its products, services, and technologies. The motivation to make sure that these three areas support the customer's requirements gives them a target to help focus and align people. In doing so, Twos take into account employees' strengths and help them work on areas that need development, while making sure that the organizational structure and systems support people in doing their best work. Two leaders may also demonstrate skill and strength in knowing the organization's structure, systems, and processes. Because they like to help others navigate the organizational system and usually are well net-worked—often having provided assistance to many people in the organization—Twos usually know how to expedite the process of getting things done.

Many Two leaders are visionary and adept at enlisting others. They often work from an intuitive mission and strategy, and their efforts are focused primarily on establishing meaningful goals and giving other people support in their tactical pursuits. Twos are likely to check in regularly with others to make sure that every-thing is going well and to ensure that people are well motivated and supported in their efforts to achieve the organization's goals.

One of Kevin's direct reports had this to say about him:

"Kevin is very experienced and works very hard, but his real gift is getting other people to do exactly what needs to be done. He has his fingers on the pulse of our industry and our customers. We just all want to do our best for him. Maybe it's because he believes in us, and we don't want to disappoint him."

However, some Two leaders, particularly early in their careers, may focus too much on pleasing customers or ensuring that the employees who work for them are happy and motivated, while underemphasizing other important factors. For example, these leaders may focus on keeping current customers happy, but lose sight of whether or not these customers are beneficial in terms of future business. Similarly, a Two may emphasize creating structures and processes that support the people who are currently doing the work, rather than creating structures and processes that best suit the work and then securing people who can work well within that framework. In addition, some Twos pay a great deal of attention to finances and financial stability, while others throw caution to the wind and concern themselves with this area only when a potential problem looms.

Vision, goals, and tactics generally come easily to most Two leaders, as they are able to mentally project themselves into future scenarios and intuitively know how to align people with these plans. At the same time, they also need to clearly articulate the mission and strategies to employees so that teams are less reliant on the leader for day-to-day guidance.

When Kevin was a less experienced leader, an employee described him this way:

> "Although I enjoy working for Kevin, I sometimes wonder whether he understands the bigger picture of the business. I have often heard the comment from my coworkers that although Kevin may know our direction, he doesn't share this with us. If we knew more about the strategy of our work unit, we wouldn't need to go to him so frequently with questions."

Development Stretches for Twos

CHALLENGE YOURSELF TO BECOME AN EXPERT IN ALL ASPECTS OF THE BUSINESS, PARTICULARLY THOSE THAT ARE NOT DIRECTLY RELATED TO PEOPLE A people orientation will always be your strength, so stretch your capabilities. Immerse yourself in the details of technology, and undertake a thorough competitor analysis. Think about the impact of these on your business and share your analyses with your bosses, peers, and employees.

PAY CAREFUL ATTENTION TO FINANCES Set the goal of knowing the financial aspects of the business. Once you have done this, ask yourself this question: *If I were going to take a conservative financial view of the key decisions I have made over the last year, would I make the same decisions?* Then think about the decisions facing you in the next three to six months (e.g., salary increases for employees, planned events, new products and services) and ask yourself these questions: *If I were to make these decisions from a primarily cost-effective perspective, what decisions would I make? How can I incorporate this fiscal perspective into my future decisions?*

MAKE YOUR STRATEGIC PROCESS EXPLICIT Write down your unit's or organization's vision so that it would be understandable to an intelligent 12-year-old. This will force you to make the vision statement clear and concise. Then write down your group's mission, identifying your key customers and articulating the value you provide them. Next, write down the three to five key strategies that are the cornerstones for achieving the mission. Finally, write down three to five goals for each strategy and three to five tactics for each goal.

Enneagram Style Threes

Enneagram Style
③ PERFORM

Leadership Paradigm:

Leaders create environments that achieve results because people understand the organization's goals and structure.

Three leaders make it their business to know the environment—the industry, the marketplace, and both current and potential customers—and it is common to find Threes at professional conferences explaining the market and industry trends to others. Not wanting to be edged out by a rival who does something better, has more clients, or knows more about the industry, Threes usually pay special attention to their business competitors. They also formulate their goals in terms of customer needs and industry and marketplace trends, then organize everything—structure, systems, people, and finances—in relationship to these goals.

Because Threes' primary focus is on well-aimed goals and efficient tactics, they like to develop work plans using the fastest route from point A to point B. They are also adept at shifting tactics on demand, and are willing to reconsider goals if they do not seem to be getting results. In addition, Threes' facility with goal setting usually becomes more intricate as they gain leadership experience. It is not unusual for a seasoned Three leader to develop a complex and intertwined set of goals with an equally elaborate set of tactics to support them.

One of Cathy's direct reports describes her this way:

> "Cathy seems to understand everything about the business, but she's also practical, and she gets results. She can read trends and shift the way we operate in an incredibly short period of time, and she is usually right. Cathy makes all this look nearly effortless, although she works long hours."

Although they learn fast, Threes also like to act fast. As a result, taking the time to get to know the organization well can be particularly challenging for Three leaders. Three leaders also are easily frustrated, feeling thwarted when a product does not meet a customer's specifications, service is subpar and customers complain, or the organization's systems, structures, people, and financial constraints present obstacles to achieving their goals.

In addition, as a result of their goal orientation and emphasis on concrete action, Threes may pay insufficient attention to developing a common vision and gaining agreements related to strategy, even misconstruing goals or tactics for a vision or strategy.

In Cathy's early years of management, an employee described her this way:

> "Cathy is extremely smart and sets very clear goals for herself and the rest of us. The problem is that we have more projects than we can handle, but no understanding of the strategy behind any of them. Cathy thinks of herself as strategic, but she thinks the work we do for our main customer is our strategy. What happens to us if we lose this customer?"

Development Stretches for Threes

TAKE THE TIME TO GET TO KNOW THE BUSINESS Even though Three leaders learn quickly, knowing the business is a complex undertaking. To get a firm grounding in the business, give yourself three times as long as you expect to need. Once you have this deep understanding, you will be able to view environmental and organizational changes within their larger context, allowing you to be even more effective at adjusting goals when you take action.

SET THE VISION, CLARIFY THE MISSION, FORMULATE THE STRATEGY, AND LEAD FROM ALL THREE When you lead from goals rather than from vision, mission, and strategy, your success will be limited to the goals you have set. However, when your leadership comes from vision, mission, and strategy, those who work for and with you will be equipped with the tools they need to reformulate goals and drive tactics. This will create less dependence on you for direct involvement in day-to-day activities, and more will be accomplished.

COMMUNICATE WITH EVERYONE FREQUENTLY The more the people who work for you understand the business, the more effective they will be. Take the time to inform and enlist people at all levels of the organization. Doing so will motivate others and help them be better performers.

Enneagram Style Fours

Enneagram Style
MOOD

Leadership Paradigm:
Leaders create organizations that give people meaning and purpose so that they are inspired to do excellent work.

Four leaders like to know and understand everything that *they* consider important. Knowing the business is usually high on their list, because Fours relish the challenges inherent in complicated and significant endeavors. Using their intuitive skills to assess industry trends and customer needs, most Fours actually picture future scenarios in full color, as though they were viewing a film projected on a screen.

Four leaders, particularly those with a great deal of management experience, also pay attention to knowing the organization. Depending on what holds their interest, Fours may know all the organizational elements in depth—that is, products, services, technology, structure, systems, people, and finances.

When it comes to thinking and acting strategically, Fours often enjoy the complexity of the process. Above all, Four leaders emphasize the creation of a shared vision, believing that being part of a large and important vision gives both them and the people they lead a sense of meaning and purpose that inspires all to do excellent work.

Dave, a director-level leader, was described by one of his employees this way:

> "At first, I wasn't quite sure if I would like Dave. It took him a while to warm up to me, but I think he was trying to figure me out. Once we got to know each other better, I realized that Dave is one of the most thoughtful, intelligent, and visionary leaders I have ever worked for. He takes the time to learn everything he can about the people and the business, and there's no one who can match him on industry knowledge and technical ability—although he rarely uses his technical skills directly anymore."

As mentioned earlier, a Four leader who is not particularly interested in the actual work of the organization may not pay attention to all aspects of knowing the business. It is particularly important to Fours that their values are aligned with those of the organization, and that the organization's work has meaning for them. This intense attraction to vision and meaning can also lead Fours to find day-to-day work pedestrian, and they may lose interest in the very activities that are required to implement the vision. In addition, Four leaders may believe that others feel and operate as they do and want the freedom to set goals and take action on their own, not recognizing that some people are not as compelled by vision and prefer to be assigned concrete goals and tasks.

While Four leaders have vivid and compelling visions, they can sometimes have difficulty putting these pictures, feelings, and experiences into words. They may measure their words or rephrase things multiple times in order to be completely clear, but in so doing, they may actually confuse the people whom they most want to inspire.

When Dave was a less experienced manager, one of his employees had described him this way:

> "We think we know what Dave wants, but when we act on this, we sometimes find that we have missed the point. I think things would go better if Dave focused less on the complexities and intricacies of the marketplace and the vision, and more on the strategies we need in order to set goals and take action."

Development Stretches for Fours

BE VERY CLEAR ABOUT WHAT YOU WANT TO COMMUNICATE Rather than being overly complex, challenge yourself to be as clear and straightforward as you possibly can, especially when you speak in front of groups. In that situation, write down in advance exactly what you want to say, and practice your speech in front of others who will give you honest feedback. Ask them these questions: *Can you repeat my main point in two sentences? Did my words inspire you to move forward? Do you have a clear sense of what action to take as a result of what I said?* If the answer to any of these questions is no, keep revising your speech until you get an affirmative response to all three questions.

BE HONEST IN IDENTIFYING WHAT YOU DON'T LIKE DOING, AND THEN GIVE YOUR FULL ATTENTION TO THOSE AREAS Write down the parts of your job that you truly enjoy. Review this list, and think about how you approach these tasks and how you feel when you do them. Make a second list of the responsibilities that you find dull or uninteresting. Review each item, and ask yourself this question: *How can I bring the same enthusiasm, satisfaction, and overall approach to these tasks that I bring to the activities I enjoy?*

CREATE AND WORK FROM A VISION, MISSION, AND STRATEGY; KEEP YOUR EYE ON STRATEGIES AND THEIR IMPLEMENTATION Write down your vision, mission, and strategies. List your goals beneath each strategy, and place your tactics below each goal. Putting this on paper will clarify your strategic elements, showing you what might be missing and needing more thought, and giving you something to discuss with those you lead. Remember that some people need explicit direction and oversight.

Enneagram Style Fives

Leadership Paradigm:
Leaders develop effective organizations through research, deliberation, and planning so that all systems fit together and people are working on a common mission.

Enneagram Style (5)
KNOWLEDGE

Because Five leaders have an enormous amount of intellectual curiosity, they feel stimulated by knowing the business from both an environmental and an organizational perspective. Not only do they take an interest in analyzing the latest trends and the needs of customers, but they are storehouses of information about the organization's products, technology, services, structure, and finances. Five leaders see the entire business almost as a gigantic puzzle, and they are fascinated by its component parts and the interconnections that exist between and among the pieces.

One of Michelle's employees describes her this way:

"Whenever I ask Michelle a question about customers, products, industry trends, or the latest technology, she always has the answers right at her fingertips. How she knows and retains all this information seems like a miracle, but she is certainly a great resource for us."

Five leaders' strength in knowing the business and thinking and acting strategically can also be an obstacle for them. It is impossible for someone to know everything about an organization and its business context, especially in a constantly changing marketplace. These realities may frustrate Five leaders, who often believe that they must understand all the data before they can take action. In addition, while intellectual analyses are a necessary component of high-level success in this competency, understanding feelings—your own and those of others—is equally critical, as is a gut sense of what is most important and what direction the organization must take.

There is also a tendency among Fives, particularly early in their leadership careers, to handle the running of an organization, business unit, or work group as one would handle project management. The Five leader's strength in understanding how pieces of the business fit together works well in project management, but it can be a limitation in running a business. An organization or a strategic business unit is far larger in scope and complexity than a project, no matter how complex the project, and there are many more unpredictable and changing variables involved in running a business.

Five leaders may also confuse tactics with strategy, since many tactics are strategic in nature—that is, they are crucial to the business. However, a strategic activity is not the same as a strategy, as it is simply one tactic rather than an overall strategy or approach from which several tactics emerge.

Five leaders may also place little emphasis on the development of a shared vision, instead working primarily from the business mission. Without a vision, however, it is difficult for employees to know what decisions to make or whether their daily activities make a difference.

Earlier in Michelle's career, one of her employees described her this way:

"Although Michelle is extremely knowledgeable and competent, she treats our business as if she's managing a project and misses the big picture. We know what we're supposed to be doing, but we have a very limited sense of the larger context of our work—for example, we don't really know why we're doing the work in a certain way. I also have no idea how my work contributes to the overall business. Maybe Michelle knows the answers, but she hasn't shared the information with us."

Development Stretches for Fives

USE YOUR FEELINGS AND GUT REACTIONS AS MUCH AS YOUR INTELLECT The deepest part of knowledge—that is, insight and wisdom—does not come from intellect alone. Increasing your capacity to trust your feelings will mean first allowing yourself to experience your emotions in real time and in depth. Work on not automatically detaching emotionally, even though you are pushed beyond your comfort zone.

In addition, pay attention to your gut reactions. Instead of analyzing as much as you do, ask yourself this question: *What does my gut say about this situation?* Allow a spontaneous answer to emerge. When you have developed your emotional capacity and your gut instincts, you will probably discover that your overreliance on mental data will decrease, because you will have access to these other information sources as well.

PUSH YOURSELF TO DEVELOP A COLLECTIVE VISION   Make sure that you have a clear, purposeful, and values-based vision from which to lead and that this vision is a collective one—that is, make sure that you have shared it with everyone whom you lead through writing, in-person conversations, interactive meetings, and teleconferences. This requires time, but you will find that it is time and energy well spent.

TALK WITH PEOPLE   Learn to use others as information sources and sounding boards. Doing so will not only help you to create a better information base, but also make others feel like partners in the process of knowing the business and thinking and acting strategically.

Enneagram Style Sixes

Ⓐ Enneagram Style
DOUBT

Leadership Paradigm:
Leaders solve organizational problems by developing a creative problem-solving environment in which each person feels that he or she is part of the solution.

Although some might think that Six leaders would avoid complex leadership situations, the opposite is usually true; most Six leaders thrive on challenge and risk. They put their analytical minds and team leadership skills to the task of understanding the business environment and knowing the organization well. More than likely, they perceive this complex challenge as an opportunity to enhance the success of the business by eliminating the potential obstacles. Six leaders want to fully understand the industry, marketplace, and customers. Sixes also make it their job to know and develop the organization, with a particular emphasis on anticipating problems and solving them before they become barriers.

Because Six leaders prefer clarity to ambiguity, they put a great deal of effort into clarifying the business charter or mission, giving special attention to lines of responsibility and authority. The development of realistic goals and concrete tactics from strategies is usually done in a team-oriented manner, with an emphasis on resourceful problem solving.

Josh replaced a senior manager who was struggling in a key leadership role. Six months into the new position, Josh was described by one of his employees in this way:

> "Our prior manager couldn't handle the complexities of the job and often retreated to his office behind a closed door. When Josh came, the product we were supposed to deliver was six months behind schedule, and we were over budget. Josh simply immersed himself in all aspects of our work, got to know each of us as individuals, renegotiated the budget with senior management, met regularly with customers, and created a team atmosphere where none had existed. The more challenging the job, the more Josh rises to the challenge."

A less experienced Six leader might find these complex challenges anxiety-producing and stressful rather than something to attack with zest. Getting to know the structure, the systems, and particularly the people in the organization can be a daunting task; building relationships takes time, and Sixes tend not to completely trust people until they have seen proof that trust is warranted.

With respect to thinking and acting strategically, less seasoned Six leaders usually focus on goals and tactics because these elements are more concrete and predictable. While Sixes often pay attention to the clarity of the mission, it can take them extra time to gain the capacity to develop comprehensive, proactive, and explicit strategies. Although they may back into strategies by extrapolating strategic approaches from chosen goals and tactics, the most useful strategies for teams, business units, and organizations are explicit ones.

Finally, Six leaders need to frame the vision, mission, strategies, and goals in positive rather than negative terms. Most people find it difficult and demotivating to put their efforts toward something that is intended to prevent something. For example, it is more motivating for a sports coach to say, "Let's beat this team," than it is to say, "Let's keep this other team from beating us." Visions, strategies, and goals are most effective when they are explained with words that imply positive action.

When Josh was new to leadership, he was described by one of his employees in this way:

> "I know Josh has a lot of experience as a project manager, but he just doesn't feel like a leader to me. While he may know what we should do, he doesn't communicate this to us very effectively. Because of this, I lack confidence in him, and I think many of my coworkers feel the same way. He appears more adept at picking apart the ideas we suggest than at helping us figure out a common direction."

Development Stretches for Sixes

TAKE PROJECTS OR JOBS THAT WILL BE PRODUCTIVE STRETCHES FOR YOU Don't undersell yourself and take on work that is too easy for you, as doing so won't push you to expand your capabilities. On the other hand, be careful not to be so attracted by the risk and excitement of a new challenge that you take a job that is more complex than your prior experience would suggest is a good career move. Give yourself the time to fully develop your skills.

MAKE SURE YOU DEVELOP A VISION AND STRATEGY BEFORE MOVING TO GOALS AND TACTICS Although you may feel more comfortable working with the concrete areas (missions, goals, and tactics), staying within this comfort zone will hurt your chances to rise in the organization. At higher levels, you will need to lead from vision and strategy.

FRAME YOUR RESPONSES IN A POSITIVE WAY   Instead of responding to the ideas of others with reasons why something *may not* work, respond first with how the ideas *could* work, then add your thoughts about potential problems. Although Sixes are often thought of as more pessimistic than optimistic, they can also be thought of as optimists with a strong sense of reality. When you think of a worst-case scenario, instead of verbalizing it, ask yourself this question: *I know what I am trying to prevent from happening, but what do I hope can happen?*

Enneagram Style Sevens

Leadership Paradigm:
Leaders get people excited and create innovative ventures so that organizations can take advantage of important business opportunities.

Seven leaders usually find that the environmental aspect of knowing the business comes easily to them. They become highly energized by keeping up with the latest trends and customers' needs, processing the data quickly, and synthesizing the information into potential business ideas.

Seven leaders are also very interested in knowing the organization's products, services, and technology, with a focus on innovation and new products. Not only will they pay attention to the organization's structure, systems, and finances when necessary (i.e., when they have to get something done quickly), but they also get to know others in the organization easily through their engaging interpersonal style.

Seven leaders embrace thinking and acting strategically, with a focus on vision and strategy. They tend to be dreamers, conjuring up possible future scenarios and becoming enthralled with the organization's potential, and their enthusiasm helps enlist others in these possibilities. Because they like to see their dreams become reality, Seven leaders pay attention to goals and tactics in order to get the job done, although they prefer to leave the implementation to others, as this frees them up to create even more possible ventures.

Maggie is described by one of her employees this way:

"Nothing eludes Maggie, whether it's an innovation in the industry, new competitors entering the field, or a shift in what our customers want. She always seems to be ahead of the rest of us, always thinking of new ways to improve what we offer. I would call her a tireless visionary."

There is also a downside to the Seven leader's boundless energy and enthusiasm for ideas and innovation. While almost all Seven leaders grasp complex information quickly, they do so by selecting what they perceive to be the highest level of information needed in order to understand a situation. This is certainly an asset when the data are vast, but it can also lead them to miss important facts and issues.

Most Seven leaders are visionary, but less experienced Seven leaders may have trouble focusing on only one vision. A vision that continually changes is extremely difficult for people to follow, and it does not provide a firm foundation from which to develop the mission, strategies, goals, and tactics. It is not the overall vision, but rather the tactics, goals, and strategies—and in that sequence— that need to change as the business and/or organization's environment changes.

In addition, the Seven's tendency to engage in internal brainstorming may cause less experienced Seven leaders to come up with a very large set of ideas for strategies, goals, and tactics. While some of these may be brilliant, others may be merely thoughts that are not clearly linked to current plans and activities. As a result, the staff may not know which ideas have simply been part of the brainstorming process and which ones they are expected to act upon.

When Maggie was near the end of her first year of senior-level leadership, she was described in this way by one of her subordinates:

"Maggie started out strong. After six months, things began to unravel. Her many ideas, which had really excited us in the beginning, never seemed to stop. We had more ideas than we had staff to implement them. Plus, some of her ideas were unrealistic. The biggest problem was that Maggie became spread too thin, and so we were too."

Development Stretches for Sevens

GO FOR DEPTH   You may be a quick study, but it's important that you become a deep study as well. Every time you scan a piece of written information, go back and read the item in its entirety. At first you may feel frustrated, but after you have finished fully examining each piece of information, ask yourself this question: *What have I learned from reviewing this item in depth that I missed the first time around?* If you have an affirmative answer, this is good. If you don't think you have learned anything new, go back and review the item again.

STAY THE COURSE   Once you have developed a vision and shared it with those who work for you, do not waver from it. Write it down and keep it posted near your desk as a reminder to stay on course. If you have an impulse to rework the vision within two years of its development, remind yourself that this may simply be related to your excitement about new possibilities and that changing the vision may not benefit the organization. In order for people to have a solid sense of direction, a vision requires constancy.

Similarly, when you think of new ideas for strategies, goals, and tactics, make sure you focus on possible changes in tactics before you even consider changing goals or strategies. When you have new ideas, let those with whom you discuss them know that they are merely ideas, not directives for a shift in action, and that your intent is solely to discuss their viability.

SLOW DOWN   The two preceding developmental stretches will be easier to do if you also slow down. That means making a conscious effort to speak less quickly and to stay with an idea and consider it from many angles before discussing it with others. It also means concentrating on the task at hand and not being distracted by external stimuli—for example, extraneous noise or a beautiful tree outside the window. Most importantly, slowing down requires focusing your attention inward and asking yourself these questions: *What am I feeling (as opposed to thinking)? What bodily sensations am I experiencing? Can I simply focus inside myself without thinking about anything or being distracted by something external?*

Enneagram Style Eights

⑧ Enneagram Style
CHALLENGE

Leadership Paradigm:
Leaders move organizations forward by leading decisively, getting capable and reliable people in the right jobs, and empowering competent people to take action.

Because Eight leaders become invested in making big things happen in organizations, they enjoy knowing the business and developing a vision from which to create a viable mission and effective strategies, goals, and tactics. They voraciously absorb all they can about industry and marketplace trends and make it their job to know the key customers. They then focus on the organization's products, services, and technologies to ensure that customers are getting everything they need, and that the whole system makes sense in terms of the structure, systems, people, and finances.

Eight leaders expend a great deal of energy making sure that the right people are in the right jobs, so that they can trust others to do their work without close supervision. Eights take pleasure in making certain that everything in the organization is directed toward making the company a leader in its field. In fact, Eights often work themselves to exhaustion to make this happen.

Eights usually lead from a vision—one that their gut tells them is aimed in the right direction—and the organization's mission is at the forefront of their minds. Their ambitions for the organization are big, and they enjoy the art of strategy. Having little time for or patience with details and misfires, Eights expect others to capably develop and execute the goals and tactics, which Eights expect will be aligned with the organization's strategy.

Richard, an Eight leader, is described by an employee in this way:

"Richard's grasp of the entire business is astounding. The man is a walking strategist, seeming to live and breathe it. Many people are intimidated by his strength and power. Because I work closely with him, I don't feel that way. I see his humility and even his uncertainty, although that is rare. I do find his brilliance daunting, but I learn from him every day."

Eights trust their gut reactions; once they believe they know the truth, getting them to change their minds can be a challenge. Although they *eventually* will respond to new data about the environment and the organization, the Eights' certainty can create problems when the organization's environment changes rapidly.

In addition, while Eights remain focused on the big picture and give a great deal of latitude to people who they believe are competent and trustworthy, they do the opposite with those they feel they must watch closely. Compounding this issue, Eights frequently form impressions of people's abilities and character early on, and they are correct often enough to reinforce their view that they are good at assessing people's strengths and weaknesses. Thus, while an employee who has exhibited problems in the past may have remedied these problems, it takes time for the Eight's impression of someone to shift. Consequently, while Eight leaders may initially be good at understanding the people component of the organization, they may have difficulty changing their opinions over time.

Although some Eights are good at detail work, very few Eights actually enjoy it, preferring to leave it to others. For most Eights, goal setting is part of the big picture, but tactics are viewed as the specifics of execution. Most Eight leaders would rather receive honest and timely progress reports than be involved in the day-to-day particulars of the work.

Finally, while Eights like to make big things happen and move quickly, without a lot of smaller, preliminary steps, they can become impatient and angry when their organizations, business units, or teams do not proceed at as fast a pace as they would like.

When Richard was younger, one of his employees had a different take on his leadership performance:

> "Although I think Richard is a great person, his expectations for himself and those who work for him are not sustainable. He works too many hours without a break, and he gets frustrated when people don't perform the way he wants or when the organization puts any kind of obstacle in our path. Nothing happens as fast or as well as he wants it to, but he can't make this happen all by himself. Details end up falling through the cracks because we are all overextended and exhausted."

Development Stretches for Eights

DEVELOP YOUR SENSE OF HUMOR You may think you already have a well-developed sense of humor, but ask yourself this question: *Do I use my sense of humor at work as a way to laugh at myself and my expectations?* If you can laugh at your foibles, you will work less excessively and enjoy yourself more at work.

BECOME MORE FLEXIBLE Make a list of all your strongest beliefs, opinions, and ideas. Next, ask yourself: *If I were to react less intensely and become more open-minded about anything on this list, would I perceive myself as being less strong?* If your answer is no, proceed to the next paragraph. However, if you answered yes, tell yourself this: *Being flexible is not the same as being weak, and* *having fixed opinions does not mean being strong. While too much flexibility is a weakness, so is too much rigidity.* Repeat these statements until you believe them.

Once you are more receptive to new ideas, review each item on your list and ask yourself: *What do I need to do to be even more open-minded about this?* Finally, pick three of the items and take the actions you have identified as ways to help you become more open.

BE PATIENT You probably drive yourself very hard, but you need to take time to relax, read, or do something that is calming, such as stretching or walking. Not only will this give you more patience with yourself, but it can actually prevent illness. Then, work on being patient with other people. Every time you become frustrated and want to confront someone for not living up to his or her commitments, ask yourself: *What might I not understand about this person and his or her perspective on this situation?*

Finally, learn to be patient with organizations. Organizations and systems are very much like people: some pressure may contribute to movement, but too much pressure creates resistance to change. If you want to use humor in learning to become more patient, remember this: *You don't change very easily, so why should the organization?*

Enneagram Style Nines

Leadership Paradigm:

Leaders help achieve the collective mission by creating a clearly structured and harmonious work environment.

Enneagram Style **9**
HARMONY

Seasoned Nine leaders take pleasure in knowing all aspects of the business. Methodical and able to perceive all points of view, Nine leaders enjoy understanding the industry, the marketplace, and their customers, and they also embrace the nuances and complexities of the organization's products, services, and technologies.

Because Nines desire harmony, they like organizations that feel unified and have logical, well-designed, and clear organizational structures and processes. Nine leaders also form relationships easily, perceiving interactions as a pleasure, not a task. In addition, they consider finances important and create processes that are aligned as much with the financial demands of the business as with the organization's products and services.

Nine leaders think and act strategically with clarity and resolve, keeping their focus on the mission. Because they enjoy the more detailed aspects of the work, Nines often immerse themselves in goals and tactical pursuits. Often, Nine leaders will back into vision and strategy from the mission, goals, and tactics, with a tacit or implicit strategy emerging intuitively through goal identification and tactical choices.

Here is a comment made by one of Liz's direct reports:

"Our organization is very complex, with multiple clients wanting something different from us, but Liz takes it all in stride. Her excellent client relationships are an asset, but she also knows the industry and the market well. More than that, she is highly analytical, and she applies what she knows to make us a first-class business. She is also easy to talk to and gives great advice."

Because Nine leaders usually focus on the details to get to the big picture, this can create a challenge for them when they are new to leadership. Starting with the details and extrapolating the big picture from this information is a viable way of knowing the business and thinking and acting strategically, but it takes longer and can thus create dilemmas for Nine leaders.

Organizations and followers may expect leaders to grasp the important items early and show them the overall direction quickly, but Nines like to take their time and do not appreciate being pressured to make a decision or to take a strong position before they are ready to do so. However, most Nine leaders learn to identify, absorb, and act on the most crucial organizational elements as they rise to higher leadership positions.

Earlier in Liz's career, she was described by one of her employees this way:

"Liz gives us assignments, but it's hard to work independently of her. She likes to see everything we do, and then work piles up on her desk. If I could give Liz one piece of advice, it would be to let go of needing to know the details and to focus more on the bigger picture. If she could do that and explain it to us, then we would understand what our priorities should be."

Development Stretches for Nines

BE STRATEGIC   Although you may be comfortable with the details, you have to force yourself to let others handle them. As soon as you are engaged in anything more than a high-level overview of other people's work, say to yourself: *I'm getting too involved in minutiae. I'm being too tactical when I should be strategic. What should I really be paying attention to?*

MAKE YOUR VISION, MISSION, AND STRATEGY EXPLICIT   Write down your vision, mission, and strategy on one page. Practice describing them to at least three other people, and ask them: *Was my explanation viable, compelling, evocative, and brief?* From the feedback you receive, make revisions and then communicate the revised vision, mission, and strategy to three other people. Ask them for feedback. Repeat this process until you receive only positive feedback. Finally, communicate the vision, mission, and strategy, together with the goals and tactics, to the people who work for you.

SET ORGANIZATIONAL PRIORITIES AND KEEP THEM   Make a list of the three to five areas that will be the most important to address in the next six months. Make four copies of this list, then put these copies in places where you will see them and read them daily. Each time you are about to spend more than a half hour on a task, ask yourself: *Does this task fit with my organizational priority list?* If the answer is no, decide whether this task really needs to be done and, if it does, assign someone else to complete it.

Development Stretches for Everyone

- Develop a two-page document for your area of responsibility. On the first page, use words and/or graphics to outline the key elements in your environment. For example, identify the following: key trends in the industry and the marketplace; current and future customers and their most critical needs; the organization's key products, services, and technologies; a brief description of the organization's structure, systems, and people; and, finally, information about the financial situation.

  On the second page, identify your area's vision, mission (including for whom you provide work and your value-added proposition), strategy, goals, and tactics. At the bottom of this page, add a statement that reflects your Balanced Scorecard; depending on your role, the scorecard would be for the organization, the business unit, or the team.

  Finally, have someone whom you consider skilled in Know the Business and Think and Act Strategically provide you with feedback; make adjustments as needed. Then share this document with your boss, the employees who work for you, and peers with whom you are interdependent. Solicit their feedback and make changes as desired.

- Read biographies or watch DVDs that reveal the thought processes and actions of leaders who mobilized people and resources to make significant changes in their organizations (for example, Mahatma Gandhi, Nelson Mandela, Franklin D. Roosevelt, Rudy Giuliani, and Oprah Winfrey). Write down what you believe were each leader's vision, mission, strategy, goals, and tactics.

- Educate yourself further by reading one of the recommended books under "Know the Business: Think and Act Strategically" in the Resources section at the back of this book; read Chapter 6, "Leveraging Your Leadership," in *Bringing Out the Best in Yourself at Work: How to Use the Enneagram System for Success*, by Ginger Lapid-Bogda, Ph.D.

Chapter 5

Become an Excellent Communicator

L eaders must communicate constantly and effectively with people at all levels, both within and outside the organization. Communicating with others can be challenging and even stressful. A great deal of skill and poise is often required—for example, when delivering difficult performance feedback, managing conflict, and dealing with issues of politics and influence.

Becoming an excellent communicator means that you are skilled in the following six competency components (see Figure 5.1):

1. Creating genuine relationships
2. Communicating clearly
3. Listening fully
4. Giving effective feedback
5. Managing conflict constructively
6. Influencing others

As you read further and reflect on the six competency components of Become an Excellent Communicator, rate yourself in each

FIGURE 5.1 **Become an Excellent Communicator**

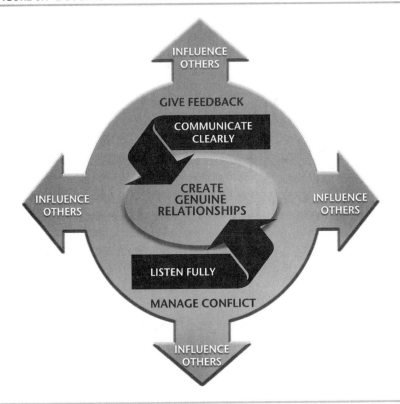

area on a scale of 1 to 5. This will help you determine both your areas of strength and the areas that need development.

The Six Competency Components of Become an Excellent Communicator

Component 1: Creating Genuine Relationships

This requires being approachable, making time for people, and putting others at ease; being warm, gracious, open, and nonjudgmental; showing empathy; having personal credibility and integrity based on congruence between action and words; demonstrating respect for diversity of thought, style, culture, skill sets, and perspectives; relating comfortably with people from diverse demographic groups and individuals from various levels in the organization; and generating trust by honoring confidences and being honest.

Low				High
1	2	3	4	5

Component 2: Communicating Clearly

This involves communicating accurately and concisely, both verbally and in writing; providing timely and accurate information so that people can make reasoned decisions and do their jobs well; and creating and using formal and informal communication vehicles, structures, and processes to keep others well informed.

Low				High
1	2	3	4	5

Component 3: Listening Fully

This means giving your full attention to others before responding; hearing what is said, with a minimum of personal bias; listening well to people with communication styles different from your own; accurately restating the opinions of others, particularly when you disagree; asking relevant questions for deeper understanding; and encouraging input from people who have a wide variety of perspectives.

Low				High
1	2	3	4	5

Component 4: Giving Effective Feedback

This involves providing employees, peers, and bosses with positive and negative feedback in an honest and respectful manner; paying careful attention to the timing, location, and delivery of feedback; and modeling receptivity to feedback by regularly soliciting feedback about yourself and responding to it constructively.

Low				High
1	2	3	4	5

Component 5: Managing Conflict Constructively

This includes anticipating issues and preventing problems; resolving disagreements early, using an issue identification and problem-solving approach; neither avoiding disagreement nor becoming overly aggressive in conflict situations; seeing conflict as an opportunity rather than a problem; knowing how to approach people who are agitated; achieving win-win outcomes by finding common ground and gaining cooperation, but also pursuing tough yet equitable agreements; and being able to manage your own anger, using your reactions as opportunities for self-development.

Low				High
1	2	3	4	5

Component 6: Influencing Others

This involves conveying a sense of competence, confidence, and engagement that enlists others; developing broad networks inside and outside the organization; identifying the concerns and needs of bosses, peers, employees, vendors, and customers; creating solutions based on accurate issue identification; having well-reasoned ideas that contain a strong business case; and knowing when to use your influence and when not to do so.

Low				High
1	2	3	4	5

The remainder of this chapter describes how leaders of each Enneagram style can become excellent communicators by forming genuine relationships, communicating clearly, listening fully, giving effective feedback, managing conflict constructively, and influencing others. Directly after the information on each Enneagram style, you will find the following: (1) real e-mails from people showing the communication patterns of that style, (2) an analysis of these e-mails, and (3) suggestions for rewriting the e-mails should individuals of that style want to use their e-mail writing as a developmental stretch.

E-mails are used as developmental stretches because much of today's communication occurs electronically. Our e-mail writing style also sheds light on who we are, how we think, and what we feel. When you use e-mails to enhance your communication skills, make sure you review each e-mail that you write before you send it, analyzing the e-mail according to the Enneagram-based communication tendencies described in this chapter. Then, rewrite the e-mail and send it. Eventually, your new writing style will feel more natural and require less effort, and it will also cause your language patterns to change during in-person conversations.

Enneagram Dimensions of Become an Excellent Communicator

Enneagram Style Ones

Create Genuine Relationships

Ones have cordial and consistent interactions with others as a result of their well-developed interpersonal manners and the fact that Ones usually say what they mean and do exactly what they say they will do. However, because Ones value politeness,

Enneagram Style
DILIGENCE (1)

they do not always say exactly what is on their minds and may at times be disingenuous—e.g., acting overly cordial to someone they dislike intensely. In addition, when Ones are interacting with someone whom they do not respect or who they believe has an incorrect opinion, they can become irritated and unintentionally dismissive.

Communicate Clearly

Because Ones tend to notice what is correct or incorrect in a situation, they use words that imply judgment—for example, *should*, *ought*, *must*, *appropriate*, *right*, and *wrong*—or that suggest remedial action. Ones also discuss tasks or ideas more than feelings, except with those to whom they feel close.

When they observe something that has been done especially well, Ones display great pleasure through both verbal praise and nonverbal signals such as smiling. However, when Ones are displeased, their nonverbal behavior usually indicates this—for example, through a stern look. If Ones feel criticized, they may react defensively with a sharp comment, a defense against their own self-recriminating tendencies.

Listen Fully

Ones listen closely to people whom they respect or perceive as knowledgeable. Tenacious about their own ideas and opinions, Ones do not listen as fully when they do not hold the other person in high regard, or when they are preoccupied with their own thoughts.

Give Effective Feedback

When Ones give constructive feedback, they are genuinely trying to help someone overcome a flaw or a deficiency. However, they can come across as giving too much detail and being picky or judgmental, the latter being manifested through word choice and nonverbal behavior that elicits defensiveness from the other person. While Ones do give sincere and thoughtful positive feedback, they also need to remind themselves that everyone (including themselves) needs recognition for good work—even if the performance is not at the highest level of excellence.

Manage Conflict Constructively

When Ones are upset with someone or someone is angry with them, they may either approach the situation logically or become short-tempered and accusatory. However, Ones usually take the time to reconsider their responses. Later, they will engage in constructive dialogue, preferring a somewhat structured, problem-solving approach that deals with issues more than feelings and produces a fair but speedy outcome.

Influence Others

Ones typically appear competent and confident and offer well-reasoned opinions, so others usually listen to them. At the same time, Ones may not solicit or listen fully to others' ideas. As a result, Ones may not integrate other points of view into their own thinking and thus may not achieve their highest degree of potential influence, since most relationships involve reciprocal influencing.

Using E-mail as a Developmental Stretch

Constance, a One, sent the following e-mail to Ian, her coworker, about a bonus that Ian had recommended for a staff person named Janice:

> I think this bonus is entirely appropriate. Janice is a treasure, and I think she needs to feel that we see and appreciate all she has done and is doing for our organization.
> Best,
> Constance

ANALYSIS This e-mail illustrates the characteristic language patterns of Ones. Although short, Constance's e-mail offers several opinions in an emphatic and unequivocal manner—for example, *I think*, *entirely*, and *all*. In addition, the e-mail uses words that imply rightness or correctness of action—for example, *appropriate* and *needs*. Ones tend to discuss thoughts (often stated as opinions) rather than feelings and to use words that imply right or wrong and refer to correct or incorrect behavior.

This e-mail is actually gracious; however, if Constance wants to use her e-mails as an aid in her self-development, she could do the following:

- Delete language that implies *should*, *ought*, *right*, and *wrong*.
- Use words that suggest more flexibility and less categorical or emphatic thinking.
- Adopt language that acknowledges and encourages multiple points of view.

Constance could rewrite her e-mail as follows:

Dear Ian,
    Your idea of giving Janice a bonus would compensate her for the extra time she has spent and can serve as a reward. This might be highly motivating, and everyone could feel pleased about the solution.
    Best,
    Constance

Although the changes are relatively minor, the elimination of emphatic words and the inclusion of less definitive words—e.g., *can*, *might*, and *could*—give the e-mail a softer tone and invite more dialogue, should the e-mail recipient disagree with Constance.

Enneagram Style Twos

Enneagram Style ②
GIVING

Create Genuine Relationships

Twos are highly relationship-oriented and are eager to listen, offer help, and give advice. They establish rapport easily, and most people believe that they can count on Twos to be available in a time of need. However, this may not always be the case, as Twos can become exhausted from constantly focusing on others at the expense of themselves. When Twos become aware that they are giving far more than they are receiving—even though their own behavior contributed to this situation—they may sever a relationship that was previously important to them.

Communicate Clearly

Most Twos ask frequent questions but talk about themselves only with people to whom they feel close. Twos also give numerous compliments for the purpose of affirming others, and they smile frequently, using a soft, responsive voice in order to encourage the other person to tell them more.

However, when Twos are upset or exhausted or when they dislike someone or something that the person has said, they become either quiet, or angry and complaining. In addition, while Twos may appear to be interested in almost everyone, in cases where they are not genuinely interested in the other person or in what he or she is saying, they can disengage from the conversation precipitously.

Listen Fully

Twos are usually excellent listeners, easy to talk to, and quite compassionate, but they listen most fully to people to whom they feel close, those they believe need and want their help, people they want to have like them, and individuals who have high status and influence. While listening, Twos may also be preoccupied with their own thoughts, even when they don't show this—for example, they may be pondering whether they (1) like the other person or the person likes them, (2) want to help the other person, (3) strongly disagree with what the person has said, or (4) feel the other person might do harm to someone the Two wants to protect. In the last situation, Twos become filled with an intense and protective concern, which they often express directly.

Give Effective Feedback

Twos are insightful and offer useful advice, but their feedback may also be only their own perception. Consequently, getting confirmation or disconfirmation of these perceptions from the feedback recipient can be helpful.

While Twos are adept at giving positive feedback and have excellent timing because they tend to read body language adroitly, they may be reluctant to give constructive feedback, avoiding saying something negative for fear of hurting the recipient's feelings or harming the relationship.

Manage Conflict Constructively

Because Twos empathize well, they bring conflicts between others to resolution easily, listening to both the rational and the emotional issues involved and searching for common ground.

When Twos feel angry, they often keep their feelings to themselves, not wanting to get into direct conflict with others. This allows them time to think through what they might want to say at some later point. On occasion, however, deeply agitated Twos may burst forth with expressions of resentment, particularly when they feel that they are unappreciated or have been taken advantage of, or when someone they care about is at risk. At these times, Twos can be very direct, accusatory, and even harsh.

Twos are usually surprised when people become angry with them. Because Twos try to please others—unless they dislike someone—and perceive themselves as being sensitive and perceptive, most Twos don't expect other people to have many problems with them. Of course, this is not realistic, but it does mean that many Twos are taken aback when they learn that someone is upset with them.

Influence Others

Twos are usually socially and politically astute, influencing others as much through their personality and relationships as through their ideas or organizational roles. It is as if Twos have antennae for what will enlist others and what will cause others to resist. However, the Two's preference for influencing behind the scenes can be less powerful than direct influence and may also be interpreted as manipulative.

Using E-mail as a Developmental Stretch

While the first e-mail illustrates the most common communication style of Twos, the second shows the typical language patterns of

Twos when they are angry; the complimentary, supportive tone then changes dramatically.

E-MAIL 1 Daniel sent this affirming e-mail to Carolina, a colleague who had given him some positive information about a mutual client.

> That's great! Thanks for letting me know.
> Hope 2005 is a wonderful year for you.
> Mexico was FABULOUS. I'm already plotting my next trip.
> All the best,
> Daniel

E-MAIL 2 Larry sent this angry e-mail to a group of 150 people regarding an upcoming project team reunion. Larry was a member of the planning committee for this event; Shirley and Marc were the event co-chairs. This e-mail was sent in response to an e-mail sent by committee member Joseph Spaulding to the entire project team questioning the $75 per person cost for the reunion.

> Here's a thought from left field, from someone who always tries to make everyone happy:
> Sure wish everyone who has NOT spent several hundred hours planning venue alternatives, food and caterers, refreshments, music, dance floor, entertainment, name tags, correspondence, invitations, cost, budget, and a couple of dozen other relatively important items would have JUST A LITTLE RESPECT for Shirley, Marc, and two dozen or so other people who HAVE spent the time, done the research, and functioned as close to a democracy as possible in coming to some conclusions. This process began in mid-2004, not yesterday; no one was excluded from involvement, participation, and opinion voicing. Joseph Spaulding's opin-

ions on food, dancing, and price were considered by several people BEFORE any firm decisions were made.

I have supreme confidence in Shirley and Marc. They've led a process that has located about 70 percent of the project team, four months before the event. No project team reunion gets that high a percentage.

Rather than second-guessing and asking the committee to start over, how about saying thanks to the chairpeople and committee members, especially Joseph Spaulding, for a job well done.

I feel a little better now . . . but just a little.

Larry

ANALYSIS Daniel's e-mail is upbeat and optimistic—for example, it uses words such as *great*, *wonderful*, and *fabulous*. Focusing more on the e-mail recipient than on personal or professional information about Daniel, the e-mail offers Daniel's sentiments about what the e-mail recipient is doing and indicates his feelings of pleasure and approval.

Should Daniel want to use e-mails to increase his awareness of his Enneagram style language patterns, he could follow these guidelines:

- Focus as much of the content on himself as on the e-mail recipient.
- Use fewer superlatives (e.g., *great* and *terrific*).
- Eliminate the flattering comments.

Daniel's e-mail could be rewritten as follows:

Dear Carolina,

Thanks for letting me know that the client is back in touch.

My trip to Mexico was so enjoyable that I am trying to figure out how to return as quickly as possible.

All the best to you in 2005,

Daniel

Both original e-mails use capital letters to emphasize particular words. In e-mail etiquette, capitalization is the equivalent of using a loud voice or yelling. None of the individuals with the eight other Enneagram styles use capitalization with the same frequency as Twos, although some Eights will write an entire e-mail in capital letters.

While Daniel's e-mail capitalized the word *FABULOUS*, Larry capitalized words that chastise Joseph Spaulding, the most obvious being the words *JUST A LITTLE RESPECT*. The other capitalized words in Larry's e-mail, when read in context (*NOT, HAVE, BEFORE*), are intended to stop Joseph—as well as others who may share Joseph's opinions—from raising these types of issues.

Like Daniel's e-mail, Larry's focuses primarily on others and events rather than on himself, with the exception being the opening and closing lines. Larry's clear agitation, stated aggressively, illustrates the common Two emphasis on having appreciation, respect, and positive regard expressed toward both themselves and others for whom they feel loyalty and concern. Daniel's e-mail shows appreciation and positive regard for the e-mail recipient; Larry's e-mail expresses anger because, in his view, respect was not shown to Shirley and Marc, or to himself, the informal leader. Twos like to orchestrate the interactions between and among people, and they often become angry when others do not behave according to *their* rules of interpersonal conduct.

The two original e-mails differ in length and detail. While Daniel's e-mail is brief, Larry's longer e-mail indicates that he put considerable effort into writing it. The sequential logic of Larry's position, combined with his use of capital letters to emphasize certain words, shows that Larry feels extremely angry and resentful, although he never states this directly. Even Larry's statement, "thanks to the chairpeople and committee members, especially Joseph Spaulding, for a job well done," is an indirect sarcastic comment directed toward Joseph. Finally, Larry's ending comment, "I feel a little better now . . . but just a little," indicates that he is still quite agitated and serves as a warning to Joseph Spaulding and others not to raise these issues again.

Larry's e-mail also communicates his displeasure with Joseph's behavior in subtle ways, such as referring to Joseph formally by using his full name, while referring to others by first name only—a more friendly and familiar way to mention or address people. Larry's e-mail would have been more productive and less of an attack if he had done the following:

- Expressed his feelings with less strident and pointed words
- Used more simple and direct expressions of his feelings
- Sent the e-mail to Joseph only, with copies to Shirley, Marc, and the other committee members, rather than sending it to the entire group of 150
- Encouraged a respectful response from the intended recipient (Joseph)

Larry could use this e-mail to examine his Enneagram language patterns and rewrite it like this:

Dear Joseph,

In response to your e-mail raising several questions about the project reunion, here are my thoughts. The issues are ones that the planning committee, of which you are a part, has wrestled with for many months, and we are now at a point where we need to move forward on what has already been decided by the planning committee. Reopening these decisions will hinder our progress and our ability to meet our deadlines.

All of us are entitled to our opinions—you as well as me—and these are mine. I felt upset with your e-mail because of all the hard work we have put into the planning of this event. It would be unfortunate if Shirley and Marc felt that their efforts as chairs of the reunion were, in effect, being called into question at this point in time. Your suggestions may be good ones; however, they have come too late in the process.

I would appreciate it if you raised any future concerns only with the planning committee instead of sending an e-mail to the entire project team. Doing that gets people stirred up, and we need to deal with these sorts of issues at the planning committee level. In the end, we all want the reunion to be a harmonious and positive event.

Hoping to hear from you on this,

Larry

Enneagram Style Threes

Create Genuine Relationships

Some Threes rely heavily on their relationships for social support and are willing to share personal information—a foundation for all genuine rela-

Enneagram Style
PERFORM ③

tionships. Other Threes are so busy with work that they don't spend the time required to develop deeper relationships. Although most Threes have well-developed social skills, they may not exercise those skills when they are overworked or feel stressed.

It is common for Threes to have their most important relationships with people they have known for a long time and/or people with whom they have work in common. Client relationships, so fundamental to the success of Threes, often come more easily to them than do relationships with people in closer proximity, such as colleagues.

Communicate Clearly

Threes speak as if they were delivering a well-rehearsed Power-Point presentation, relaying their thoughts in a clear, efficient manner, even when they are speaking extemporaneously. While Threes prefer advance preparation, they seem to be able to summon the words and confidence they need, even in times of uncertainty.

Threes prefer to discuss topics about which they feel confident, and they look at their audience frequently in order to assess the group's reaction to what they are saying. If they perceive that others are not responding favorably, Threes change the topic or adjust their style of delivery.

Listen Fully

Threes like to listen, but only in short spurts, wanting to get the information and then get back to work. If the other person speaks in concise phrases rather than in complete sentences, he or she will perceive the Three as an effective listener. However, if the other person talks at length or in abstract terms, Threes become frustrated and impatient. In these situations, Threes let others know when their time is up by going back to work or ending the conversation with a sudden closing comment. When this occurs, Threes may be perceived as cold or abrupt.

Threes feel challenged when the other person wants to discuss feelings, particularly if these feelings are about the Three. Because they tend to put their feelings aside or bypass emotional discussions by overfocusing on work, emotional conversations—even if the content has nothing to do with the Three—can make Threes very uncomfortable; they often don't know what to say or do.

Give Effective Feedback

When Threes give feedback, it typically is clear and honest. They consider what goals the other person is trying to achieve, think through concrete examples of behavior that do not match these goals, and give their time and effort to help the other person become more successful. All of this is done in an efficient way that keeps the conversation short.

Goal-focused feedback can be highly effective if Threes also allow room for feelings—both their own and those of the other person. When the Three has strong suppressed feelings, the feedback recipient may sense this and respond to the unexpressed emotions. In addition, feedback recipients often have emotional responses to what they are hearing, and these reactions often require as much discussion as the content of the feedback. If the emotional responses are not discussed, these feelings can lead the recipient to be unwilling to accept the information and make changes. Threes also need to remember that while honesty is good, so is gentleness, since people receiving constructive feedback often feel vulnerable.

Finally, Threes need to provide an equal balance of constructive and positive feedback. The latter builds relationships and lets people know not only what they need to improve, but also what they are already doing well.

Manage Conflict Constructively

Threes can get angry, particularly when obstacles to goal accomplishment arise—for example, work delays, the withdrawal of resources, or someone's poor performance. Threes also become agitated when they have a great deal of work to do, perceive that another person is wasting their time, or believe that they are not receiving credit for work that they have done.

Threes may not express their distress directly, but may instead burst forth with a rapid fire of questions aimed at eliciting the facts or telling the other person what he or she has done wrong. If the conflict does not get resolved quickly, Threes unconsciously speed up their speech and sharpen their tone, and may become brusque. At the same time, Threes are usually skilled at resolving conflicts between other people. They sit down with the parties involved, enable them to air their feelings (but not for very long), and then use problem-solving techniques to achieve a resolution.

Influence Others

Threes make it their job to know both the formal power structure and the informal influence networks within the organization and to develop relationships with the key individuals in both systems. They rely on their competence, self-confidence, and well-honed social skills to enlist others and influence them to take action.

Threes may find that some people in the organization resist their influence because of these individuals' past experiences with or perceptions of the Three. For example, Threes may be perceived as overly competitive, ambitious, abrupt, and too political. These perceptions lessen the Three's influence and heighten resistance to his or her wishes.

Using E-mail as a Developmental Stretch

Alex sent the following e-mail to his coworkers regarding a project plan that the team—of which he is a member, but not the leader—has been struggling with for several months.

> Dear friends,
>
> I am writing this e-mail from a small town near Portland, Maine, where I am participating in a conference on risk management. I will be making a presentation on the strategic implications. I have given several presentations like this before that have been well received, so I am optimistic that this one will also go well.
>
> After reading the useful contributions of other project team members, I wanted to put in my two cents for the discussion. I think we should consider . . . [The e-mail continues with Alex's doing an outstanding job of outlining the project plan—one that the team had been struggling with for months.]
>
> Peace to everyone, from the East Coast—Alex

ANALYSIS In this friendly e-mail, Alex boasts about his past accomplishments and talks about what he is currently doing—where he is, why he's there, and the fact that what he is doing is a high-status activity (i.e., presenting on a sophisticated topic at a conference).

The last part of Alex's e-mail reflects the value that Threes place on competence and capability, as well as their ability to read an audience well. In the part of this e-mail, which is not included here because of its length, Alex does an excellent job of laying out a logically sequenced action plan. However, he is also sensitive to the fact that several of his colleagues have already tried to do this and failed. In an effort not to offend others in the group, he compliments their efforts ("useful contributions") and refers to his own work as adding "two cents," thereby downplaying his own contribution. Some recipients of this e-mail, however, might find Alex's self-deprecating comment insincere (false humility), since he presents a plan that is so obviously well thought out.

If Alex wanted to use e-mails to heighten his awareness of his Enneagram style language patterns, he could do the following:

- Talk less about his own actions and achievements.
- Use language that focuses more on the specific task and the other people involved.
- Neither inflate nor dismiss the importance of his performance and actions.
- Present his ideas in a more straightforward way.
- Invite a response.

For example, Alex could rewrite his e-mail in the following way:

Dear friends,

I'm away on business, yet I wanted to offer some thoughts about our project, ideas that came to my mind after reading the contributions several of you have already made. [Continue outlining the project.]

I will look forward to hearing your reactions to these ideas and to the discussion we will have.

Alex

Enneagram Style Fours

Create Genuine Relationships

Fours like nothing better than to develop genuine relationships, which most Fours would call authentic relationships. With little patience for what they perceive to be superficial conversations, Fours enjoy deep bonds with others, and their ability to help people discuss difficult issues cements relationships both inside and outside of work.

Enneagram Style ④
MOOD

However, while Fours develop intense relationships, they do so primarily with people with whom they feel an emotional resonance. Fours are more challenged in building relationships with individuals who take longer to develop connections, who don't want to form relationships based on deep personal sharing, or with whom the Four does not feel an immediate affinity. In such situations, Fours can come across as overly intense or remote, depending on whether the Four moves toward the person for more contact or away from the person to create distance.

Communicate Clearly

Fours use emotionally expressive words, share stories about personal experiences, and often use self-referencing words such as *I*, *me*, and *mine*. Although their word choice may sound deliberate or contrived, they do this because they want to be understood. Fours also tend to analyze and reanalyze conversations, including how they came across and whether or not the other person valued and empathized with what they said and felt.

Most Fours have a special gift for communicating symbolically through the use of imagery, symbols, and metaphors. When they fully grasp the nuances of a concept or experience, Fours can explain a complex idea or feeling in a way that communicates its essence. However, when they are grappling with the meaning of a multifaceted issue or are in the throes of a personal experience and are trying to sort out a myriad of feelings, they may talk about the subject for prolonged periods of time. This gives them a way to think out loud and sort out what it is they really mean to say.

Listen Fully

Some Fours talk more than they listen, others listen attentively far more than they talk, and still others talk and listen equally. Fours listen best when they find the other person deeply interesting or when the speaker is talking about something that is extremely important to the Four. When someone is emotionally distressed, Fours will usually listen to the person for extended periods and with great compassion.

In contrast, commonplace conversations bore Fours, who then have trouble staying focused. In addition, when Fours listen, they may redirect a conversation to themselves by sharing a personal experience, one that has been elicited by what the other person is discussing. Although the Four's intention is usually to deepen the dialogue and enhance rapport, others may perceive the Four as being self-oriented and failing to listen.

Give Effective Feedback

When giving constructive feedback, Fours are typically empathetic and truthful. They anticipate another's reaction, consider what the other person truly wants, think through instances when the person's behavior and desires have not matched, and try to understand how and what the other person thinks and feels. All of this occurs in the Four's mind before he or she even meets with the feedback recipient.

Because of this, Fours need to be careful not to presume that they know what another person has in mind or that everyone is as sensitive as they are, and they need to be especially careful not to presuppose that the feedback recipient wants to discuss feelings and issues in the same depth that Fours relish.

Manage Conflict Constructively

When Fours are directly involved in conflict, they usually feel unsettled. Fours worry about the potential damage that the conflict may cause to the relationship, and they become highly upset when they feel dismissed, slighted, or chronically misunderstood.

When upset, Fours either become extremely quiet or say something in a surprisingly blunt way. In either case, they become internally agitated, with multiple feelings, thoughts, and sensations occurring simultaneously. They often use their rational minds to analyze their emotional reactions, as if understanding strong feelings will somehow lessen them. In fact, the opposite is sometimes true; after the Four has dissected the nuances of his or her feelings, those feelings often become more intense. Typically, Fours don't let go of their anger easily, and their hurt feelings and anger play off each other until the Four experiences a sense of closure, which can take a prolonged period of time.

Fours can be quite skilled at mediating conflicts with others. People find Fours easy to talk to about emotional concerns, adept at identifying the complex issues involved, and intuitive about what it will take for the parties involved to reach a satisfying resolution.

Influence Others

When Fours are effective influencers, it is usually a result of their thoughtfulness, deep introspection, strong relationships, values orientation, and deep commitment to the issues they believe are important. When Fours are less influential, it is because they are too intense, overly emotional, or overly insistent on their positions, or because they overemphasize values at the expense of practical concerns.

Using E-mail as a Developmental Stretch

In the following e-mail, Althena informs her coworkers that she will miss a conference call.

Hi Everyone,

First, I'd like to let you know I'm healing well from my surgery. It didn't quite go as I had hoped, and I ended up needing a transfusion and had a couple of other postsurgical complications. I was home in two days, and out taking a walk on the fourth. I'm feeling quite good considering everything; the pain is manageable, and now and then I forget and have to remind myself to slow down and not do too much.

That said, there are doctor's appointments, including Monday at 10:00. I remember our discussion about moving to this time, but it's the only time of the day I'm unable to participate. I want to say thank you to all of you who sent me e-mails and cards inquiring about my health.

With regrets—Althena

ANALYSIS   Althena's e-mail uses the words *I*, *my*, *me*, and *myself* 14 times. In addition, most of the e-mail discusses Althena's experience with a recent surgery, although the e-mail's ostensible purpose is to apologize for having to miss a business call. As a result of Fours' frequent use of personal words and stories, they are often perceived as being "self-referencing"—that is, continually bringing the conversation and attention back to themselves.

Although this e-mail is personal, warm, and informative, Althena could increase her self-awareness by doing the following:

- Reducing the number of self-referencing words (*I*, *my*, *me*, *mine*, and *myself*)
- Using language that is less personalized and more objective
- Focusing the e-mail more on others than on herself

Here is a possible way Althena could rewrite her e-mail:

Hi everyone,
   Thank you all for your concerns about my recent surgery. The healing has gone remarkably well, and the biggest challenge right now is to slow down and let the recovery process take its course.
   Unfortunately, a doctor's appointment will prevent me from attending the scheduled conference call.
   With regrets,
   Althena

Enneagram Style Fives

Create Genuine Relationships
Fives develop respectful relationships because they honor people's privacy and make it their goal to provide relevant information to those who need it. Fives also create intellectual rapport with others, providing thoughtful perspectives and intellectual stimulation.

Enneagram Style ⑤
KNOWLEDGE

Fives have deeper relationships with those they trust, and they are highly selective about those with whom they form strong bonds. As a result of this cautious way of relating, Fives can initially appear aloof, which can be an issue with people who prefer more warmth. In addition, Fives have little patience for small talk, finding it frivolous and a drain on their energy.

Communicate Clearly

Fives usually share data more than feelings and often speak succinctly, all in an effort to maintain their privacy and conserve their energy. However, when Fives are extremely knowledgeable about a topic, they may talk at length, expounding on all aspects of the issue. At these times, they can get so caught up in ideas that they may not notice that some people feel overloaded with so much data.

When Fives speak, they typically appear self-controlled, rarely using animated body language, and they prefer more physical space between themselves and others than individuals of the other Enneagram styles. However, when Fives feel relaxed and are with someone they know very well, they can be highly spontaneous, both verbally and physically.

Listen Fully

Fives can be excellent listeners, although most Fives listen more for content than for feelings. When Fives perceive another person as being overly emotional (which may be an average degree of emotionality by the standards of others) or when a person seems to Fives to be standing or sitting too close, they usually want to back away or close off the conversation. This can give the other person the impression that the Five doesn't want to listen.

Curious and investigatory, Fives listen closely when they are interested in the content of what someone is saying or when the information includes data that directly affect them. Fives are also accurate reporters, able to recount most information exactly as stated.

Give Effective Feedback

Fives usually give feedback that is precise, concise, and clear. In general, they are more likely to give negative than positive feedback, simply because they prefer to conserve their emotional reserves for feedback that is essential to improving performance.

It can be helpful for Fives to allow others to express feelings as well as thoughts, even if that makes them feel awkward or uncomfortable. Practice and success with allowing emotionality into the feedback process also helps Fives develop their own emotional capacity and become more comfortable with feelings in general. Through body language, questions asked, and comments made, feedback recipients can easily sense whether the feedback giver is comfortable with feeling-level responses. Consequently, it is important for Fives to encourage other people to discuss delicate issues and vulnerabilities.

Manage Conflict Constructively

Fives are generally calm and methodical when managing conflict because they understand that conflict is a natural and inevitable part of organizational life. When they mediate conflict, Fives are more interested in facts than in feelings, an approach that can be an asset in some circumstances but a limitation in others.

When Fives become angry themselves—for example, when they feel that their privacy has been violated, when they have trusted someone who proves unworthy, or when they feel overwhelmed by tasks or situations that they didn't expect or agree to—they are most likely to withdraw. Although it may be obvious that something is awry, it can also appear that nothing is disturbing them, as most Fives are well practiced at saying little and controlling their facial expressions. Occasionally, Fives do show their anger outwardly. When this happens, they can be extremely direct, highly intense, and very passionate.

Influence Others

Most Fives prefer to keep to themselves, influencing others only when the issues directly affect them. When they attempt to influence others, they do so through strategizing and sharing expertise more than through relationships.

Because Fives are typically reservoirs of knowledge but talk less frequently than individuals with other Enneagram styles, people often take notice when they do speak up and try to influence others directly. When Fives try to influence others indirectly, by going to individuals behind the scenes, their attempts are sometimes perceived as covert and thus are viewed with suspicion. Fives also tend to be less engaged than others in the numerous social networks within organizations, thus hindering the full realization of their influence.

Using E-mail as a Developmental Stretch

The Five's language patterns and core issues are clearly reflected in the following series of e-mails. The correspondence begins with an e-mail from Sarah to her coworkers in which she discusses the possibility of carpooling to a staff party. The subsequent e-mails are between Martin (a Five) and Sarah (a Two):

E-MAIL 1, FROM SARAH, REGARDING AN UPCOMING STAFF PARTY

This party sounds like so much fun. I wonder if anyone would be coming from the Southside who might like to make the drive with me. That probably only includes Martin and/or Trish, but who knows?
  Sarah

E-MAIL 2, FROM MARTIN TO SARAH

Hi Sarah,
  I can pick you up, no problem.
  Martin

E-MAIL 3, FROM SARAH TO MARTIN

Hi Martin
  Or I can pick you up! Either way. Where do you live, or would you be coming from work?
  Sarah

E-MAIL 4, FROM MARTIN TO SARAH

Hi Sarah,

Looking forward to it. I live and work in Southfield . . .
okay, so I live in my car . . . what's the big deal? Just kidding.
I get off from work at about 5:00 p.m., so we could be fash-
ionably late.

Martin

E-MAIL 5, FROM MARTIN TO SARAH

Hi Sarah,

Well, I've got this new Blazer, and you know about my
trust issues already, so what the heck, I'll pick you up. What's
your address?

Martin

E-MAIL 6, FROM SARAH TO MARTIN

Hi!

I forgot about the privacy and autonomy issues involved!
Forgive me!!

Sarah

ANALYSIS This e-mail series illustrates several Five language patterns: (1) expressing thoughts succinctly, (2) needing to preserve
autonomy and privacy, (3) being self-reflective (in a wry way), and
(4) engaging in moderate self-disclosure (the sharing of information about self) when the Five knows someone well.

In e-mail 2, Martin immediately suggests that he pick up Sarah,
and he makes it clear in the subsequent e-mails that he wants to drive
(thus preserving his autonomy) and does not want to give Sarah his
address or have her pick him up (thus preserving his privacy). Martin's self-reflection and self-disclosure can be read in e-mail 5 as he
explains why he prefers to pick her up (his "trust issues").

Martin could use the following guidelines to work on his Five
language patterns:

- Elaborate on each idea.
- Include real feelings with thoughts.
- Be more forthcoming about his desires at earlier stages of the communication.

Martin could have written Sarah only one e-mail (saving them both a great deal of time) saying the following:

> Hi Sarah,
>   I would be happy to drive to the party with you. That day, I will be getting off work about 5:00 p.m., which might make us fashionably late. My preference is to pick you up, and I hope this is okay with you. Why don't you e-mail me your address?
>   See you soon,
>   Martin

Enneagram Style Sixes

Enneagram Style
DOUBT

Create Genuine Relationships

Above all, Sixes like relationships in which they feel they can count on and trust the other person. Insightful and sociable, Sixes create genuine relationships with groups as well as with individuals, feeling more certain and supported when there is a group behind them. However, when Sixes feel wary or distrustful of someone, they may question that person's motives and assume that their negative assessment of the other person's character or behavior is well founded. Thus, Sixes can end up with a bad relationship or, at best, an ambivalent one.

Communicate Clearly

Sixes like to develop relationships and communicate in a reciprocal way, with talking and listening being given equal importance.

Sixes usually start their conversations with analytical comments, but they can move swiftly into emotional discussions when needed.

Although the Six's conversational style can be confident and bold (the counterphobic Six), it can just as easily become hesitant and uncertain (the phobic Six). Most Sixes, however, alternate between the two. Most Sixes appear somewhat serious, and they talk about "what-ifs" as part of their anticipatory problem solving. Sometimes this comes across as pessimism, but from the Six's point of view, it is really a matter of being idealistic and realistic simultaneously. In addition, Sixes have quick reactions to events and ideas that concern or surprise them.

Listen Fully

Sixes give others what they would most like to get themselves: they listen fully, especially to friends and colleagues who are in need. However, they have a tendency to project their own thoughts, feelings, and behaviors onto others, assuming that others function exactly as they do. Because most Sixes do not confirm or disconfirm their perceptions, they can believe they have listened fully to someone when they actually have not.

In addition, Sixes may filter or distort what they hear when they distrust the other person, imagining negative intentions where there are none. This can be especially true with authority figures, whom the Six may imagine to be either more malevolent or more benevolent than they actually are.

Give Effective Feedback

Giving positive feedback is usually easy for Sixes, but giving constructive feedback can cause them to engage in extensive anticipatory planning. When they do this, Sixes review numerous details and examples, anticipate how the feedback recipient may react, and develop strategies for minimizing the negative consequences of the interaction. Although this preplanning is helpful, Sixes also need to make sure that they bring calm, clarity, and hope to the interaction, focusing on concrete behaviors and finding out from the feedback recipient why she or he did something rather than making assumptions.

Manage Conflict Constructively

Because Sixes have a keen sense for issue identification and problem solving, are easy to talk to, and often give insightful advice, others like to talk to them about distressing issues. Sixes are often able to defuse or resolve issues merely by sharing their perspective and suggestions.

When they are directly involved in a conflict, Sixes either face it head on or avoid it altogether. In either case, conflict causes them to feel anxious. When Sixes feel pressured by others—and they often feel pressured because they put so much pressure on themselves—or when they perceive someone as being untrustworthy, abusing authority, or disregarding his or her commitment to the group, Sixes can become furious. They may not say anything right away, but when they do, Sixes can be quite harsh. In either case, the issues will undoubtedly be recycling in their minds.

Influence Others

Sixes like to influence others to come around to their way of thinking, and they do this by identifying potential problems, discussing issues with group members, and building support for what the Six thinks is important.

Sixes can feel that their perspective is not receiving adequate attention when others act without addressing these obstacles. However, when their timing is right (i.e., when they do not identify problems too early) and when they frame problems as issues with solutions rather than as negatives, Sixes have a strong impact on others.

Using E-mail as a Developmental Stretch

Two e-mails from Sheldon, an attorney in a large law firm, were sent to a human resource staff member in charge of an employee morale survey. Sheldon sent the second e-mail within an hour of having sent the first, although the human resource staff member had not yet responded to the first query.

E-MAIL 1

I am slightly confused. Our group has only four employees in Chicago. One has been there only a year. How can we have a 64.7 percent response rate?
Sheldon

E-MAIL 2

I certainly don't believe new employees' responses have any meaning. My recollection, though, was that we were not going to survey them.
Sheldon

ANALYSIS While Sheldon raises legitimate concerns, a contextual issue may help clarify why these e-mails reflect Six language patterns. The survey to which Sheldon refers was sent to several thousand employees. Of the 70 attorneys in management positions comparable to Sheldon's, he is the only person to scrutinize the preliminary response rates from the survey and send an e-mail requesting clarification.

The words that Sheldon chooses in these e-mails, combined with his action of sending two consecutive e-mails before even seeing the results, reflect his worry.

If Sheldon wants to use his e-mails to practice new language patterns, he can do the following:

- Use the recipient's name at the start of the e-mail, thus communicating more warmth.
- Collect his thoughts and send only one e-mail, thus conveying less anxiety.

- Reduce the amount of concern and fear implicit in his words.
- Imply that the recipient of the e-mail will effectively handle the issues he raises.

Sheldon could have collapsed his two e-mails into one and written the following:

Dear Shannon,

When I received the e-mail about the response rates for our Chicago group, I did the math and wondered about the 64.7 percent response rate. That group has four employees, one of whom has been there only one year.

My recollection is that we were not going to survey employees who are new because they have had limited experience with the firm.

Your answers will be very helpful to me in understanding this process and yielding data that will be useful.

Regards,
Sheldon

Enneagram Style Sevens

Enneagram Style
OPTIONS

Create Genuine Relationships

Upbeat and engaging, Sevens usually charm people with their friendly demeanor, stimulating ideas, and versatile intellects. Because their interests are broad, it is easy for Sevens to find a common ground for conversation.

Genuine, enduring relationships can be more challenging for Sevens. First, when they stop feeling stimulated by either the topic or the other person, Sevens lose interest in the interaction, and this sudden lack of interest is usually obvious. Second, Sevens move toward the pleasurable and exciting but avoid situations in which they feel uncomfortable. Discussing feelings tends to make

Sevens uneasy, and they are reluctant to discuss such feelings in depth even with people they trust.

Communicate Clearly

Quick and spontaneous, Sevens usually talk fast and change topics quickly. To the listener, these topics may seem unrelated, but to the Seven, the association of ideas seems perfectly logical. When talking, Sevens are also easily distracted by a new thought or by something in the environment that stimulates them and diverts their attention.

Sevens often convey their ideas through storytelling, with the main point being left for the listener to discern. Their language is usually optimistic and vivid, and they keep other people's attention through their smiles, effervescence, facial expressions, gestures, and animated body movements.

When they experience emotions such as sadness, fear, or anger or receive negative feedback, Sevens tend to reframe it as something positive. For example, if they hear criticism of themselves, Sevens will provide a context so that their behavior can be seen in an affirmative way. When highly displeased, Sevens can be sharp and sarcastic.

Listen Fully

Sevens perceive themselves to be good listeners and adamantly want to be heard, but to Sevens, listening means quickly absorbing what the other person is saying and then commenting on the topic or something related to it, usually before the other person has finished what he or she is saying. While the Seven's listening style is effective with some people, others may simply feel that they have been interrupted and were not being listened to at all.

Give Effective Feedback

Sevens are more likely to give positive than negative feedback, since their intention is to uplift rather than discourage. However, they will give constructive feedback when they need to, citing many examples and offering multiple possibilities for changes in behavior.

When offering constructive feedback, Sevens need to make sure that their optimism doesn't obscure the seriousness of the message, and that they keep the focus on the single most important point. Adding more detail or including related issues can confuse or distract the feedback recipient.

Manage Conflict Constructively

Because conflict elicits anxiety in most Sevens, they often use humor or a positive reframing of the situation as a way to defuse the conflict. These techniques can be helpful in relieving tension, but they can also interfere with a thorough discussion of the issues involved.

Sevens become frustrated and angry when they feel that they are being forced to participate in nonstimulating or routine tasks, perceive that someone is limiting their choices or criticizing them unfairly, or feel that they have been dismissed. Although dealing with these feelings can be difficult for many Sevens, doing so helps them to understand and accept their emotional reactions.

Influence Others

Sevens easily inspire and influence others through their innovative ideas, optimistic personalities, and engaging conversations. Sevens can also become so enthralled with an idea that they may not notice the reactions of others. In addition, Sevens can present so many ideas that others may have difficulty giving each idea full consideration. Finally, although most Sevens know the power and authority relationships within an organization, they often ignore these dynamics, thus interfering with their ability to fully influence others.

Using E-mail as a Developmental Stretch

Leslie, a Seven, sent this e-mail to a former colleague, a person who had left the company two years earlier and had recently contacted her via e-mail to rekindle their friendship.

I would love to talk to you—I know you are busy too—home
phone: 318-277-3993—weekends are best
   Daughter is getting married on April 7 to a New
Zealander—wonderful man—in Glasgow, Scotland—small
wedding, only the two of them—more later
   Take care,
   Leslie

ANALYSIS   Leslie's e-mail illustrates the Seven's tendency to think, talk, and move at a rapid rate. Leslie talks about herself, offers her phone number, and highlights her daughter's wedding plans, all in a brief e-mail. Many details, however, are not included—for example, why Leslie is so busy, who will initiate the telephone call, and why the wedding is taking place in Scotland when the bride is from the United States.

Leslie's e-mail uses phrases rather than complete sentences, uses a dash rather than a period at the end of a thought, and some capital letters and commas are missing. Leslie's optimism is evident, as she implies that everything is going well in her life and mentions that her prospective son-in-law is "wonderful."

Although the e-mail is short, Leslie's primary focus is on what *she* is doing, with limited reference to the recipient of the e-mail. While individuals with several Enneagram styles can exhibit this same tendency to focus on themselves, giving the impression (almost always unintended) that their own life and activities are more interesting and important than those of others, Sevens do so using an upbeat tone.

Leslie could use her e-mails to become more conscious of her Enneagram style language patterns by following these guidelines:

- Elaborate on problems or concerns as well as positive information.
- Use complete sentences.
- Pay more attention to punctuation.
- Focus on the e-mail recipient as well as on herself.

Leslie could rewrite the e-mail this way:

Dear Linda,

It was a pleasure to hear from you, and I would love to talk to you soon. My home phone number is 318-277-3993. I still have your number. Perhaps we can talk sometime this weekend; I'll give you a call.

Thank you for asking about my daughter. She is marrying a wonderful man from New Zealand this coming April. They want to have a tiny wedding in Scotland—just the two of them; unfortunately, my busy work schedule does not allow me to be there, and I also want to respect their wishes for the idea of just running off together.

Work has been hectic, but challenging. I can share more about this and other things when we speak by phone, and I want to hear about what is going on in your life, too.

Take care,

Leslie

Enneagram Style Eights

Enneagram Style
CHALLENGE

Create Genuine Relationships

Eights develop honest relationships, having little tolerance for relationships that are not candid and direct. Because Eights demand truthfulness from themselves and others, and because they like to decide the terms of the relationship, they often have excellent relationships with people of their choosing. However, their relationships with people they don't respect or trust are generally more tenuous.

Communicate Clearly

Eights use a bold, authoritative communication style, knowing how to grab other people's attention by raising the volume of their voices, emphasizing key words, moving closer to their audience, or increasing their overall energy level. Eights may also say little, sit back, watch everyone else's interactions, and then decide whether to enter the conversation to either add a missing point or turn the entire conversation around to another perspective. However, when Eights are quiet for extended periods, it usually means that they are bored, angry, or extremely fatigued.

Listen Fully

Eights can be excellent listeners, particularly with those whom they like or respect, or with individuals who have information that is very important to the Eight. However, Eights also detest having their time wasted and usually just want the answers. They may listen for a short time, but then show their impatience through short, direct verbal messages (for example, saying, "So what's the point you're making?") or through intense body language, starting other work, or frowning. Eights also stop listening when they perceive that the other person is (1) being untruthful, (2) directly or indirectly asserting unauthorized or poorly executed control, or (3) when they feel blindsided and/or blamed.

Give Effective Feedback

Eights usually give feedback in a straightforward way, specifying what the other person should do instead. This can be helpful because the other person then knows exactly what to change, why change is needed, and how to accomplish the change. However, the Eight's forthrightness and intensity can be intimidating to those who need more warmth when discussing vulnerabilities. It helps when Eights show positive regard for the other person and remind themselves to give positive feedback and constructive feedback with equal frequency.

Manage Conflict Constructively

Eights expect others to deal with conflict directly, but will take sides if they believe that one of the parties is right and the other wrong. Although this sort of bravery earns them respect, it also gets them embroiled in disagreements that are not fundamentally their own.

Eights become very angry if another person blames them unfairly, lies, makes them feel vulnerable, or acts abusively toward others. When angry, Eights usually take immediate action. Occasionally, angry Eights become silent, but this usually happens either when they believe that there is no effective action they can take or when they have already disengaged from the other person or the organization.

Influence Others

Eights enjoy political strategizing and anticipating likely outcomes, and they know how to function effectively within influence networks. They expect to have influence, and when they lose any power—for example, if their position shifts in a reorganization or if some key allies leave the organization—Eights sense this loss of power immediately and dislike it. They then turn inward to determine what to do next. When Eights feel thwarted in their ability to remedy the situation, they may become more visibly upset and angry, remain withdrawn, or do both in an alternating fashion.

Using E-mail as a Developmental Stretch

The following two e-mails, the first from a man and the second from a woman, both contain identical language patterns, showing that these patterns are the same for male and female Eights. The first e-mail, from Raymond, was sent in response to an e-mail from a longtime professional colleague.

> Good to hear from you. All is well. I will call you when I next come to San Francisco.
> Raymond

The second e-mail, from Martha, the CEO of a midsize company, was sent in response to an e-mail that was originally intended for the firm's chief operating officer, Ken, regarding the directions and logistics for a forthcoming meeting.

> Greetings!
> Unfortunately, Ken is out sick today. Gloria will forward directions to the parking structure for our office. You are scheduled for the Senior Staff meeting agenda tomorrow. The Senior Staff consists of six seniors and myself, for a total of seven.
> Our Senior Staff meeting is scheduled to begin at 12:00 p.m. We are scheduled to have that meeting at one of the local restaurants, so we'll be walking. Plan on arriving at 11:55 a.m. I would allow 45 minutes to get here at that time of day.
> Martha

ANALYSIS Both e-mails get right to the point. Raymond acknowledges the person who e-mailed him and says exactly what he, Raymond, will do next—he will make contact with the recipient when he is in San Francisco. Martha gives direct and precise answers—what will happen next, who will do what, who will be at the meeting, what time the meeting will begin, what time to arrive, and how long the drive will be. Both e-mails contain complete, concise information and are directive and action-oriented.

These e-mails contain no extra words and few pleasantries, and both are no-nonsense. Still, they are friendly: Raymond says, "Good to hear from you," and Martha begins her e-mail with "Greetings!" The directness of both e-mails results partly from the sentence structure. Together, they contain eleven complete sentences, nine of which use the same sentence structure—subject (noun) and predicate (verb), with very few adjectives or adverbs.

Both Raymond and Martha could increase their awareness of their Enneagram style communication patterns by rewriting their e-mails following these guidelines:

- Changing thoughts or statements that convey ways to organize, structure, and control events to statements that are less directive and more contingent
- Acknowledging and inviting a response from the other person
- Including more variation in sentence structure
- Using more adjectives and adverbs
- Being more personal

For example, Raymond could revise his e-mail like this:

Dear Joe,

It was good to hear from you. All is well at the office. We have new projects coming in all the time, ones that are demanding a great deal of my time and attention. I will call you when I next come to San Francisco, but when that will be is unclear. Hopefully, it will be soon.

Looking forward to talking with you,

Raymond

Martha could rewrite her e-mail this way:

Greetings, Arnold!

Unfortunately, Ken is out sick today, so he is unable to return your e-mail. In answer to your request, Gloria will forward you directions to the parking structure for our office. You are scheduled for the senior staff meeting agenda tomorrow. I, along with the six other senior staff members, am looking forward to meeting with you tomorrow at 12:00.

It would be helpful if you arrived around 11:55 a.m., because we will be walking to a local restaurant. It may take you 45 minutes or so to get here at that time of day.

Please let me know if there's anything else you need.

Regards,

Martha

Enneagram Style Nines

Create Genuine Relationships

Open, affable, and able to converse on a variety of topics, Nines develop relationships that last a lifetime, even when they don't see the other people very often. However, Nines' reluctance to say

Enneagram Style ⑨
HARMONY

exactly what they think and feel for fear of creating tension or conflict also hinders the development of deeper relationships.

Communicate Clearly

When Nines speak, they either affirm the other person's point of view or describe their own ideas and experiences in a highly detailed, sequential manner—for example, instead of reporting only the results of a meeting, Nines are likely to explain the structure and outcomes of the meeting in exact order so as to not forget anything important. Wanting to be fair to all sides, they either elicit differing ideas from others or express an alternative view themselves, without making it clear whether they agree with that perspective. This makes it difficult for others to know what the Nine is truly thinking and feeling.

Listen Fully

Nines make especially good listeners because they listen in a way that does not make others feel judged. However, Nines' affirming responses, such as nodding their heads at the right moments and saying "Uh-huh," can give the impression that they are in full agreement when this may not be the case.

While Nines do listen, it is not always with the complete attention they appear to be giving because Nines are not entirely nonjudgmental. They do have opinions and judgments, but they tend to keep these to themselves or express them indirectly toward the end of a conversation.

Give Effective Feedback

Giving positive feedback can be easy for most Nines, who especially like to offer supportive comments in public. This has the effect of strengthening both group harmony and individual relationships.

Although Nines can be very effective in giving constructive feedback, they have to work up to doing this by thinking through what they want to say, finding the inner courage to risk saying something negative, and calculating how to achieve the most positive outcome. All of this reflection can produce excellent results, but for this to occur, Nines have to make themselves actually give the feedback, staying focused on the central point they want to make and making it clearly.

Manage Conflict Constructively

Known as the mediators of the Enneagram, Nines relish bringing harmony and unity to interpersonal situations. Because they are easy to talk to and can easily see each person's side of the problem, most people appreciate it when Nines step into the middle of a disagreement and bring it to resolution.

However, when Nines feel angry, they may not know they are angry until they are livid. Being ignored repeatedly, being told what to do without having a say, and being confronted directly can ignite their fury, although it usually takes them a long time to express it. When others are angry with them, Nines become agitated and unsettled, and they try to appease the other person or avoid a confrontation if they can.

Influence Others

Nines' extended network of relationships, easy-to-relate-to interpersonal style, and ability to see various viewpoints all contribute to others wanting to hear their perspectives and know what they think. Because of this, Nines do have quite a bit of influence, which often surprises them. At the same time, Nines exert less influence than they could because they may not state their opinions directly, or because they communicate their concerns and ideas in such an even-toned way that people don't really know what they think or how strongly they feel about an issue.

Using E-mail as a Developmental Stretch

The first of the two e-mails that follow shows the language patterns used by Nines when they want to affirm others; the second illustrates their language pattern when they are angry.

Belinda, a Nine and a board member of a nonprofit company, sent this e-mail to the entire board after a board of directors' conference call.

> Thanks for the fine minutes, Sheila.
> Welcome President Jeremy.
> Thanks Madame President, Alicia. [Alicia was the past board of directors' president.]
> A good weekend to all.
> Warm regards,
> Belinda

Byron (also a board member) sent Jeremy (the current board president) the following e-mail. In it, Byron expresses his anger about Jeremy's request that the board commit two days to an in-person meeting, which is to occur six months later.

> Jeremy,
> I am of the opinion that you cannot ask people who have ongoing work responsibilities to give up nearly two whole days for this meeting. My suggestion is to try to carve out three hours on Monday night, meet all day Tuesday, and make the meeting as focused and productive as possible.
> Byron

ANALYSIS In the first e-mail, Belinda's explicit intention is to compliment and honor specific individuals; consequently, she sent the e-mail to the entire board of directors. This affirms these three individuals in front of the whole board, reflecting the Nine's sensitivity and orientation to goodwill.

The second e-mail illustrates how Nines communicate when they are deeply angry and ready to share their feelings. Because most Nines are not readily aware of feeling angry and are also reluctant to express these feelings openly, their anger can be manifested as controlled eruptions. Byron's strong criticism of Jeremy is clear, as are his unequivocal prescriptions for remedying the situation. He expresses anger about being compelled to do something against his will—spending two full days in a meeting. Although Nines appear flexible, they can also become immovable objects when they feel pushed. If Byron had expressed his real feelings and needs earlier, his e-mail to Jeremy would probably have had a less strident tone.

Although both e-mails serve their intended purposes, Belinda and Byron could use e-mails to enhance their awareness of their Enneagram-based communication patterns by following these guidelines:

In situations of goodwill:

- Alter the use of overly affirming language.
- Use language that states a clear position and message.
- Be clear for whom the e-mail is really intended.

Belinda could have rewritten her e-mail as follows:

Dear board members,

I thought our recent conference call went very well and that everyone contributed to its success. I also want to extend my appreciation for the work that Alicia has put into this organization as our president and to welcome Jeremy into his new role as current president. Sheila, the minutes look great, so thank you for your effort.

Warmly,

Belinda

In situations of conflict:

- Stop the use of strident and overly formal language.
- Express concerns more thoroughly, using a respectful tone.
- Consider talking in person or by phone instead of writing an e-mail.

Byron could have rewritten his original e-mail in this way:

Dear Jeremy,

When I learned that you would like the board meeting to last two full days, I became concerned about the amount of time this would require from all of us. I don't have two full days available at that time. Why don't we spend three hours on Monday night and a full day on Tuesday? I think we can cover what is needed if we have a clear agenda and keep our discussions focused.

Please let me know what you think.

Byron

Developmental Stretches for Everyone

In addition to the e-mail writing suggestions that are specific to each Enneagram style, the following tips can be useful to everyone:

- **Include a salutation, such as "Dear David" or "Hi Janet."** This personalizes the e-mail and makes the recipient more responsive.
- **Use an appropriate ending, such as "Looking forward to your response" or "Regards."** This helps e-mail recipients to not speculate about what you are thinking or what they should do next.
- **Include your name at the end of the e-mail.** This personalizes the e-mail and makes it easier for recipients to refer to later if they save it to a desktop file.

- **Use CAPITAL letters sparingly; for emphasis, use bold font.** Remember that while you may not mean to shout what you capitalize, many people read capitalization this way.
- **Use complete sentences whenever possible.** This simply makes your statements clearer to the recipient.
- **Do not use e-mail for all your communications.** Sensitive conversations are usually best done in person, or at least by telephone. Remember that any e-mail you send can be forwarded to hundreds of people.
- **Reread your e-mail before you send it.** Rereading helps you be more conscious of your Enneagram-based communication style, and you are likely to catch words, tone, or statements that don't reflect what you really want to say.

To Learn More . . .

Read one of the recommended books under "Become an Excellent Communicator" in the Resources section at the back of this book; read Chapter 2, "Communicating Effectively," Chapter 3, "Giving Constructive Feedback," and Chapter 4, "Managing Conflict," in *Bringing Out the Best in Yourself at Work: How to Use the Enneagram System for Success*, by Ginger Lapid-Bogda, Ph.D.

Chapter 6

Lead High-Performing Teams

*T*eams—groups whose members have common goals and some degree of interdependence in achieving these goals— are the foundation of contemporary organizations. As a result, the ability to create and Lead High-Performing Teams is essential to every leader's success. All teams—senior teams, management teams, task forces, steering committees, matrix teams, project teams, and intact work teams—require their leaders to create team-based structures and processes that support a skilled and motivated workforce in delivering seamless, high-quality goods and services to their customers.

Having the ability to Lead High-Performing Teams means being skilled in the following seven competency components (see Figure 6.1):

1. Providing team leadership
2. Creating a team vision
3. Attracting and developing team talent
4. Designing a team architecture
5. Establishing effective team processes
6. Building a team culture
7. Assuring quality products and services

FIGURE 6.1 **Lead High-Performing Teams**

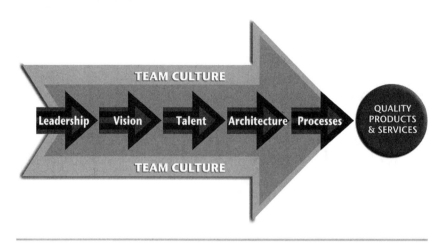

As you read further and reflect on the seven competency components of Lead High-Performing Teams, rate yourself in each area on a scale of 1 to 5. This will help you determine both your areas of strength and the areas that need development.

The Seven Competency Components of Lead High-Performing Teams

Component 1: Providing Team Leadership

This includes believing in the value of teams and being willing to empower team members to do their jobs; sharing power appropriately so that some aspects of leadership can be rotated among team members; being able to play numerous roles as needed (e.g., facilitator, "orchestra" conductor, coach, mentor, and disciplinarian); inspiring excellence and commitment within the team through your words and actions; being perceived as making wise decisions; treating all team members fairly; establishing clear boundaries, rules, and authority structures that enable the team to do its work effectively; having organizational credibility and being well networked; and both obtaining resources for the team (e.g., information, time, and money) and running interference between the team and the organization when needed.

Low				High
1	2	3	4	5

Component 2: Creating a Team Vision

This involves developing a collaborative, compelling, and shared team vision based on both a strategic analysis of the environment and a set of core values; creating a team mission and a set of strategies and goals that are aligned with both the team's and the larger organization's vision, mission, strategy, and philosophy; ensuring that the team's subunits support the larger team vision, mission, and strategy; and being able to translate the team's vision, mission, and strategy into reality through the team's commitment to take action.

Low				High
1	2	3	4	5

Component 3: Attracting and Developing Team Talent

This involves developing a team that is so highly regarded that it attracts the best talent; recruiting talent from sources that are likely to generate excellent new hires; hiring new team members whose capabilities are matched to both current and anticipated business needs; using interviewing processes that accurately assess which candidates have the best skills and can also thrive in a team environment; orienting and integrating new team members so that they can perform quickly and effectively; providing a variety of ongoing development opportunities and honest feedback—both positive and negative—so that team members are supported, challenged, and continuously learning and growing; and coaching or mentoring team members so that each individual can contribute his or her personal best.

Low				High
1	2	3	4	5

Component 4: Designing a Team Architecture

This includes structuring work in a flexible and effective way and reorganizing the work and/or specific jobs as needed; providing clarity about individual and team roles and expectations so that all members understand both their own and one another's jobs, with enough role flexibility provided to foster creativity, innovation, and initiative; establishing individual and team accountabilities and metrics, and regularly monitoring individual and team performance; and establishing a reward system that reinforces both the individual and team behaviors required for success.

Low				High
1	2	3	4	5

Component 5: Establishing Effective Team Processes

This involves designing effective and efficient work-flow processes; ensuring that work between and among team members is well coordinated; creating multiple communication vehicles that are efficient, accurate, and timely so that information flows freely within the team and between the team and other parts of the organization; providing clarity regarding the team's scope of authority and its decision-making processes; communicating information about decisions in a clear and timely manner; planning and facilitating meetings that encourage participation, make the best use of time, and produce important results; and ensuring that differences and conflicts are responded to in a timely and constructive manner.

Low				High
1	2	3	4	5

Component 6: Building a Team Culture

This includes creating a positive, collaborative environment in which employees feel valued, respected, and appreciated; developing an inclusive culture in which diversity of perspective, style, and background is perceived as value-added; designing an atmosphere in which individual strengths are leveraged, and in which the synergy within the team creates even higher performance levels than would be achieved by individual team members alone; creating a vibrant sense of *esprit de corps*; recognizing and celebrating both individual and team milestones and successes; and fostering a culture of innovative problem solving, continuous learning, and well-calibrated risk taking.

Low				High
1	2	3	4	5

Component 7: Assuring Quality Products and Services

This means creating a quality-focused culture in which everyone strives for excellence; identifying, designing, and delivering products and services in accordance with customer needs and, at the same time, working collaboratively with customers to help them understand when their requests are not realistic; setting up multiple feedback channels between the team and its customers, vendors, suppliers, and distributors; and building quality and improvement into every aspect of the team's products, services, and ways of working together.

Low				High
1	2	3	4	5

Enneagram Dimensions of Lead High-Performing Teams

Enneagram Style Ones

Enneagram Style Ones create teams that focus on producing the highest-quality products and services. Their high standards apply to the team's ultimate goals as well as to the team's ongoing work products. For example, One leaders find typos, poor grammar, incorrect information, lack of

Enneagram Style
DILIGENCE ①

timely delivery, subpar analyses, and lack of follow-through deeply troubling.

With a vision of quality and a high regard for talent, One leaders establish well-organized teams that are focused on practical, clear, realistic, and purposeful goals. One leaders also prefer teams in which roles are unambiguous, so that each member clearly understands his or her area of responsibility. Because this is how One leaders themselves prefer to operate, applying these same principles to team leadership enables them to keep their teams well organized and to maintain individual accountability.

One leaders place great emphasis on self-improvement; as a result, their team culture is usually one of learning and growth. Ones usually create processes that allow work to be coordinated in a smooth manner, with quality measures set up at key milestones, and they lead their teams by example, demonstrating the most flawless execution possible.

Following is a description of Tim, a well-respected One leader:

"Tim's team is exceedingly well organized, and all members know the team's goals as well as their own specific objectives. Because Tim is such an exemplary leader, new team members are sometimes initially intimidated by his capabilities. Once they get to know him, however, they see his humility. Tim definitely places the team's well-being above his own, which makes the team members respect him even more."

One team leaders know that they are not perfect. They may sometimes unintentionally appear to be overly critical—for example, using a sharp tone of voice when giving feedback to a team member about a minor issue. A related area is the One leader's tendency to offer opinions quickly, which may discourage some team members from voicing their own ideas, particularly if the One leader's opinion is negative.

In addition, although One leaders usually value fairness, they may rely more on certain team members whom they know they can count on, or overlook objectionable interpersonal behavior on the part of a team member who the One leader believes is highly talented. Both responses may be viewed by other team members as favoritism.

Finally, because One leaders like doing concrete, day-to-day tactical work, they sometimes have difficulty staying at the strategic level of team leadership—i.e., strategic planning, providing oversight and mentoring, and interfacing between the team and other parts of the organization.

The reluctance of Ones to delegate detail work that they enjoy is illustrated by the following story:

> During a meeting with his staff, Tim expressed some reluctance in a discussion of whether the team should take on a new project. His response to the idea was to say, "I have so much work on my desk that we can't take on one more project!" When the team members offered to take over some of his work, Tim surprised everyone by exclaiming, "You can't do that! I like what I'm doing, even though I know some of you could do it equally as well."

Development Stretches for Ones

LET GO OF TACTICAL WORK Make a list of all your team-related tasks. Next to each item, write either *T* for tactical work or *S* for strategic work. Unless you are a "working supervisor" (that is, one who is expected to do some of the hands-on work), you need to relinquish as much tactical work as possible to members of your team. Strategic work is always the team leader's responsibility. For all tactical work that can be delegated, write down the names of the team members you believe are capable of performing specific tasks, then assign the work to them.

TAKE TIME TO RELAX AND ENJOY YOURSELF One leaders can become curt, on edge, and resentful when they have too much to do for too long a period of time. They are often able to relax while on vacation, but they have a hard time doing so on other occasions. Every day, give yourself permission to spend 15 minutes just relaxing. Listen to music you like, read a magazine that is unrelated to work, or go for a walk by yourself and enjoy the experience of feeling unburdened.

PAY ATTENTION TO THE UNINTENDED CONSEQUENCES OF YOUR BEHAVIOR FOR YOUR TEAM   Remind yourself that each individual relationship you have with a team member—whether more positive or more negative in nature—can have unintended consequences for other members of the team or for the team as a whole. For example, when you tolerate the difficult interpersonal behavior of a talented team member, others may perceive this as your condoning the behavior and feel disempowered in terms of dealing with this individual.

Enneagram Style Twos

Enneagram Style Two leaders focus on the following three areas: (1) the assessment, motivation, and professional development of team members; (2) the creation of a positive team-based culture; and (3) the development of just enough organizational processes to get the work done without stifling individual creativity and initiative. Two leaders believe that when these factors are present, the team will produce high-quality goods and services. More than leaders with any other Enneagram style, Twos take time at the beginning to allow team members to get to know one another and develop trusting, supportive relationships. They then focus on creating moderate to highly interdependent teams whose members work together to ensure a high-functioning work unit.

Twos are people-oriented and tend to lead their teams through a collective vision that focuses both on the team itself and on the customer. Encouraging participation and acting as the team's cheerleader, they coach, urge, and challenge team members on a one-on-one basis, preferring not to say anything negative to someone in public for fear of damaging the morale of the individual, the team, or both.

Anne is an example of an excellent Two leader:

> Anne's greatest strength as a team leader is in bringing together a group of talented people and transforming them into a community. Her team produced the best conference in the organization's history thus far, with a strong team spirit that was dedicated both to producing a high-quality event and to the members' supporting one another in the process. For example, Anne dedicated the first half hour of every team meeting to a check-in, with team members being given the opportunity to share what was happening in both their work and their personal lives. With this foundation of openness and mutual understanding, the team thrived. Although Anne's leadership style was to allow team members to take the initiative and do their jobs well, her behind-the-scenes influence could be felt in all aspects of the work.

Although Twos can be quite forceful in setting direction, many are uncomfortable with being in highly visible leadership roles and having attention focused on them for extended periods of time. When Two leaders receive commendations for work they have done, they typically deflect the praise to their team as a whole, saying that the achievement would not have been possible without the efforts of the entire team. While this statement may be true, it also minimizes the contribution, diminishes the stature, and reduces the visibility of the Two leader. Twos prefer to work behind the scenes, even when they are in fact at the center of activity. However, every team needs a leader who willingly acknowledges and accepts a visible leadership role.

Twos may also minimize their importance as team leaders by becoming too involved in the detail work, usually to help team members who have requested assistance or who are overloaded. In doing so, Twos reduce their impact as leaders in three ways: (1) people both inside and outside the team begin to see the Two as a worker rather than a leader, (2) it becomes more difficult for the Two leader to find the time to focus on the larger picture of where the team is going, and (3) Two leaders can become so overworked that they become short-tempered, thus undermining their effectiveness in leading the team.

Here's an example when Anne slipped into the role of team member:

> The 45-page conference program was written and required editing. Although a team member named Shawn had volunteered for this job, he asked Anne's assistance in editing a portion of the program. Anne immediately said yes, although her leadership responsibilities more than filled her day. When confronted by her boss about why she was doing work at this level rather than other higher-level activity, Anne admitted, "I like helping people out, and I enjoy doing this type of work. I can't say no now, after I've already committed to doing it. Besides, it gives me a way to know the program better."
>
> Her boss replied, "You're leading this team well, but maybe you don't want to be the real leader. You could just read the final program! Get someone else to help Shawn."

Development Stretches for Twos

STEP INTO VISIBLE LEADERSHIP It is important for you to claim both the authority that goes with the leadership role and the personal influence that you can have. Doing so makes it easier for others to follow your lead; it also creates more respect for the leadership role, and this increased level of recognition is important, both for the team's success and for your own professional growth. In public settings, refer to yourself as the leader of the team. Run your own team meetings rather than having someone else facilitate them. Pay attention to ways in which you minimize your leadership role.

DEVELOP THE TEAM ARCHITECTURE TO THE SAME DEGREE AS THE TEAM PROCESSES Two team leaders know how to set up processes that enable people to work together effectively, but they tend to put less emphasis on clear team structure, roles, and specific accountabilities. Greater clarity helps team members work more effectively and reduces unnecessary dependence on the team leader. Design the team architecture in the same way you design the team processes—that is, make it slightly *under*organized, so that team members will still have the freedom to take the initiative and be innovative.

AVOID DOING TOO MUCH OF THE DAY-TO-DAY WORK Discipline yourself to neither offer assistance nor automatically say yes when you are asked for it. Each time you are about to involve yourself in detail work, say no and remind yourself that there is something more important that you are neglecting.

Enneagram Style Threes

Three team leaders organize their teams around concrete results and a team architecture that has both clearly delineated roles and a structure that is directly connected to the team's goals. Three leaders develop specific, measurable goals, visibly linked to both team and individual performance. This reliance on goals and structure is reflective of how Threes operate best: they like to know where they're going and have a plan for getting there efficiently.

Enneagram Style
PERFORM

As a result, Threes try to create teams that are made up of highly talented and self-motivated individuals who are receptive to feedback and who put customer satisfaction first. Because Threes become frustrated with what they perceive as unnecessary obstacles to both their own and the team's success, they develop clear team processes to eliminate confusion whenever possible.

Most Threes assume a team leadership role with ease, with efficiency and effectiveness as their primary operating principles. For this reason, their willingness to take charge of a team is rarely in question.

The following example describes Noreen, a Three project team leader:

> Noreen was known as a take-charge leader. Even when her team wasn't sure what direction to take, its members had faith that Noreen would never let the team fail. Although she was eager to hear the ideas of team members, Noreen was also able to help them maintain their focus on the ultimate goal and on a positive result for the customer. Her certainty was reassuring to the team.

Their intense focus on tasks and deliverables can cause Three leaders to miss some of the human-related process issues that are at work. For example, team members may not know one another well or understand one another's working styles. As a result, they may not have built the team relationships they need in order to function effectively when the inevitable unanticipated problems and time pressures arise.

Three leaders may also be unaware that their high activity level and strong sense of direction may overwhelm some team members or create too much reliance on the leader for direction. Threes may want team members to show more initiative, yet be unaware that their own strong leadership prevents members from feeling empowered enough to assert their own ideas more or to disagree with the direction of the team.

Here's an example of some feedback that Noreen received from her team:

Noreen thought her team members worked well together, so she was surprised when she sensed tension among them during a project staff meeting. When she asked about this, the team members told her that they didn't feel they had enough influence on the team's direction because Noreen always stepped in to tell them what they should do. They added that although they appreciated her dedication and clarity, they wanted her to solicit their ideas more, as well as not react to those ideas so quickly, so that members would feel freer to bring up and discuss alternatives.

Development Stretches for Threes

ENJOY THE TEAM MORE If you relax at work and enjoy the team more, team members will follow your lead and will work more effectively and with less stress. When you explicitly emphasize both the task and the pleasure in working with others, so will your team.

PAY AS MUCH ATTENTION TO HUMAN PROCESSES AS YOU DO TO THE WORK STRUCTURE AND PROCESSES Just as you pay attention to the team structure and how work flows between and among team members, give equal attention to the human processes that are at work—e.g., motivation, rewards, team morale, coaching and mentoring, and interpersonal relationships. Teams actually involve two systems: the task system and the social system. The development of both systems allows the two systems to reinforce each other; people work better at a task when the social system supports that task, and social systems work more effectively when the task system supports people working together productively.

RESTRAIN YOURSELF FROM PROVIDING TOO MUCH DIRECTION TO THE TEAM While providing your team with clear direction is an asset, you also need to be clear about how much of the team's road map and route you should provide and how much should be developed within the team itself. Giving too much direction too early or too often impedes the team's ability to develop self-reliance and self-confidence. Share your ideas, but be genuinely open to others' reactions and to ideas. Involve team members more directly, and be willing to shift course as a result.

Enneagram Style Fours

Enneagram Style
MOOD

Four leaders enjoy the thrill of aligning a team behind a common and compelling vision, utilizing and bringing out the talent within the team, and developing a team architecture to match the team's deepest intentions—all in order to help the team deliver high-quality goods and services. Fours embrace team goals that are important and meaningful to them, and they prefer to break down big projects into smaller pieces so that the team's efforts do not feel too daunting. The Four leader's team architecture and processes are usually designed to maximize creativity and self-expression at both the individual and the team levels. For this reason, Four leaders tend not to overstructure or overorganize work for others.

Fours usually manage their teams in such a way that issues that need attention are expressed and dealt with. They feel comfortable helping a team discuss difficult issues in a constructive way, and they believe that every team member is important as an individual. Fours also develop close one-on-one relationships with all team members whenever possible.

The following story about Don illustrates a Four team leader in action:

Don adores leading what he describes as "messy" teams. He develops new teams well, but he is most excited when he takes over a team that is in disarray. Don understands that teams with undiscussed issues and unresolved conflicts do not perform effectively. He takes a dysfunctional team and enables its members to discuss the previously undiscussable, thereby removing a key obstacle to their ability to become a high-performing team. Don then refocuses the team on its task and on working together toward the team's goals.

A focus on discussing personal experiences, feelings, and process issues can also be a detriment to a Four's ability to lead teams. While teams do need to discuss issues that may impede their progress, the team leader must know when to discuss these items, how to discuss them, and for how long. Four leaders may err on the side of discussing issues too soon or discussing issues in too much depth for the team's level of trust and comfort.

In addition, Four leaders enjoy having work that has meaning to them and doing so within a team that is high-functioning. If the team's tasks become too mundane or the team's issues seem insurmountable, Fours may either lose interest or become discouraged.

Finally, the deeply felt sensitivity of Fours can be both a strength and a liability, as Fours can become disheartened when either they or the team is treated in a dismissive or unappreciative manner by others in the organization.

Here's an example from Don's experience:

Don had built a cohesive, high-performing team that produced high-end, innovative programs for its customers. All of this ended when Don's new boss seemed more interested in making money than in the quality of the work produced by Don's team. After several months of trying unsuccessfully to convince his boss that program excellence was of greater value than generating large profits, Don became so discouraged that he quit his job, even though he had no position waiting for him elsewhere.

Development Stretches for Fours

PUT YOUR STRENGTH IN WORKING WITH TEAM PROCESSES INTO PERSPECTIVE While it is important to honor and utilize your sensitivity to underlying team issues, it is equally important to remember that issues need to be discussed only to the point where they no longer impede the team's progress, not to the point at which every issue has been thoroughly examined. Practice your ability to facilitate issue identification and resolution using methods that are efficient as well as effective.

WHEN YOU FEEL DEEPLY DISCOURAGED, USE THIS AS A SIGNAL TO WORK ON CHANGING YOUR PERSPECTIVE When you feel discouraged, this can permeate and demoralize your team. Whenever you begin to feel disheartened and concerned, intercept these reactions by gathering an ad hoc team of trusted advisors. These people can help you gain a different perspective and assist you in developing innovative ways of addressing the organizational factors that are triggering your concerns.

BE MORE PLAYFUL Four team leaders can be intense and serious. While this is not necessarily a negative characteristic, it does need to be balanced with some lighthearted fun. Find the humor in adverse circumstances, laugh at the absurdity of situations that you might normally perceive as negative, and try to balance your seriousness with some levity.

Enneagram Style Fives

Enneagram Style
⑤ KNOWLEDGE

Fives bring their analytical and logical orientation to team leadership, constructing team goals that are precise and concrete, with each team member having a specific role and clear accountabilities. Five leaders often say that being able to trust their team members is crucial to having good working relationships; in this context, Fives define trust as being able to count on individual team members to deliver first-rate work products on or before the due date. With capable and efficient team members, particularly individuals who don't waste the Five leader's time, Fives focus their teams on the task at hand, with the end product in mind.

Fives particularly enjoy discussing important ideas with intellectually agile and knowledgeable team members. They do their best to establish rational, consistent, and systematic work processes that enable all team members to use their time productively. Because Fives take satisfaction in understanding how all the parts of a task or project fit together, they enjoy the puzzle aspect of issue identification and problem solving. They also enjoy coaching team members using this same approach—providing a systems perspective on how everything works, taking a rational view of turbulent issues, and finding just the right concept or development activity to help people learn and grow.

Following is an example of a Five leader at work:

> At a team meeting in which self-development planning was being discussed, Barbara listened eagerly as team members shared what each would do for his or her six-month development plan. During this discussion, Barbara took careful notes and said little except to positively reinforce individuals who had selected an appropriate and challenging area, or to gently push those who she believed could challenge themselves even more. When someone asked Barbara why she was taking notes, she laughed and said with a wry smile, "So I can remember to remind you of what you have just committed to do."

Because Fives prefer to work on teams with low interdependence among team members and high levels of individual autonomy, they often develop a team architecture based on these same characteristics. While this architecture works well when team projects require low interdependence, other team projects require members to work more interdependently in order to be successful. For example, a golf team works best when team members function with low interdependence, but a soccer team requires moderate to high interdependence among its members.

The Five's belief that team members are there to work and not to get involved in one another's emotional lives has merit. At the same time, people do have feelings at work that can either support or derail the work effort. Interpersonal issues, if not dealt with constructively, can erode the productivity of the team. For this reason, team leaders need to be both willing and able to lead the team in resolving issues that might impede its progress. Because Fives experience most emotional interactions as draining, they tend to stay away from them if they can.

Barbara received feedback about her interpersonal style:

> The topic of the team's interpersonal relationships arose at a staff meeting. One team member said, "Barbara, I can never tell how you are. In the morning, I say hello and ask how you are, but you rarely say anything in return. In fact, I hardly ever know how you are reacting to something."
>
> Barbara replied in an unusually animated voice, much to the surprise of her team, and said, "If you want to really know how I am, I might tell you! But when you ask how I am after saying hello, it is merely a pleasantry. I don't get the feeling that you are really asking how I am, and because of this, I am not inclined to say anything."

Development Stretches for Fives

EXPRESS YOUR FEELINGS USING MORE THAN JUST WORDS Fives usually control their body language and rely on words to communicate, but your team needs more information from you than this. Videotape yourself talking about something that is important to you. Watch the tape with a coach or someone you respect, and solicit his or her feedback about how you come across. Finally, practice communicating your feelings during a staff meeting, with an emphasis on making your words and body language congruent.

BE EXPLICIT ABOUT NEEDING TIME TO CONSIDER YOUR TRUE REACTIONS It is perfectly fine for you to tell individuals or groups that you want time to think about a situation. Both you and they deserve your most heartfelt and well-considered responses. In fact, being clear about your need to take time to consider your reactions is preferable to acting as if you have no response at all. During your time of reflection, go beyond an initial identification of feelings by asking yourself: *Yes, but why do I feel that way?* The deeper you go, the more deeply you will connect with your truest feelings. You may or may not choose to share these with others, but at least you will know what they are.

LEARN TO READ BODY LANGUAGE CLEARLY Pay as much attention to others' body language as to their words so that you can become expert at reading nonverbal cues. An excellent way to learn this skill is to watch 15 minutes of a DVD you have not seen before, with the sound on mute. As you watch, write down what you think is occurring, what you imagine the characters are feeling, and the film's general feeling or atmosphere. Then review the same 15-minute segment with the sound on. Assess your accuracy in reading the nonverbal behavior. If you were not very accurate, watch the segment again to determine what you missed. Repeat this activity with the same and/or other DVDs until you feel more knowledgeable in the art of reading body language.

Enneagram Style Sixes

Most Six leaders value teamwork almost as much as they value group loyalty. They believe that anything is possible with a like-minded, capable, and committed team that has purposeful goals. Once Six leaders have aligned team members around a common vision and developed the team's architecture and

Enneagram Style ⑥
DOUBT

processes—which they often do in a collaborative manner—they support the team in producing quality products and services.

Because they enjoy risk but don't like surprises, Six leaders develop strong team cultures that embrace and respond to big challenges and simultaneously emphasize honesty and responsibility. Sixes provide guidance and support to team members who do their jobs well, are loyal to the team, and raise issues before they become problems. At the same time, Sixes are wary of team members who have known of a problem and failed to bring it to the leader's attention, or who act as though they are solo players rather than members of a team.

Here is how Matthew, a team member, described Karl, a successful Six leader, to members of a new team during a meeting:

> "I've worked under Karl's leadership on several other teams, and I will tell you this: don't make the mistake of taking Karl's low-key leadership style for a lack of strength or decisiveness. He knows exactly what he wants from us, but he also values our ideas and teamwork in setting the team's direction. He will, however, make decisions when he should or when we can't, and he makes them fast when he needs to."

Six leaders may also demonstrate ambivalence about being in a leadership role. While they want to set the direction for the team and make sure that members are well supported, they may not feel completely comfortable with the authority and power that go with the leadership role. Almost all Sixes focus on the motivation and behavior of those in authority, hoping that those in authority will use their power fairly and effectively, yet being simultaneously concerned that these individuals will not act equitably or constructively. When Sixes become leaders themselves, they are earnest about wanting to do the best possible job, but they may also have doubts about their ability to meet this complex challenge.

Sixes truly appreciate the power of positive teams, but are aware that team dynamics can be complicated and volatile. For this reason, some Sixes prefer to watch teams from a distance than to be highly involved with them. This is not as problematic when Sixes are employees, but it creates a dilemma for them when they are in team leadership roles, as it is very difficult to lead a team effectively from the sidelines.

Finally, Six leaders often understate (even to themselves) their numerous leadership assets.

In the same new team meeting referred to previously, Karl demonstrated the somewhat self-deprecating quality of Six team leaders:

> When asked to describe his leadership style so that the new team members might understand how to work well with him, Karl answered, "I believe I am steady and don't panic in even the most challenging situations. I am also fair, or at least I try to be."
>
> It took Matthew, the team member who had previously worked for him, to explain Karl's leadership style more fully: "Karl is available, easy to talk with, and assertive when he needs to be. He does not like to micromanage people, and when he sees that you can do your job well, he gives you every opportunity to do it. If he starts to micromanage you, it is only because you have failed to deliver on your commitments."

Development Stretches for Sixes

BECOME INCREASINGLY COMFORTABLE WITH POWER AND AUTHORITY
Examine your relationship to power and authority, with a focus on understanding that most authority figures are not completely positive or negative, but are usually a mixture of both.

Take a piece of paper and make three columns: positive authority figures, negative authority figures, and mixed authority figures (those who are both positive and negative). Make a list of all your prior bosses and place each name in the appropriate column. Next to each name, write down that person's most prominent leadership qualities. Then review each column. Do you have more names in the positive column, more in the negative, more in the mixed, or some other pattern? For each individual in the positive column, write down some of his or her negative qualities; for each individual in the negative column, write down some of his or her positive qualities. Then write down your own name, listing your positive and negative leadership traits. You will find that most leaders have both positive and negative attributes.

SAY POSITIVE THINGS ABOUT YOURSELF TO YOURSELF   You may have a tendency to underestimate yourself and to understate your positive qualities. Write down all your positive attributes, both as a leader and as a person. Put at least 20 items on this list. Pick one item each day to focus on and to appreciate in yourself. Look in the mirror a minimum of three times per day and say out loud: *I really like that I am . . .* (fill in the blank with your word or phrase of the day).

ASK FOR POSITIVE FEEDBACK FROM OTHERS   Don't go fishing for compliments, but do seek genuine positive feedback in order to understand how others perceive your favorable attributes. During the first week, select three people whom you know well and respect, and ask each of them to give you one item of positive feedback regarding something they believe you might not know about yourself. Write it down. During the second week, select three more individuals and follow the same process. Continue this for two more weeks so that you have at least 12 items of positive feedback. Review these nightly to remind and encourage yourself to appreciate your assets.

Enneagram Style Sevens

Enneagram Style
OPTIONS

In a sense, Sevens can be thought of as eternal visionaries, always stimulated by new ideas and new possibilities. Their love of innovation and their energetic spirit often attract talented people who also want to think outside the box. Sevens are more inclined to ask "Why not?" than to ask "Why?"

Seven leaders foster fast-paced, energetic, and stimulating team cultures focused on delivering exceptional products and services to customers. Most often, Sevens create team cultures that are egalitarian; the Seven leader regards all team members as equals, with each individual being entitled to voice an opinion. Sevens also expect each member to contribute ideas, to say what is on his or her mind, and to deliver high-quality work products.

Here is an example of a Seven team leader in action:

> Francesca was engaging, bright, and full of new ideas. She had been hired to work with a 75-person team that had been performing adequately but that was entirely lacking in innovation. Francesca had also been asked to reduce staff by 30 percent because a number of team members were not carrying their weight or had a negative or "can't-do" attitude. Within three years, Francesca had completely transformed the team into one that was highly productive and innovative. In the process, she had gained the admiration and loyalty of the remaining team members, who described her as pure energy in motion.

While Seven leaders emphasize vision and team culture, they just as often underemphasize team architecture and processes. It is not that they purposely ignore these areas, but simply that they themselves prefer to work in underorganized teams. To Sevens, too much structure or process restricts their freedom of thinking and movement. While this relaxed organizational style may work well for some team members, others may require more structural and process guidance.

In addition, while the Seven's emphasis on vision can be highly stimulating to a team, the Seven leader may continuously add new ideas to the original vision. From the Seven's perspective, these new ideas are embellishments, augmentations, or just simply different activities related to the vision. However, these continual additions may feel overwhelming to team members and may cause the team to lose focus on essential work.

Finally, Seven leaders may feel that they end up supplying all the new ideas for their teams and may hunger for their team members to take more initiative. The irony is that team members may not be contributing ideas because the Seven leader has so many new suggestions and presents them so quickly that members do not have time to think through their own ideas or find it difficult to get "air time."

Here is Francesca's report of her own idea-generation process:

"I get so excited by new ideas—once I think of one idea, more keep on coming. Two weeks before a team project is due, I have 12 items on my to-do list, which I write down but rarely use. Two days before the project is due, I have 20 items on my list. I just can't say no to a good idea. My team members say I wear them out with last-minute changes and additions, and that I delay projects. Sometimes I even wear myself out!"

Development Stretches for Sevens

ACCEPT THAT YOUR JOB IS TO LEAD FROM A CLEARLY DEFINED LEADERSHIP ROLE Although you may prefer teams that are egalitarian, they can still be egalitarian with you in a clear leadership role. Embrace a leadership role from the start. Many Seven team leaders act more like team members in the beginning; this can make the inevitable and necessary shift to a more authoritative role more difficult.

CREATE MORE TEAM STRUCTURE AND PROCESSES THAN YOU YOURSELF NEED Encourage the members of your team to tell you how much structure they need beyond what you currently provide. By honoring these requests, you'll create more safety in the group and will probably see an increase in the team's innovation and productivity.

KNOW WHEN TO STOP This suggestion applies to many areas of a Seven team leader's development. Do you know when to stop sharing your own ideas and to start listening to others? Do you know when to stop creating new ideas and focus on the most important ones that have already been developed? Do you know when to disengage from a fascinating conversation because there are critical meetings to attend or items on your desk that need action? In general, it is helpful to think in terms of shortening everything you are involved in to one-third. For example, talk one-third of the time, and listen two-thirds. Stop when one-third of the ideas have been generated and decide which of the ideas are the most actionable. Limit your work conversations to one-third of their usual length.

Enneagram Style Eights

Eights like to lead high-performing teams that engage in big-picture, high-impact work. They enjoy taking chaotic and uncontrolled situations and turning them around quickly. When they sense talent in people and these individuals demonstrate capability and reliability, Eight leaders give them an

Enneagram Style CHALLENGE ⑧

abundance of autonomy to perform at their best. Eights lead primarily through a vision and secondarily through their robust personalities. Most team members appreciate the certainty provided by the Eight leader as well as the honest feedback and encouragement they receive.

Some Eight leaders focus heavily on designing team processes and architecture, while others may pay less attention to this, preferring to set up systems on an as-needed basis. In either case, Eight leaders challenge both themselves and their teams to do extraordinary work, and they enjoy the intensity of working collectively and interdependently to get the job done beyond expectations.

Here is an example of how Marshall, an Eight, works to challenge his team:

> Although Marshall was new to the organization, he picked up the corporate culture at lightning speed and moved forward quickly, challenging his team to make increasingly larger contributions to both the customer and the organization. For example, at a team meeting, the members were reviewing their relationships with customers. Two members of the ten-person team spoke of their frustrations with customers whom they described as extremely demanding. Marshall then challenged them to examine their own reactions rather than to focus on the customers' behavior, saying, "I know the expectations of these customers can feel excessive, but what I need to do and you need to do is to look at our own reactivity, which can make the situation worse. I get impatient, you get impatient, and the customer feels this. We need to stop this, and stop it now!"

There are three ways in which Eight leaders' attraction to cleaning up chaos can also have a negative impact on the teams they lead: (1) their team may be too underorganized; this keeps the Eight leader stimulated, but the result can be that everything becomes a crisis; (2) after too long a period of too much under-organization, things feel out of control, and the Eight leader then steps in to organize everything, becoming overly controlling of the structure; and (3) the Eight leader may have everything so well under control that he or she becomes bored and disengages from the team by not being very involved or available, or by finding another job.

Eights also may not solicit sufficient input from their team members in situations where doing so would result in better decisions and encourage team members to take more initiative. Eight leaders keep their own counsel and seek advice only when they are uncertain of what to do (which is rare), and then only from team members whose opinions they respect. This can have the impact of unintentionally disenfranchising others on the team.

Finally, many Eights like to protect their team members. While that can breed loyalty, it can also create unhealthy dependencies.

Here's an example of Marshall's leadership in a prior job:

> Marshall prided himself on protecting his people, viewing this as one of his greatest team leadership strengths. In his mind, the team wanted and needed him to be strong and able to remove any obstacle. Team members became very committed to him and to their joint work. What Marshall came to realize was that he really got along well with those who wanted his protection, and that he had a more difficult time relating to team members who wanted more independence. After much self-reflection, Marshall realized that the underlying issue was really his need to feel strong, and that this need was hurting his team more than it was helping it.

Development Stretches for Eights

ORGANIZE YOUR TEAM AT THE OPTIMAL LEVEL OF STRUCTURE AND PROCESS In collaboration with your team, discuss the current team structure and processes. Ask for members' reactions to the way in which the team is organized, solicit their ideas for improvement, and then organize accordingly.

BE MORE CONSISTENT IN YOUR ATTENTION TO DETAIL Most Eight leaders do not like to delve into detail unless they absolutely have to do so. When they do, Eights can be relentless. Be more balanced and consistent in your approach; become more involved than you would normally be when work is running smoothly, and become less micromanaging when things feel out of control.

EXAMINE YOUR ISSUES WITH DEPENDENCY AND AUTONOMY This stretch can be challenging, because you may not see yourself as creating dependency or as offering too much autonomy to those whom you regard highly. Start by asking yourself this question: *How have I become overly reliant on my strength?* Next, ask yourself this question: *How am I overly reliant on my autonomy?* Discuss your answers with someone whom you know well and respect. Finally, examine how you may be demonstrating these same tendencies in your team leadership by asking yourself these questions: *How am I causing some members to become dependent on my strength? How am I acting overly reliant on the strength of a few team members? What is the downside of my giving some team members so much autonomy?*

Enneagram Style Nines

Enneagram Style
HARMONY

Nine leaders build collaborative and cohesive teams by aligning them around a common purpose and concrete goals, expecting each person to contribute individually and interdependently to both the work of the team and a harmonious team climate.

Nines usually dislike elaborate or highly structured team architectures, perceiving them as too demanding and rigid. However, Nines do like structured work processes that are predictable and routine. Consequently, Nine leaders tend to clearly define team processes in order to (1) let team members know what is expected of them, (2) provide appropriate support for getting the work done, and (3) minimize potential disagreements.

Nine leaders also contribute to the morale and well-being of their teams through their easygoing and nonjudgmental interpersonal style. These same characteristics also help team members feel comfortable voicing their opinions to Nine leaders, whether in one-on-one conversations or during team meetings. The Nine's approach to leadership tends to be more facilitative than authoritative, as Nine leaders are prone to drawing upon the ideas of others and to making sure that everyone gets heard.

Here's an example of Diane, a Nine leader:

> When Diane joined the board of directors of a nonprofit organization, she immediately recognized that the board's bylaws were outdated. She also saw that its working processes—e.g., its financial reporting systems and the process for electing new board members—were either old or inadequate for the current size of the organization. Within a year's time, Diane had organized a subcommittee and led it in making a complete revision of the organization's major processes.

The Nine leader's reliance on process over structure can also be a shortcoming. Some team issues are resolved more easily by changing organizational structure than by changing organizational processes. For example, when a team is having numerous ongoing coordination problems, redesigning the team structure to maximize information flow may be far more efficient and effective than developing elaborate communication vehicles.

The Nine's facilitative style, which works well in many circumstances, may be an impediment in others—for example, when quick action is required, when a tough position must be taken, or when disagreements can't be resolved through discussion. Although Nine leaders can assert themselves in these situations, doing so is usually stressful for them.

Finally, Nine leaders often focus on details rather than on the broader vision. Because they tend to lead from goals and a common mission, Nines may fail to articulate the team's vision and the strategic approach it must take.

Here's an example of Diane's work in leading a committee of the board of directors:

> Once Diane had completed developing the board's new systems, she was ready to deal with its 10-year-old Web site,

which was antiquated and was constantly breaking down. After spending more than 100 hours speaking with vendors and developing elaborate documents for the board to review, she presented her findings and recommendations. Although the board appreciated Diane's efforts, her recommended solution was deemed too costly. Diane felt deeply angry and unappreciated. However, from the board's perspective, Diane had gotten so involved in the details of the effort that she had neglected a strategic concern: the availability of funds for this project, given the board's overall direction and numerous initiatives.

Development Stretches for Nines

LEARN TO LEVERAGE TEAM STRUCTURE AS WELL AS PROCESS It is a challenge to determine whether changing the team's structure—for example, its organizational chart, design of jobs, roles, and task force structure—or redesigning the team processes is the best approach to dealing with issues and creating higher team performance. Depending on the circumstances, either might work, or one might be better than the other. Every time you are about to change a team process, ask yourself this question: *Before I change a team process, what structural changes could I make instead?* If you have no answer, solicit ideas from peers, then experiment with structural changes until you become as comfortable with these as you are with process changes.

PRACTICE BEING CLEAR Although being very clear and explicit with others about what you think and what you want from them will feel strange at first, once you start doing it, you are likely to end up feeling exhilarated by it. When you are communicating with others, ask yourself: *What do I really think? What do I really want them to do?* Then tell them—kindly, nicely, but firmly.

DON'T DIG INTO THE DETAILS Team members look to you for guidance, feedback, support, and resources; they want you to remove obstacles from their path, but not to dig deeply into the details. Although you may enjoy details, your team needs you to operate at a higher level so that you will have time to deal with the more important issues.

Development Stretches for Everyone

- Observe four different sports teams and assess their effectiveness along the team dimensions described in this chapter:
  - Leadership (coach, team captain)
  - Vision (focus)
  - Talent (players)
  - Architecture (roles, rules)
  - Culture (morale, team values, team spirit)
  - Processes (strategy, communication, rewards, sanctions)
  - Quality products (results)

  These can be professional, amateur, or even children's teams. Write down your observations. Once you have observed all four teams, review your notes and answer these questions: *What differentiated a winning team from a losing one? If you could coach the coaches of the losing teams, what advice would you give them?*

- Assess what you really think and feel about teams by answering the following questions:
  - *Do you like teams? Why or why not?*
  - *What team leaders have you encountered in the past that brought out the best in you and your teammates? List the characteristics of these leaders.*
  - *What sorts of work activities can teams accomplish more effectively than individuals by themselves, and vice versa?*
  - *In what ways do you excel as a team leader?*
  - *What is your greatest development challenge as a team leader?*

- Educate yourself further by reading one of the recommended books under "Lead High-Performing Teams" in the Resources section at the back of this book; read Chapter 5, "Creating High-Performing Teams," in *Bringing Out the Best in Yourself at Work: How to Use the Enneagram System for Success*, by Ginger Lapid-Bogda, Ph.D.

Chapter *7*

Make Optimal Decisions

ecision making is one of the most crucial tasks facing today's leaders. Leaders must make decisions about issues both large and small on a daily basis. Globalization has added new complexities to decision making, and leaders no longer have the luxury of time in which to consider their options. Today, leaders are frequently required to make wise decisions very quickly.

Having the ability to Make Optimal Decisions means that you are skilled in the following seven competency components (see Figure 7.1):

1. Understanding the organizational culture
2. Honoring the organization's decision-making authority structure
3. Factoring in the context of the decision
4. Using your head to make rational decisions
5. Using your heart by listening to yourself and others
6. Using your gut by trusting your instincts
7. Making wise decisions by integrating your head, heart, and gut

As you read further and reflect on the seven competency components of Make Optimal Decisions, rate yourself in each area on

FIGURE 7.1 **Make Optimal Decisions**

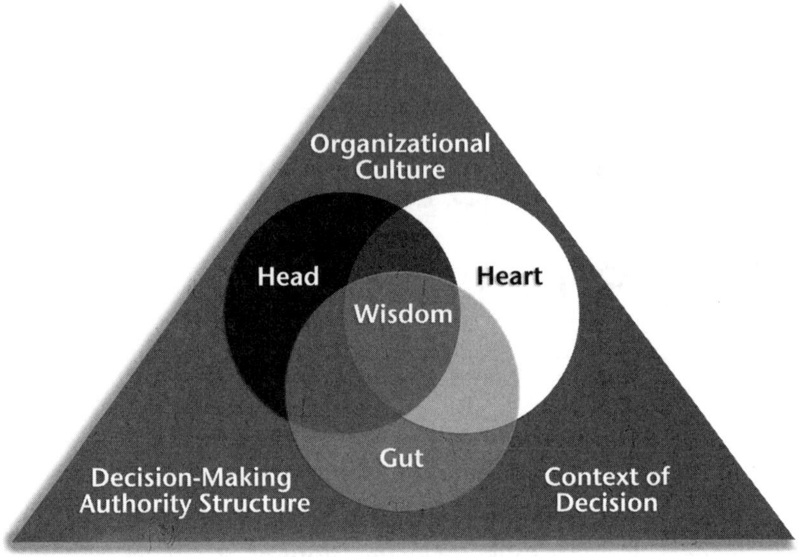

a scale of 1 to 5. This will help you determine both your areas of strength and the areas that need development.

The Seven Competency Components of Make Optimal Decisions

Component 1: Understanding the Organizational Culture

This involves meeting organizational expectations about how decisions are made (e.g., are they collaborative, consultative, or authoritative); explaining honestly how and why decisions are made (within the boundaries of how much open disclosure is allowed within the organization); understanding organizational politics, such as who must be consulted before, after, and during the decision-making process; and being able to sell decisions to key individuals and groups within the organization.

Low				High
1	2	3	4	5

Component 2: Honoring the Organization's Decision-Making Authority Structure

This includes respecting the lines of authority within the organization; understanding and adhering to your scope of decision-making authority; clearly defining decision-making roles, boundaries, and processes for those who report to you in order to foster compliance and accountability; delegating decision-making responsibilities according to people's skill level and knowledge of the issues; and escalating complex or volatile decisions to higher levels in the organization when necessary.

Low				High
1	2	3	4	5

Component 3: Factoring In the Context of the Decision

This includes knowing when a decision is required immediately and being able to respond quickly; understanding when a decision is not urgent and time is available for consideration of options; being able to calculate risks and take action in the face of continuous uncertainty; knowing which decisions require extensive input and which can be made without a high level of involvement from others; understanding how a decision affects other decisions and being able to set priorities among multiple decisions that must be made; and making decisions with a broad context in mind so that the solutions benefit the entire organization and its customers, not just one area or business unit.

Low				High
1	2	3	4	5

Component 4: Using Your Head to Make Rational Decisions

This involves collecting accurate data, including soliciting the most current and relevant information from groups and individuals inside and outside the organization; methodically analyzing situations and probing for the underlying root causes of issues; detecting inaccuracies and flaws in both your own reasoning and that of others; specifying the decision-making criteria with which to evaluate alternative courses of action; being able to accept and integrate information that doesn't support your own ideas or your preferred choice of action; and anticipating and weighing the impact of the decision on the organization's systems, structure, processes, and resources.

Low				High
1	2	3	4	5

Component 5: Using Your Heart by Listening to Yourself and Others

This includes getting buy-in for decisions from key stakeholders, even when doing so takes additional time; seeking advice and input from others and factoring their reactions into your decisions; anticipating and weighing the potential impact of a decision on individuals and on groups such as employees, leaders, work groups, customers, and vendors; helping people feel that they are part of the decision-making process; being responsive to people's actual or anticipated feelings about decisions and developing constructive ways to respond to these; and making decisions that are congruent with both your own and the organization's core values.

Low				High
1	2	3	4	5

Component 6: Using Your Gut by Trusting Your Instincts

This includes resolving problems efficiently and removing obstacles quickly; making timely and effective decisions, even when deadlines require that the decision be made with incomplete information; quickly sensing what decisions will help or hinder the accomplishment of the organization's goals; knowing the right or best decision by consulting your gut; using your decision-making power and authority fairly and justly; and being able to readily translate decisions into plans and then transform plans into actions.

Low				High
1	2	3	4	5

Component 7: Making Wise Decisions by Integrating Your Head, Heart, and Gut

This involves factoring in logic, compassion, and gut reactions when making decisions; being able to use intuition as well as facts, feelings, and a desire to take action quickly; understanding your own personal biases and guarding against allowing these to influence your decisions; using a fair, consistent, and transparent decision-making process; making wise decisions that will stand the test of time, while simultaneously balancing such factors as risk, speed, difficult trade-offs, and uncertainty; having the courage to stand by a tough decision in the face of opposition; holding yourself and others accountable for the decision-making process and for the outcomes of decisions; and being flexible enough to reconsider decisions when new information becomes available, as well as knowing when to do so.

Low				High
1	2	3	4	5

Making optimal decisions really means making wise decisions using your head, heart, and gut in an integrated way, while also taking into account the organizational culture, its expectations with regard to decision making and scope of authority, and the particular requirements or context of the decision itself.

Before examining the Enneagram style dimensions of Make Optimal Decisions, it is helpful to understand how the three Centers of Intelligence—the Head Center, the Heart Center, and the Body (Gut) Center—relate to making wise decisions.

We all have Head, Heart, and Body Centers, and we can use our centers in productive or unproductive ways. For example, the Head Center's productive use is for analysis, insight, and planning, but its misuses can be overanalyzing, projection, and overplanning. The Heart Center, which is supposed to be used for empathy, authentic relating, and compassion, can be misused for emotional manipulation, playing roles, and oversensitivity. The Body (Gut) Center's most productive uses are for taking effective action, steadfastness, and gut knowing, but it can be misused by taking excessive action, passivity, and reactivity.

Imagine having to decide whether to reduce your staff by 35 percent in anticipation of a possible decrease in customer demand. To make a wise decision, the decision maker would do the following: (1) use the Head Center to analyze the relevant data, gain insight into the trends, and prepare a tentative plan; (2) use the Heart Center to consider the impact on both employees and customers; and (3) use the Body (Gut) Center to answer these questions: *Is a staff reduction the right thing to do? If yes, what would be the best timetable for implementation? Can I stand behind this decision 100 percent?*

However, if a leader made this decision without using his or her three centers productively, the decision would be flawed. The decision might (1) be based on the supposition that there is a need for a reduction in staff rather than on facts (e.g., no rigorous trend analysis was done); (2) be based on insufficient consideration of its impact on people (e.g., there were no discussions with employees about possible transfers within the organization); or (3) suffer from ineffective execution (e.g., there was no sense of the best timetable for the staff reduction). To make wise decisions means integrating the information you receive from the productive use of all three Centers of Intelligence.

Individuals with all Enneagram styles can use and misuse their Centers of Intelligence in the ways described in the preceding paragraphs. In addition, each style misuses its own Center of Intelligence in a specific way. Fives, Sixes, and Sevens have specific misuses of the Head Center; Twos, Threes, and Fours have specific misuses of the Heart Center; and Eights, Nines, and Ones have specific misuses of the Body Center.

The productive uses and misuses of each Center of Intelligence, as well as the common Enneagram style–specific misuses, are described in Chart 7.1. This chart is followed by the Enneagram dimensions of Make Optimal Decisions and specific developmental activities for each Enneagram style that support the productive use of each center.

CHART 7.1 Centers of Intelligence: Uses and Misuses

Center of Intelligence	Productive Uses of This Center	Enneagram Style–Specific Misuses
Head Center	**Objective analysis** Understanding data without bias	**Overanalyzing (Fives)** Obsessive collection and examination of data
	Astute insight Understanding the true meaning and implications of data	**Projection (Sixes)** Attributing one's own thoughts, motives, and behavior to other people
	Productive planning Structuring sets of activities effectively	**Overplanning (Sevens)** Excessive planning; overscheduling
Heart Center	**Empathy** Identifying with and understanding another person's feelings	**Emotional manipulation (Twos)** Attempting to control others through the calculated use of feelings
	Authentic relating Relating without pretense	**Playing roles (Threes)** Relating through an image or role
	Compassion Heartfelt kindness toward another person	**Oversensitivity (Fours)** Excessive emotionality
Body (Gut) Center	**Taking effective action** Taking well-chosen and timely action	**Excessive action (Eights)** Taking too much action

(Continued)

CHART 7.1 *(Continued)* **Centers of Intelligence: Uses and Misuses**

Center of Intelligence	Productive Uses of This Center	Enneagram Style–Specific Misuses
	Steadfastness Being firm and resolute	**Passivity (Nines)** Being inert
	Gut knowing Having a clear and trustworthy instinctive response	**Reactivity (Ones)** Reacting too strongly or too quickly

Enneagram Dimensions of Make Optimal Decisions

Enneagram Style Ones

Enneagram Style
DILIGENCE

The possibility of making the wrong choice and then having to live with the consequences causes Ones a great deal of concern. As a result, One leaders typically use their Head Center to analyze the information they receive and their Body (Gut) Center to sense the right course of action and execute a well-conceived plan. At various points during the process, they use their Heart Center, consulting their own value systems to make certain that the decision and the plan of action are congruent with their core principles.

Because One leaders usually trust their own judgment, they tend to make most decisions on their own. They will solicit input from those whom they respect, but only when necessary. It can be difficult for Ones to acknowledge that they don't know how to do something, and they usually perceive asking someone for help as an imposition. At the same time, because One leaders like to be aligned with the organization's decision-making rules and roles, they will try to use a more participatory decision-making style if the organization's culture values collaborative decision making.

When Ones make decisions, they try to do the following: (1) understand the organization's decision-making authority structure,

(2) clearly delineate the decision-making framework for their subordinates, and (3) make decisions that they believe fall within their span of control.

Here's an example of Pat, a One leader, making an effective and timely decision:

> Pat was asked to lead a 10-person team in which three team members had serious performance issues. Pat developed a plan that involved her doing the following: (1) taking no action for 90 days so that she could observe the performance of all team members; (2) investigating the past performance of the three poorly performing individuals, using employee records and conversations with their prior bosses; (3) analyzing the reasons for the subpar performances to determine what, if anything, she could do to improve the skills and attitudes of the individuals involved; and (4) taking appropriate action. At the end of 90 days, the performance of one of the three had improved dramatically, one was moved to another group where there was a better skill match, and the third employee was terminated.

When faced with the need to make a decision, Ones may err by making a precipitous or overly strident decision when a more temperate decision would be more effective. In addition, Ones can become confused when the decisions they must make involve a great deal of emotionality. Ones prefer to make rational decisions that their gut tells them are the best alternative, rather than dealing with the many interpersonal issues involved. As a result, when confronted with emotionally charged issues, Ones can start to doubt their minds and their guts.

The following story illustrates a One's behavior when deciding whether to fire an employee:

> Pat was extremely concerned about Keith's current performance. Although Keith had once been an excellent employee,

his performance and his interpersonal interactions had slipped in the past six months. Had Pat not seen Keith's prior excellent performance, she would have terminated him without hesitation. However, because she knew Keith's capability, she refused to give up on him. Because of this, she failed to recognize that Keith's sudden fall was the result of a home-related problem that was beyond her ability to solve.

Pat engaged in six months of emotionally draining conversations with Keith, during which time he blamed her rather than taking responsibility for himself. After each encounter, Pat blamed herself for not being able to remedy the situation. Eventually, she realized that, being a One, she had a very difficult time accepting the fact that she could not fix the situation; Ones believe that they should be able to fix anything and anybody. Pat also recognized that she had ignored her initial gut reaction that Keith had problems that only he himself could solve.

Development Stretches for Ones

CHART 7.2   Ones: Development Stretches

Center of Intelligence	Activities for Ones That Develop That Center
Head Center	**Objective analysis** Be careful not to let your positive or negative opinions about another person overshadow the objective data; don't overthink your decisions. **Astute insight** Go beyond the facts to the patterns implicit in the facts; understand the themes derived from these patterns. **Productive planning** Make sure you don't overplan a decision or overorganize its execution; allow room for new information and activities to emerge.
Heart Center	**Empathy** Consider both your own and other people's feelings in depth. **Authentic relating** Be willing to share deeply held feelings when discussing issues.

(Continued)

CHART 7.2 *(Continued)*   **Ones: Development Stretches**

Center of Intelligence	Activities for Ones That Develop That Center
	Compassion Make certain you don't become too emotionally involved when making hard decisions, but don't be too cerebral either.
Body (Gut) Center	**Taking effective action** Turn decision making into an art form; use just enough action to get the results you want.
	Steadfastness Hold firm in your decisions, but not to the point of rigidity.
	Gut knowing Learn to honor your gut reactions by asking yourself what it is that you know very deeply to be true; watch out for reacting too quickly.

Enneagram Style Twos

Because Two leaders have highly developed intuitive skills, they can usually anticipate which decisions will be readily accepted and which ones will meet with resistance. Twos rely primarily on their Heart Center to understand the desires and inten-

Enneagram Style ②
GIVING

tions of others, and also pay attention to the organization's norms and values in both making decisions and executing them.

In addition, Two leaders focus on the organization's decision-making authority structure in order to fine-tune their ability to orchestrate people and events. However, they don't always abide by the formal decision-making structure. For example, a Two might say, "This decision lies in another person's area, but I'm going to make the decision myself because it needs to be made, and no one's going to get too upset." On the other hand, when Twos anticipate a strong negative reaction, even if the decision falls within their area of authority, they will say, "I want to find out what this other person thinks before I make the final decision."

When asked about Paul's decision-making style, one of his senior employees described him this way:

"When Paul makes a decision, he does ask for our opinions, but he is more than willing to make the decision himself. What is most remarkable is that most of Paul's decisions are good ones. He seems to know when he needs to take fast action and when to take his time. Everyone knows what the decision is and, just as importantly, why it was made."

Twos can feel anxious when they initially assume a leadership role, as they are often more comfortable influencing decision makers than making the decisions themselves. In addition, Two leaders can become even more concerned when the decision's risk level is high and the probability of its widespread acceptance is low. At these times, Twos can lose all contact with what they feel is the right thing to do, becoming overly attuned to what others think of them and feeling anxious about the possibility that people will be displeased with the decision they make. Twos care most about the reactions of authority figures and those whom they like or respect, but they also care about the reactions of those whom they must lead. Twos believe that if their followers become too frustrated or angry with them, their ability to lead will be diminished. In part, this results from the Two's belief that people follow leaders to whom they are positively inclined, but it is also a by-product of the fact that Twos often lead through building positive relationships.

For Twos, *fully* utilizing the analytic (Head Center) and instinctive (Body Center) aspects of decision making is an important development area. While Twos do use rationality and instinct in their decision making, these two aspects are usually secondary to their intuition, which generally comes from their Heart Center. A Two leader is more likely to say "I feel this is the right thing to do" than to say either "I think this is the right thing to do" or "My gut tells me we should do this."

The following example shows how Paul anguished over a decision concerning an employee, Greg:

Although Paul knew that he had to tell Greg about his decision that Greg would not be receiving a raise, he was having difficulty reconciling how he felt with what he knew he must do. Logically, Paul knew that Greg's performance was only average and that the company did not have the money for anything other than merit raises. At the same time, he knew that Greg had two young children and needed the extra income. Because Paul and Greg were friendly and often went to lunch together, Paul knew that this was going to be a tough conversation. Although Paul eventually had this difficult discussion with Greg, it took him three more weeks to actually initiate the conversation.

Development Stretches for Twos

CHART 7.3 **Twos: Development Stretches**

Center of Intelligence	Activities for Twos That Develop That Center
Head Center	**Objective analysis** Do not let your personal feelings for other people bias your decisions; strive to be objective. **Astute insight** Base your decisions more on objective information than on perception. **Productive planning** Don't overplan when you're anxious or underplan when you're tired; don't overschedule yourself.
Heart Center	**Empathy** Examine your motivations for needing to know exactly what others are thinking and feeling. **Authentic relating** Be completely honest with others about your reasons for making a decision. **Compassion** Realize that offering too much compassion can make people unable to stand up for themselves.
Body (Gut) Center	**Taking effective action** Learn the art of timing so that you will know when to act, when to wait, and when to do nothing.

(Continued)

CHART 7.3 *(Continued)* **Twos: Development Stretches**

Center of Intelligence	Activities for Twos That Develop That Center
	Steadfastness Have the courage of your convictions so that you will neither back down nor become defensive when others disagree with your decisions. **Gut knowing** Learn to trust your gut as much as your heart.

Enneagram Style Threes

Enneagram Style
③ PERFORM

Three leaders are aware that making a good decision and then implementing it will lead to success, and that a poor decision—no matter how well executed—inevitably results in failure.

When Threes make decisions, they usually consider the organization's culture, their own scope of decision-making authority, and the context surrounding the particular issue. Although Three is the core style of the Heart Center, Threes tend to rely more on the Head Center than on the Heart Center when making decisions. They process the relevant information in order to determine the most rational choice, make their decision, and then proceed to implement it.

However, this does not mean that Threes ignore their Heart and Gut Centers. They are likely to use the Heart Center to assess how key individuals in the organization might respond to one option versus another, and they are most likely to use the Body Center in choosing how to implement a decision. Because Three leaders are so focused on execution, they factor this into their decision making, imagining different implementation scenarios and most often choosing the one with the greatest probability of success. Threes like to have a plan and to know where it will take them.

The Three's decision-making process can be seen in this example:

Marie, the owner of the company, was certain that she could do anything she set her mind to achieve. When confronted with the need to decide whether to expand her company's business by establishing another office in a location two hours away by car, Marie analyzed the situation. She determined that establishing a new office would require a large capital investment and would involve far more risk than would be incurred if the firm simply provided services in the new city by flying employees back and forth. Although Marie herself wanted the firm to expand into this new location because she believed it had great potential, her decision was clear: the company would advertise and build up its client base in the new location before making the commitment and incurring the risk of opening an office.

Although Threes usually like to make decisions, as doing so makes them feel that they are in charge of important outcomes that will directly affect them, they can also experience anguish if the outcome is uncertain or if people's deeper feelings are involved. In the former case, Three leaders analyze these situations as though they were looking for more detail to remove the uncertainty, even in cases where it is clear that there will always be ambiguity. When the decisions involve strong feelings, including their own, Threes—normally quick decision makers—can become frozen, as their head, gut, and heart all tell them to take different paths. However, there is a good lesson in this situation: quick decisions are not always the best ones. When quick action is not essential, taking time to gain more input and reflect can help Threes make not just good decisions, but wise ones.

This issue was apparent when Marie was trying to make an important personal decision:

Marie had run her own business successfully for 10 years, but she had always wanted to go back to graduate school for an advanced business degree. However, she was about to be married, and she planned to have a family. Marie was used to setting goals and being successful in everything she did, but how could she do it all? While this situation would cause most women to wonder what their next step should be, Marie became completely paralyzed by this issue for over a year. Her well-tuned analytical skills could not give her a ready answer because both her feelings and her future husband's had to be discussed and considered.

Development Stretches for Threes

CHART 7.4 **Threes: Development Stretches**

Center of Intelligence	Activities for Threes That Develop That Center
Head Center	**Objective analysis** Consider data, including feelings, that may not lead directly to the result you intend, but that can help you make the best decision. **Astute insight** Make certain that your desire for efficiency doesn't cause you to spend insufficient time analyzing the meaning of the data. **Productive planning** Be realistic about time frames, remembering to account for unforeseen obstacles.
Heart Center	**Empathy** Spend time considering your own feelings and those of others; factor them into your decisions. **Authentic relating** Share your real feelings (including anxieties) related to the decisions you must make; this will help dismantle the overly confident image you have created that serves as a barrier between you and others. **Compassion** Make decisions that are not just expedient but also compassionate.
Body (Gut) Center	**Taking effective action** Work on making most of your decisions less quickly so that new insights have time to percolate. **Steadfastness** Explore your deeper values and hold firm on values-based decisions. **Gut knowing** Become more aware of your body's signals when you are considering alternatives.

Enneagram Style Fours

When Four leaders make decisions, they use their Head and Body Centers, but, above all, they trust their Heart Center. Fours have feelings about many things: the facts of a situation, the alternative choices they might make, the people involved, the likely outcome, and even their feelings about their feelings. Fours usually have strong opinions about  their decisions, and they become particularly passionate when a decision is related to their most important values.

Enneagram Style
MOOD
④

Because many Fours are highly analytical, they gather information (including information about feelings); scrutinize the issues; talk to others about their thoughts, feelings, and prior experiences; and then reanalyze the information to determine the best course of action. Fours also factor the organization's culture and decision-making authority structure into the equation, and they stand behind the decisions they make.

Here's a story about Jacob, a Four leader faced with an important strategic decision:

> Jacob was proud of the research center he had created. In five years, he had led the center from infancy to its current status as an institution that was well respected for doing first-rate academic research that could be applied in real-world settings. In addition to hiring the top talent in the field, Jacob had decided that the center would do only research that had practical applications. Because of Jacob's clarity about his values—making a difference by conducting research that could be used to improve people's lives—the center has thrived.

Four leaders can err by making decisions that overemphasize their values and/or are overly focused on personal experiences and feelings, both their own and those of other people. For example, a Four may decide to raise an employee's salary because that individual has personal issues that cause him or her to need additional financial resources. However, the Four may pay insufficient attention to the fact that this employee's work performance is far below that of other employees who did not receive raises. In an effort to be compassionate, the Four may unintentionally be unfair and damage employee morale.

Many decisions don't have obvious answers, and Fours can become distraught when a decision is complex and none of the alternatives seems ideal. A Four leader will also experience angst over a decision where one choice, though profitable, may hurt some employees. Because Fours are so sensitive themselves, they tend to put themselves in the shoes of the other person—or in what they imagine to be the other person's shoes—and they have a difficult time making a decision that they believe will cause someone to suffer.

Here's an example of a time when Jacob had a very hard decision to make:

> Jacob knew that if the center was to grow, the older research
> scientists had to mentor the younger scientists. However, the
> two most senior scientists were unwilling to do so, believing
> that their job was only to do research. They also had no
> interest in developing the skills of the scientists who had just
> recently received their graduate degrees. Jacob knew that (1)
> without these two scientists' support, he would never get the
> mid-level scientists involved in mentoring; (2) if he pushed
> the issue and alienated the senior scientists, they might
> resign over this issue; and (3) if he ignored the problem, the
> work of the center would be hurt. Jacob was unable to deal
> with this issue for two years, until he sought guidance from
> a consultant, who helped Jacob develop an incentive system
> that was successful in motivating the mid-level scientists to
> become mentors.

Development Stretches for Fours

CHART 7.5   **Fours: Development Stretches**

Center of Intelligence	Activities for Fours That Develop That Center
Head Center	**Objective analysis** Don't let your personal experiences and feelings bias your view of the facts; become more objective in your decision making. **Astute insight** Develop insights of the mind in addition to insights of the heart. Ask yourself: *What do I think is true?* in addition to *What do I feel is true?* **Productive planning** Think through your decisions, using a logical as well as an intuitive approach; if you get two different answers, ask yourself which decision will provide the best result.
Heart Center	**Empathy** Examine your perceptions about what other people are feeling about issues and decisions; make sure you are not projecting your own emotional reactions onto others. **Authentic relating** Let others tell you their real thoughts and feelings about a decision; be open to whatever is said. **Compassion** Remember that excessive emotionality does not help either you or others when making decisions.
Body (Gut) Center	**Taking effective action** Don't let feelings immobilize you and prevent you from making a decision; action is one way to move through emotional reactions. **Steadfastness** Being adamant and overly tenacious about a decision rarely enlists people, but neither does being overly compliant or passive. Find the middle ground. **Gut knowing** Ask yourself on a regular basis what your gut reactions are to these questions: *What do I really want? What should I do here?*

Enneagram Style Fives

Enneagram Style
KNOWLEDGE

Five leaders approach decision making from an analytical perspective, accumulating facts and piecing them together in a logical fashion. Their decisions are usually well thought through because Fives take the time to make sure they do the necessary research, assessing the pros and cons and the potential impact of each alternative before making their final decision.

Because Fives pay a great deal of attention to the organization's decision-making authority structure and culture, they rarely overstep their lines of authority, and they usually make decisions that are consistent with the operating practices of the company.

Fives primarily make decisions using their Head Center. Although they do use their Heart and Body Centers, they are likely to do so only as a feasibility check for a decision they have already made based on rational data. However, Five leaders who have done self-development work to help them avoid disengaging from their emotions will use all three centers, and their decisions can be very powerful ones.

Here's an example of Beth, a Five leader, using an integrated head, heart, and gut approach:

Beth was in a senior team meeting listening to the company president outline his strategy proposal. He indicated that professional development was crucial to the organization's success, and he proposed that employees who did not take advantage of the development opportunities available to improve their performance levels could not be assured of ongoing employment at the company.

Just as the team was about to approve the strategy, Beth said the following: "Wait a minute. We are about to make a decision that will enlist no one. This is way too harsh. What about people? It's true that we need to change the strategy to emphasize development, but the way this proposal currently is worded will be taken as a threat. This is not the best decision."

The president and the other team members sat in stunned silence, because they knew she was right. The fact that this was coming from someone who was *not* perceived as making decisions based primarily on their potential impact on people made the others pay even more attention. Beth's comments caused the team to review the strategy and change the intent and wording entirely.

Five leaders tend to make decisions on their own, relying on their own understanding and analyses rather than involving others in various stages of the decision-making process. This can be an asset, because Fives often stand firmly behind their decisions. However, this approach can also be a liability, particularly when a decision requires input from a variety of sources or when participation in the process would encourage people to accept the decision more readily.

Unlike Beth in the preceding example, Five leaders tend to place insufficient emphasis on others' reactions when making a decision. Because most Fives don't normally have strong emotional responses themselves—which might be thought of as their having an underexplored Heart Center—they often assume that other people will or should have the same nonemotional types of reactions. In addition, the unfamiliarity or discomfort that some Fives have with in-depth feelings can make it more difficult for them to anticipate and/or empathize with the emotional reactions of others.

Finally, many Five leaders do not move to action quickly enough because they want to be sure that they have secured all of the relevant information and analyzed it extensively before making a decision. However, some decisions require quick action, while others involve such large quantities of data that it is impossible to know everything in advance.

The following example involving Beth illustrates the potential pitfalls:

Prior to joining her current company, Beth had spent 10 years working as a consultant in a large consulting firm. After a year with that firm, Beth wanted to leave. She did not respect the owner, she felt limited by the firm's rules on how consultants must function with clients, and she detested the constant firm meetings. Still, she also reasoned that the money was good, the firm had prestige, and she didn't know what else was available. She would have to research her options, but the time she had for doing so was limited by her workweek of 50+ hours. Beth worked unhappily in the firm for eight more years, until she finally realized that she was relying solely on logic and ignoring her heart. This had immobilized her and prevented her from taking action.

Development Stretches for Fives

CHART 7.6   **Fives: Development Stretches**

Center of Intelligence	Activities for Fives That Develop That Center
Head Center	**Objective analysis** Remember that logical analysis is not necessarily objective; logic can have its own bias, depending on the logic used. **Astute insight** Make sure your insights include information about feelings as well as facts. **Productive planning** Don't overplan or overstrategize; remember, it is not always possible to know everything before you develop a plan.
Heart Center	**Empathy** Learn to feel your own feelings in real time, not after the fact. This will enable you to read other people's feelings more accurately and to use this information in decision making. **Authentic relating** Create fewer communication barriers between yourself and others; people will then give you more truthful information.

(Continued)

CHART 7.6 *(Continued)* **Fives: Development Stretches**

Center of Intelligence	Activities for Fives That Develop That Center
	Compassion Tell people how you reached your decision, and also share your feelings about it. Be kind when delivering tough information.
Body (Gut) Center	**Taking effective action** Make decisions in a timely manner, using information from your mind, heart, and gut.
	Steadfastness Hold firm on decisions you have made using your mind, heart, and gut in an integrated way; be flexible and reconsider decisions you have made using your mind only.
	Gut knowing Learn to read your body's signals so that you can trust your gut; doing so will enable you to make better and faster decisions.

Enneagram Style Sixes

In the Six's mind, effective leadership involves making constant decisions about which course of action best solves the problem. However, Sixes don't usually make unilateral decisions; they often think of decision making as creative problem solv-

Enneagram Style ⑥
DOUBT

ing, with the best solution involving ample input from other people. Making decisions this way offers Sixes more assurance that they've considered all contingencies, and that there will be support for the decisions they make.

Sixes attempt to identify all the potential issues that could arise, calculate the pros and cons of each possible course of action, and then decide on the best alternative. Because they have finely tuned imaginations, most Six leaders can project vivid future scenarios, anticipate the consequences of each one, and then make a decision about what to do. Although these projected future scenarios arise from the Six's Head Center, they also involve the Heart Center (that is, through the Six's imagining people's emotional reactions to the various choices) and the Body Center (for example, through the Six's imagining the activities that people would be engaged in doing in each scenario).

Like the other two Head Center styles—Enneagram styles Five and Seven—Sixes pay attention to the organization's decision-making authority structure and culture. This does not mean that Sixes always comply with the organization's explicit and implicit rules; it means that when Sixes do not make a decision according to the rules, they are usually aware that they are not doing things exactly as expected, but they feel compelled to do so anyway.

In the following story, Sharon, a Six leader, had to decide whether to take a high-risk assignment:

> Known as a turnaround specialist, Sharon was asked to take a new position as the senior leader of a poorly functioning 200-person division whose previous leader had been fired for poor performance. Sharon was told that she would have three months to transform the division. The challenge excited Sharon, but it also caused her anxiety. Although she understood the kind of work these employees did, she had no familiarity with their customer base, nor did she know the managers who would be reporting to her. While many people would agonize over such a high-risk decision, Sharon decided to take the position within three days of its being offered to her. In those three days, Sharon learned as much as she could about the new group, met with its key managers to assess their attitudes and competence, and utilized the expertise of several colleagues who were familiar with the group's customer base. Having gained this information, Sharon also looked inside herself to determine whether she truly wanted to accept this challenge.

When Sixes doubt their own judgment, do not feel that they have the support of their organization or its leaders, or cannot imagine positive outcomes from a decision that they must make, Six leaders can exhibit a great degree of uncertainty and ambivalence. They may waver between alternatives for a long period of time, make a decision and then undercut their own authority by not fully implementing it, or make no decision at all.

When Sixes are uncertain, their minds have a tendency to create negative projections about what could happen next and whom they can trust to support them. These negative projections, some of which may be accurate and some of which may not be, confuse not only the Six leader, but also those who work for this person, the Six's boss, and his or her peers. It can be challenging to sort out what is real and what is a projection of the Six's imagination.

The Six's decision-making style is seen in the following story:

> Sharon had learned a hard lesson early in her career as a manager at another company. She had developed a hardworking, high-functioning team, then learned that there was going to be a reorganization that would result in the transfer of several of her team members to other departments. Both Sharon and her staff were highly displeased with the decision. When she attended an all-manager meeting to discuss implementation of the reorganization, Sharon decided to speak up. In front of all the managers, she told the company president that both she and her staff believed that the decision was a poor one, that it would have a negative impact on productivity and morale, and that it had to be reversed. Because Sharon did not select the best time or place to articulate her concerns, she angered the president, offended the other managers (most of whom did not agree with her), and hurt her career prospects in that company.

Development Stretches for Sixes

CHART 7.7   Sixes: Development Stretches

Center of Intelligence	Activities for Sixes That Develop That Center
Head Center	**Objective analysis** Slow down your analysis of the data related to a decision, particularly when you are anxious or notice that you are repeating the same thoughts.

(Continued)

CHART 7.7 *(Continued)* Sixes: Development Stretches

Center of Intelligence	Activities for Sixes That Develop That Center
	Astute insight Learn to differentiate your projections from objective insights by honestly examining your own feelings and motivations. This will help you clarify your intentions and allow you to make better decisions. **Productive planning** Plan for both positive and negative scenarios and know when to stop planning and take action.
Heart Center	**Empathy** Remain empathic even when someone's behavior bothers, hurts, or angers you. **Authentic relating** Be true to yourself even when you need or want something from another person; don't engage in ingratiating behavior. **Compassion** Be as compassionate to yourself as you are to others; factor you into your decision making.
Body (Gut) Center	**Taking effective action** Make decisions that are good risks, not just exciting ones; take action using your gut as a way to bypass overanalysis. **Steadfastness** When you are sure of a decision, believe in yourself and hold your ground in the face of opposition; make sure you do this in an approachable rather than a reactive manner. **Gut knowing** When you are unsure of what to do, engage in physical activity (such as walking) and ask your gut for the best alternative.

Enneagram Style Sevens

Enneagram Style
OPTIONS

Like Sixes, Seven leaders have extremely active minds. Unlike Sixes, however, Sevens make most decisions so fast that their decision making may appear nearly spontaneous. However, it is the result of their ability to process large quantities of information extremely quickly.

Sevens usually make decisions that push limits or encourage innovation. Ideally, they like to involve others in decision-making discussions because more possible alternatives are likely to be generated. Although Sevens often refer to themselves as egalitarian or democratic leaders, this does not mean that they believe that all decisions should be made by consensus or by a majority vote. Sevens simply want everyone to join the conversation and express an idea or opinion.

When Sevens know that a decision requires considerable forethought and input, they will take the time to make the best decision possible. Seven leaders may also assemble an informal set of respected advisors and use their input as additional data upon which to base their decision.

Here's an example of a Seven leader who sought the counsel of others:

> Steven, the leader of an important division of a large company, had abundant ideas for strategic activities, but his management staff complained that they were going in too many directions and that their priorities were unclear. Steven decided to convene a group of consultants and coaches who had worked with him in the past and ask them these three questions: *What do you know about my organization that might be affecting its ability to become more strategic? What actions would you advise me to take? What do I need to change in my own behavior?* Although Steven never revealed his reactions to their comments, he made several important decisions following this meeting that had a highly positive impact on his division.

Sevens' quick processing time can also interfere with their arriving at the best decisions, for the following reasons:

- Sevens may believe that they have all the information required, but in fact they may be missing critical data or may not have sufficient depth of information.

- Others may need more time than the Seven to process the information related to the decision.
- Sevens may omit important information when they explain a decision, assuming that this information is obvious to everyone.
- Sevens may express ideas that are not intended to be decisions, but that may be misunderstood as such by others, who start implementing them.

Since theirs is a Head Center style, Sevens can become so stimulated by their own thoughts or by an interchange of ideas that they have difficulty calibrating the reactions and feelings of others. It is as though the Head Center is turned on at these times, but the Heart Center is switched off and thus is unavailable as a source of data. Decisions based on what the Seven thinks others are feeling (a cerebral speculation) rather than on feeling what someone else is feeling (empathy) can lead to less than optimal decisions.

Finally, Sevens may not pay enough attention to the organizational politics surrounding the decision. Most Sevens consider politics to be an annoyance that impedes their ability to make decisions and take action. Unfortunately, many excellent ideas have been lost precisely because decision makers did not get the right people in the organization involved in the right way and at the right time.

Steven had learned this lesson the hard way earlier in his career:

Steven perceived himself as a model manager and began implementing new projects in his department immediately. He constantly made recommendations to his immediate boss about ways to improve the division, and he offered the company president unsolicited opinions about the organization's strategic direction. After six months, Steven's boss sat him down and said, "You've been implementing projects that require prior authorization, indirectly criticizing me by making numerous suggestions about how to change the division, and telling the president how to run the organization. If you want to continue working here, you're going to have to learn to show a little more respect for other people's jobs."

Development Stretches for Sevens

CHART 7.8 **Sevens: Development Stretches**

Center of Intelligence	Activities for Sevens That Develop That Center
Head Center	**Objective analysis** Make sure you really have all the data, not just the highlights. **Astute insight** To have insight takes time and reflection; allow yourself both of these in order to get a deeper view of the issues. **Productive planning** Make a decision and a plan, and stick to them; focus your mind.
Heart Center	**Empathy** Examine your feelings and read your internal cues; this will help you to read others' body language. **Authentic relating** Relate through more than your mind alone; when you relate through your heart as well, your decisions will be better. **Compassion** Think about the potential impact on people of every alternative you consider.
Body (Gut) Center	**Taking effective action** Slowing your pace will help you make wise decisions, not just decisions that intrigue or stimulate you. **Steadfastness** Become confident in your depth of knowledge and in your capacity to feel; this confidence will enable you to make the best decisions and to stand by them. **Gut knowing** Bypass your tendency to overthink and overplan by developing your gut knowing. When considering options, ask yourself: *Which of these options does my gut tell me will lead to the best outcome?*

Enneagram Style Eights

Enneagram Style
CHALLENGE

Eight leaders perceive making decisions as an essential part of their job, and they view themselves as being highly skilled in this area. Eights' certainty and courage come from their gut, since they process information instinctively and usually respond swiftly to issues that confront them.

More than people with any other Enneagram style, Eights sense power and authority dynamics, being highly attuned to the organization's decision-making authority structure and culture. This doesn't mean that Eights always follow the existing authority structure or make decisions in accordance with the organizational culture. When Eights break the rules, they do so intentionally, and they know that there may be consequences.

In addition, Eights factor the context of the decision into the process, focusing particularly on the urgency of the decision. Most Eights utilize their Head Center to process information (although they tend not to need as much data as the Head Center styles, Five, Six, and Seven) and to integrate this information with their gut reactions. Some Eights also utilize their Heart Center to do the following: (1) anticipate other people's likely responses to a decision, (2) assess the impact of a decision on the people affected, or (3) make a tough decision that may hurt someone and then feel guilty or remorseful afterward.

The following story about Renee shows the bold, action-oriented confidence of Eight decision makers:

> One of three attorneys leading a global law firm, Renee believed that the firm's success required greater leadership capability among the practice managers (all of whom were working attorneys with no management training) and a greater emphasis on business development. The other two leaders, one of whom was the firm's chairman and the other a peer of Renee's, agreed to let Renee take the lead

in this effort because Renee was passionate about its importance.

Renee decided to bring in two consultants, a business development expert and a leadership expert. The business consultant worked first with Renee's practice area; the result was a revenue increase of 30 percent, thus demonstrating the value of doing strategic business development. The leadership consultant worked first with the chairman and then with Renee's peer, which increased their levels of competence and confidence. Because of Renee's strategic choices, she was able to convince the chairman and her peer to expand these efforts to the entire firm.

Because Eights trust their own opinions more than those of other people and trust their gut when it comes to taking action, they can make decisions that others perceive as being unilateral. In addition, their decisions can be flawed, as no one has a perfectly calibrated gut.

Eights also like to make things happen fast, sometimes paying insufficient attention to detail as a result. They have an internal sense of urgency, wanting to get things done quickly in order to achieve the impact they desire so that they can move on to the next big challenge. However, some decisions are best made using more input, reflection, and time, while other problems may simply disappear on their own if a leader is patient and learns the art of timing.

Finally, some Eights do not take constructive criticism well or become combative when faced with what they perceive as opposition. Eights can encounter resistance because other people in the organization view them as having made decisions that overstep their lines of authority, or because others have different ideas as to the best course of action. For some Eights, changing their minds or admitting that they have made a mistake or made a less than optimal decision can be challenging.

The following example illustrates Renee's decision-making style:

After the success of the efforts described earlier, Renee decided to use both consultants in her practice area. Peter, the business development consultant, was hired to develop a comprehensive business development plan; Sandy, the leadership consultant, was hired to help Renee reorganize her 75-person practice group, with a focus on efficiency and customer service.

Sandy then learned—and told Renee—that the business development consultant was planning a major reorganization based on business development needs. Sandy advised Renee that the two different reorganizations based on different goals—one on efficiency and client service, and the other on business development—needed to be coordinated or the consultants would be working at cross-purposes.

Because Renee was busy and had little time for direct involvement, she decided to continue with the business development reorganization only. The result was that Renee ended up with an organization design that was too expensive to implement and that actually hurt current client relationships because too few resources were allocated to current client work.

Development Stretches for Eights

CHART 7.9   Eights: Development Stretches

Center of Intelligence	Activities for Eights That Develop That Center
Head Center	**Objective analysis** Question your assumptions; ask the opinions of others; take in multiple viewpoints when making decisions.
	Astute insight Honor your insights, but ask yourself what insights you might be missing that could alter your decisions.
	Productive planning Maintain your ability to do big-picture planning, but make sure you also plan for the operational aspects of implementation.

(Continued)

CHART 7.9 *(Continued)*   **Eights: Development Stretches**

Center of Intelligence	Activities for Eights That Develop That Center
Heart Center	**Empathy** Take the time to sense the feelings of other people, even when you don't respect the individuals. **Authentic relating** Become more aware of presenting yourself as bold and confident; when you allow yourself to be more vulnerable, people will support you and your decisions more. **Compassion** Consider the impact of your decisions on everyone, but don't make decisions to avoid guilt.
Body (Gut) Center	**Taking effective action** Don't rush into decisions; don't make overly complex decisions when a simple solution would work just as well. **Steadfastness** Be clear, but be careful not to become inflexible or unresponsive. **Gut knowing** Trust your gut, but when your reaction seems too strong or quick, pause and reexamine your decision.

Enneagram Style Nines

Nine leaders usually make thoughtful decisions, using a methodical process that is based on well-researched data. Because Nines place a high value both on consensus and on giving people an opportunity to present their perspectives, they generally

Enneagram Style ⑨
HARMONY

include others in the collection and analysis of the data that go into the final decision.

Because Nine leaders want to avoid conflict and also appreciate routines, they are usually explicit about how decisions will be made, and they follow a rigorous process of collecting all the relevant data. Among those data are information about the culture, including how decisions are made and the lines of decision-making authority.

Having genial social skills, Nine leaders also establish excellent rapport and are able to discuss important issues in a nonthreatening way. Nines will listen openly when someone disagrees with a decision that the Nine has made as long as the other person is not overly antagonistic or critical in doing so.

The following story about Brandon shows the Nine's decision-making style:

> Brandon, the new manager of a customer service help desk, realized immediately that the people who staffed the telephone help lines had serious skill deficiencies. Rather than immediately warning the worst-performing employees to improve their performance, Brandon instead spoke privately with each employee in order to understand his or her perspective and to develop rapport. Brandon also spoke with his boss, his peers, and the help desk's customers. In addition, Brandon benchmarked similar help desks in other companies and observed his company's help desk employees as they worked. Brandon took his time, developed relationships, and learned exactly what was causing the problem—a mismatch between the questions that help desk staff were expected to answer and the level of their technical expertise to do so. When he decided to divide the department into service specialists and technical specialists, his decision was met with widespread acceptance.

Most Nines have access to their Head and Heart Centers, using the former to collect and absorb information and the latter to engage others in the decision-making process and to anticipate their reactions to decisions. Although Nine is a Body Center style and many Nines trust their gut knowing when they sense it, most Nines do not have *full* access to their Body Center. Because Nines are uncomfortable with feeling angry, they often ignore the physical cues that let them know that they are experiencing distress, which in turn keeps them out of touch with other useful information from their Body Center.

Nines' tendency to avoid conflict also affects their decision making. Nine leaders may prolong the decision-making process as a way of avoiding tension, disagreement, or anger, or they may become confused about what course of action to take. In addition, many Nines are more cognizant of what they *don't* want to do than they are of the action that they *do* want to take.

Finally, because many Nines generally prefer making decisions with a great deal of input, they can be challenged if the organizational culture or a particular decision requires a more authoritative style. In addition, there are some instances in which Nines prefer to make a unilateral decision, especially when they believe that they know far more about the subject than anyone else and when they feel that they have the authority to do so. On these occasions, when someone seriously disagrees with them or tells them that they need to involve others more, Nines can become livid, feeling that their ideas and authority are being dismissed or undermined.

Here's an example of the Nines' difficulties with decision making:

For the task of selecting new computer software for the redesigned help desk, Brandon created a committee, but he did most of the investigatory work himself. He did so in part because he was familiar with the software and in part because he felt frustrated with the committee members' lack of expertise and impatient with the time it would take to educate them. Although he kept the members informed of his findings via e-mail and conference calls, in the end, Brandon chose a system that his committee felt was too complex for the help desk personnel to use.

Development Stretches for Nines

CHART 7.10 **Nines: Development Stretches**

Center of Intelligence	Activities for Nines That Develop That Center
Head Center	**Objective analysis** Remember that you can collect too much data and then overanalyze a situation; this creates confusion about which information is the most relevant. **Astute insight** Honor your insights related to decisions you are making and be willing to verbalize them. **Productive planning** Keep to your deadline dates by planning your time schedule carefully and then following through.
Heart Center	**Empathy** Make sure to maintain your empathy, even with people you perceive as negative and complaining. **Authentic relating** Share how you really feel about different aspects of a decision and the decision-making process early in the discussion. **Compassion** Maintain an attitude of kindness, even toward people who stridently disagree with your decisions.
Body (Gut) Center	**Taking effective action** Figure out why you procrastinate; err on the side of taking action too quickly, rather than too slowly. **Steadfastness** Without being stubborn, hold firm on decisions that you believe are best, even in the face of opposition and conflict. **Gut knowing** Every time you make a decision, consult your gut for additional information.

Development Stretches for Everyone

- Think of three personal and/or work-related decisions you have made in the past year. Write each one down on a separate piece of paper. Underneath each decision, make three columns and label them Head, Heart, and Gut. For each decision, write down how you used that center to make that particular decision. Next, review all three decisions and look for patterns related to how you used your head, heart, and gut. Finally, assess how you could use each center better to make optimal decisions.

- The next time you need to make a decision and have already collected the relevant information, ask yourself: *What does my head tell me to do? What does my heart say? What does my gut tell me?* If you have the same response to each question, you probably have an optimal decision, as long as you have also factored in the organizational culture, the organizational decision-making authority structure, and the context of the decision. If you have different answers to two or more of the questions, ask yourself why. Your answer will give you excellent guidance regarding what to do next.

- Educate yourself further by reading one of the recommended books under "Make Optimal Decisions" in the Resources section at the back of this book.

Chapter 8

Take Charge
of Change

*I*n contemporary organizations, change has become a way of life. Companies are now operating in increasingly complex environments, with more competition, fewer resources, less time to market, higher customer expectations, increased regulation, more technology, and greater uncertainty. Organizations need to be flexible, innovative, cost-conscious, and responsive if they want to succeed, particularly in the global marketplace. As a result, managers at all levels need to be able to Take Charge of Change and lead their teams in directions that they may not have anticipated.

First, leaders need to *manage change* by (1) systemically assessing the current situation that is driving the change, (2) designing the desired future of the organization in sufficient detail to allow for successful implementation of the change, and (3) developing a comprehensive master plan, along with subplans, that will enable the organization to make a smooth transition into the future. In addition, leaders need to be both symbolic and real champions of change while also running the day-to-day business. The leader's areas of responsibilities in managing change are shown in Figure 8.1.

FIGURE 8.1 **Manage Change**

Taking charge of change also requires a comprehensive *change strategy* that includes the following:

1. Increasing the Demand and desire for change
2. Creating a compelling Vision for the change
3. Developing a systematic Plan and process for the change initiative
4. Reducing Resistance to the change
5. Anchoring the Change in the future organization

These five elements of the change strategy are overlaid on the elements of managing change, as shown in the Take Charge of Change graphic (Figure 8.2).

FIGURE 8.2 **Take Charge of Change**

The Change Strategy Formula

The change strategy is actually a formula for taking charge of change and looks like this:

$$D \times V \times P > R = C$$

where D = demand, dissatisfaction, and desire for change
V = the vision or model for the change
P = the plan and process for the change
R = resistance to the change
C = results of the change

When using the change strategy formula to Take Charge of Change, D, V, and P must be greater than R in order for C (change) to occur. In addition, the strategy elements to the left of R (resistance) are multiplied rather than added, which means that each of these elements—namely, D, V, and P—must be greater than zero in order for change to be achieved. If there is a vision and a plan for a change, but no one cares about the change effort ($D = 0$), the change will have no support and will not take place.

Similarly, a change effort may be based on a great deal of demand and dissatisfaction with the status quo (high D) and have a sophisticated plan and process (high P) for the change, but lack vision ($V = 0$). In this case, people want to change and have created a plan and process to do so, but they do not know where they are going; thus, the change will not succeed.

Having the ability to Take Charge of Change means that you are skilled in the following six competency components:

1. Being a champion of change
2. Understanding the current situation and developing the desire and demand for change
3. Creating the change vision
4. Managing the transition: developing and implementing a change plan and process

5. Reducing resistance to change

6. Designing the future organization and anchoring the change

As you read further and reflect on the six competency components of Take Charge of Change, rate yourself in each area on a scale of 1 to 5. This will help you determine both your areas of strength and the areas that need development.

The Six Competency Components of Take Charge of Change

Component 1: Being a Champion of Change

This involves fostering change by identifying and actively pursuing innovative products and/or ways of doing things; being known throughout the organization as a visible and committed change leader; and understanding and integrating learning from past change initiatives in order to translate these insights into future change efforts.

Low				High
1	2	3	4	5

Component 2: Understanding the Current Situation and Developing the Desire and Demand for Change

This means deeply understanding and communicating the opportunities inherent in the change; using a systems-thinking approach to analyze the current situation and identify the root causes; motivating people to support the change by using multiple communication vehicles to make the need for change highly public; making a persuasive case for change using statistics and reason, feelings (such as hope, concern, despair, or frustration), and evocative symbols and stories; and energizing the change effort by creating a shared sense of urgency.

Low				High
1	2	3	4	5

Component 3: Creating the Change Vision

This involves creating a collaborative, compelling vision of the future; passionately communicating the vision using multiple media, selective storytelling, compelling metaphors, and testimonials; articulating the values underpinning the vision and making sure that all aspects of the change reflect these values; using organization models and examples from other companies to sell the vision; and enlisting top management, natural leaders, and other key individuals and groups to support the vision and influence others to join the change effort.

Low				**High**
1	2	3	4	5

Component 4: Managing the Transition: Developing and Implementing a Change Plan and Process

This includes developing a concrete yet flexible master plan that is aligned with the vision; creating and implementing supporting subplans (for example, plans for communication, finances, and logistics); documenting and monitoring timetables, key milestones, and accountabilities; creating one or more planning teams and making sure that these teams have the requisite time, resources, stature, and expertise; ensuring that communication vehicles are timely, frequent, and accurate; training, empowering, and rewarding or sanctioning people in ways that support the change; and regularly monitoring progress using agreed-upon measures.

Low				**High**
1	2	3	4	5

Component 5: Reducing Resistance to Change

This involves accurately identifying the sources and causes of resistance; developing strategies for reducing resistance; building positive relationships with the key influence leaders and groups; setting up formal and informal participation structures, and encouraging involvement by clarifying when input is helpful and when it can't be utilized; listening to feedback and demonstrating publicly how and when input is being used; and helping people deal with the attachment and loss that is a natural part of change.

Low				High
1	2	3	4	5

Component 6: Designing the Future Organization and Anchoring the Change

This requires articulating what the change will achieve and why this is important; engaging others in honest dialogue about the change; basing the future organizational design on a rigorous root cause analysis of the current situation and the identified vision for the change; creating design criteria for each element of the future organization in sufficient detail to allow smooth implementation, making sure that all elements support one another; understanding and communicating whether the change is developmental (i.e., small and incremental), transitional (medium to large, without shifts in culture or paradigms), or transformative (fundamental shifts in culture, paradigms, and work); specifying which parts of the organization will be directly and indirectly affected by the change; making the change sustainable by highlighting short-term wins and long-term gains; and anchoring the change in the new organization through culture change, reinforcement of changed structures and systems, and continuous communication.

Low				High
1	2	3	4	5

Enneagram Dimensions of Take Charge of Change

Enneagram Style Ones

One leaders enjoy taking charge of change because they are as deeply committed to organizational improvement as they are to lifelong self-improvement. In addition, Ones relish the act of breaking large tasks into manageable pieces, then organizing the elements into a complex plan that gets the whole job done. The more experience the One leader has, the larger the change efforts that he or she likes to manage.

Enneagram Style
DILIGENCE 1

One leaders bring their discerning minds to taking charge of change, determining whether or not they believe a particular change is a good idea. If they believe that it is, Ones fully embrace the change and are bolstered by their belief that nothing that is worth doing is impossible. Ones carefully analyze the current situation to make certain that all the issues are defined, design the future scenario in sufficient detail that the target is clear, and then develop a practical transition plan and process that are rigorously implemented. Further, Ones excel as change champions, explaining not only the need for change but also what the change should look like in concrete and compelling terms.

Here's an example of Alan explaining the reorganization to his staff:

> Alan, a senior manager in charge of quality assurance, knew that his team would feel overwhelmed when he told them about the need to reorganize the division. In making this announcement at a team meeting, Alan said, "As effective as we are, we can be even more effective if we reorganize ourselves along internal customer lines rather than quality functions. I know you're all working at full capacity already, so I'm going to need all of you to help determine how we can maintain the same level of excellence while we reorganize ourselves."

The One's sense of practicality can, however, also be a liability. If Ones believe that the work involved in executing the change far outweighs the likely positive outcomes, they may not fully commit to the change effort. They may even be viewed as resisting change, although they do not perceive themselves as doing so.

In addition, while One leaders frequently excel at implementing change, they may not pay sufficient attention to creating a shared and compelling vision. Some Ones believe that if the details of the future state are clearly defined and the need for the change is obvious, a shared vision isn't necessary. However, many people need a strong vision to keep them aligned with the change, because this allows them to disagree with details without abandoning their support of the overall effort.

Ones may also become impatient when others fail to support changes that the One perceives as obvious and important. As hard as Ones may try to hide their irritation, their feelings often show in their quick verbal responses and/or nonverbal behavior.

Finally, Ones may do too much of the work involved in the change themselves. Ones like to make sure that all the details are under control, and they enjoy accomplishing concrete tasks. Thus, they may delegate less than they should and end up with more work than they can handle.

Alan learned this lesson from past experience, as seen in the following example:

When the organization had to move to a new location several miles away from its current offices, Alan agreed to be the project manager for the entire effort. He created the plan, managed the logistics, and interfaced with the architects, movers, and computer consultants. However, the difficulties of both overseeing the move and maintaining the day-to-day business overwhelmed him. Although everything went well, Alan's family life was disrupted, and he was exhausted. In retrospect, he realized that one person really couldn't do it all and that he would have paid less of a personal price if he had enlisted others more effectively.

Development Stretches for Ones

ASK FOR HELP   Although you may enjoy doing most of the work yourself, delegate 50 percent more than you do normally. Taking charge of change means relying on others and overseeing the effort, not becoming overly involved in the details.

NOTICE HOW YOUR REACTIONS CAN BE READ AS RESISTANCE Because you have strong opinions, believe that you are correct most of the time, and react quickly to other people's comments, you may be seen as resisting change even when you are simply asking a question or disagreeing with a detail. When you listen fully and make an effort to integrate other points of view into your own, you are more likely to be perceived as an effective problem solver rather than as a resistor.

LINK ALL ASPECTS OF THE CHANGE TO THE VISION   Spend time developing the vision for the change, and link all aspects of the change to the vision—for example, the assessment, the transition plan and process, and specific details related to the results of the change. By doing this, you will help keep others focused and committed.

Enneagram Style Twos

Two leaders wholeheartedly support and enjoy leading a change effort if they believe that the change will be beneficial for both people and the organization. However, Twos have trouble embracing a change that, although good for the organiza- *Enneagram Style* **②** GIVING tion, would cause people to suffer. In this situation, Twos become creative, stretching themselves to find an agreeable middle ground.

Twos also take pleasure in organizing a complex set of tasks and bringing them to fruition on time. Twos are particularly adept at managing the numerous forms of communication involved in complex change efforts. They usually deal with resistance to change in a productive way. Two leaders take the time to listen to others' opinions and concerns. Although they do not always do what others want them to, they give people their full attention and consideration, making dissenters feel respected, even if their ideas are not ultimately implemented.

The following story shows how Twos accomplish a challenging change effort:

> Sally, the president of a nonprofit organization, was busy coordinating the work of the board, supervising two full-time staff members, and working on strategy development. The organization needed an interactive Web site that would enable it to track information, sell merchandise, and provide the latest information to customers, along with other functions. Although Sally's knowledge of Web sites was limited, she was the only person on the board with any experience with them at all.
>
> Not only did Sally lead the change effort related to the new Web site, but she simultaneously changed the related components of the organization's infrastructure. She enlisted the board members and staff in the design and writing of the site, as well as in developing the supporting organizational infrastructure. They all contributed because they believed in the organization's vision, and they knew how hard Sally was working on this effort and wanted to support her.

Many Twos like taking charge of change because orchestrating people, tasks, and events appeals to their desire to play a key role in organizing and implementing complex activities. However, Twos can also feel overwhelmed by large change initiatives; there are so many different demands on the Two leader's time and so many people with different agendas to consider that the Two worries that there is no way to satisfy everyone. If the tough decisions they make generate anger in the organization, Two leaders may feel that they haven't done a good enough job or that their hard work was unappreciated. This scenario is aggravated when Twos believe that others are inappropriately influencing the change effort or are undermining decisions that they have made.

Most change efforts involve both positive and negative unanticipated consequences. For Twos, who emphasize the impact of change on people, the negative outcomes can be extremely disheartening, especially if the Two leader has publicly vowed that these negative outcomes would not occur. While some Twos are equally adept at managing people and managing tasks, others focus more on the former. As a result, employees may be very well informed about and aligned with the change effort, but the Two may pay less attention to the details of execution. Finally, Twos often work themselves to exhaustion in the service of others, but repress their feelings of fatigue until they either get sick or become angry about all the demands placed on them.

Here's an example of what happened when Sally was the human resources manager for a small retail firm in her previous job:

Sally was part of a steering committee authorized to change the company from a function-based organization to one based on teams. At first, she supported the change 100 percent and used her enthusiasm to enlist others. However, the company then brought in efficiency experts who decided that the new change had to include a 15 percent reduction in staff. Not only did Sally perceive these outsiders as preempting the steering committee's work, but she had to lead the part of the change process that involved laying off existing workers. Angry and frustrated, Sally did a mediocre job of implementing the staff reduction process and quit two weeks after the whole ordeal was over.

Development Stretches for Twos

MANAGE YOUR ENERGY AND STRESS LEVELS   When you first realize that you are overworking yourself, or when you notice that you are chronically fatigued, *stop*. Get more rest, eat more healthfully, exercise more, and do something nice for yourself, preferably something that is not expensive. (As a way of being nice to themselves, some Twos purchase items that are beyond their budgets, thus creating more stress.)

DEVELOP A MORE BALANCED APPROACH TO DIFFICULT ISSUES   When faced with extremely complex issues, you may feel more frustrated and emotional than usual. Examine why this is so—for example, it may be related to your sense that you are responsible for everyone and everything or that others are not supporting your efforts despite your consistent support of their endeavors. Acknowledging such beliefs can be difficult, but once you do, it can be extremely freeing.

DEVELOP THE WORK IN SUCH A WAY THAT OTHERS CAN EXECUTE TASKS WITHOUT YOUR GUIDANCE   Without intending to do so, you may be making other people dependent on you. While this may make you feel needed and involved, people may begin to feel that they are unable to perform a task without your involvement. You can help people most by allowing them to be independent.

Enneagram Style Threes

Enneagram Style
③
PERFORM

Being future-focused, Three leaders know how to prepare their endeavors for success. They analyze the current situation, set goals, develop a road map for the transition, and expect results. Threes like to have a plan that both they and others can follow, and they monitor performance and progress throughout. When they have a capable team behind them, Threes keep themselves and others focused on the objectives, and their enthusiasm and willingness to do hard work are often contagious.

Typically adept at communicating the need for change, Three leaders pay a great deal of attention to how others—particularly customers, bosses, and subordinates—respond to their efforts, and they adjust their plans accordingly. The can-do attitude of Threes also makes them credible change champions. Most change involves a leap of faith into the future, and Three leaders convey a sense that any worthwhile goal can be achieved.

Here's an example of Taylor's leadership of a 360° feedback process for his organization:

> When Taylor was asked to take charge of an elaborate feedback process for the 100 senior managers in his company, he perceived this as an exciting challenge. It involved the development of a questionnaire, the creation of systems to identify who would be providing anonymous feedback to each manager, interfacing with the online survey vendor, overseeing the report distribution, and developing the manager coaching process. Because this would be the first time any of the managers had received this type of feedback, the process would also involve a major cultural shift. Taylor created multiple high-functioning teams, and his design and implementation of this initiative was seen as a major success.

Because Threes value efficiency and effectiveness so highly, they can become extremely frustrated when they encounter obstacles. Threes expect everyone to keep their agreements and to do their assigned work well. Consequently, if someone they have counted on for support changes his or her mind, or if someone who has agreed to contribute work either doesn't do so or produces an inferior product, the Three can become short-tempered, abrupt, or angry.

In addition, Threes often do not take into account the inevitable time delays or unanticipated tasks that arise during change efforts.

Because obstacles and delays were not part of *their* plan, Threes become agitated and may do one of three things: (1) become even more focused, putting in longer hours with the expectation that others will do the same; (2) become frustrated and resentful, and do less than a stellar job; or (3) become withdrawn, make an attempt to do the work, and then stop working completely, as if to say, "I don't care anymore; I'm not doing this." The latter two behaviors can be especially troubling to those who are counting on the Three to take charge of change even in times of stress.

This can be seen when Taylor encountered problems implementing the 360° feedback process:

> Although the feedback initiative went well from the feedback recipients' perspective, a problem arose with the vendor that was providing the survey results. Each leader was to receive a hard copy of his or her results on a Monday, and when Taylor received these reports on the prior Wednesday, his random sample quality check found miscalculations in almost every survey report sampled. Working with little sleep, Taylor nonetheless enlisted employees to redo the calculations and, with their help, prepared 100 new reports. Just before the reports were to be assembled, however, Taylor went to his boss, threw up his hands, and said, "I'm done. I'm leaving." As a result, his boss and several other project staff members who were unfamiliar with the details spent all of Sunday putting the final reports and supporting materials together. Although they completed the project successfully, Taylor's behavior caused a major rift between Taylor and his boss.

Development Stretches for Threes

ALLOW 35 PERCENT MORE TIME THAN YOU ANTICIPATE NEEDING
Most Threes function efficiently and expect change initiatives to run smoothly. However, change efforts are far more complex than

projects and involve many more people. It is unrealistic to expect everything to run according to plan. Make sure to build in 35 percent more time to cover contingencies.

MAKE SURE YOUR DRIVE DOESN'T TURN INTO OVERDRIVE You may be thinking: *How can I not go into overdrive when the work requires it?* Remember that other people get work done without going into overdrive, and so can you. When you see signs of overdrive, such as sleeplessness, anxiety, and anger, recognize that it's time for you to stop pushing yourself and others, to start enlisting help, and to take some time for rest and/or physical activity.

WHEN YOU FEEL STRESSED, TALK TO SOMEONE YOU TRUST Threes can be enjoyable to be around when they are relaxed, but when they are under pressure, they seem to lose a large portion of their well-developed social skills. Ironically, this is the time when their social skills could serve them especially well. As soon as you feel frustration or stress, talk to someone you trust. Discuss how you really *feel*. Focus on what you can do, not on what someone else should do or how the situation ought to be changed.

Enneagram Style Fours

Four leaders enjoy leading large-scale change efforts because the intricacies and complexities involved stimulate them and call forth many of their strengths. This is particularly true when the change involves something that the Four cares about deeply, because it allows the Four to work from an inner vision, creatively design a  collective future, enlist others in the cause, and directly manifest his or her sense of the organization's greatest potential. From a Four's perspective, work doesn't get more pleasurable than this.

Four leaders utilize their sensitivity and intuition about people when taking charge of change. Doing so enables them to understand the causes of resistance and to respond in creative ways. Fours treat change as a large jigsaw puzzle in which all the pieces will eventually fall into place. However, they are also willing to create new puzzle pieces in the event that some are missing or just do not fit.

Transition planning can be stimulating for Fours, as long as they have reasonably free rein in the design. It's not that Fours actually have to do things their own way; it's that they need to *feel* that the design is their own. They like to think big, breaking large initiatives into manageable milestones that they can then implement.

The following story describes how Libby, a Four leader, took charge of change:

> Libby was the chief technology engineer in a high-tech start-up. An outside consultant had been hired to conduct an organizational assessment of the company and to help the senior leadership team design improvements that would take the company beyond the start-up stage.
>
> After collecting and analyzing the data from individual interviews, the consultant met with Libby and shared the following information: although the engineering function that Libby led was perceived as being high-performing with respect to product design, it was also perceived as being siloed—that is, being unwilling to share information or staff and reluctant to coordinate with other functions, such as customer support services or manufacturing.
>
> Libby understood the far-reaching organizational implications of this and became the organization's chief change champion. She led the organizational improvement efforts by (1) increasing coordination with her peers in other organizational units, (2) setting up formal and informal communications between the engineers and other groups, and (3) changing the performance expectations and reward system

for engineers—for example, by basing their salary increases and bonuses, in part, on their ability to collaborate with other groups.

When Fours are fatigued, either by overwork or by personal issues, they tend to overpersonalize resistance to change. Unfortunately, when resistance to organizational change occurs, it is sometimes expressed as personal criticisms, unfair speculations about a leader's motivations, and worse. Whether these accusations are public or private—and the latter is often more painful than public criticism, as it is more insidious—they are especially hurtful to Fours, who often have few filters or defenses with which to protect themselves from such criticisms.

The Four's sensitivity can also limit his or her ability to take charge of change in another way: Four leaders can be especially sympathetic to employees with whom they have strong bonds, whom they perceive as having suffered, or with whom they identify in some regard. If one of these employees is going to be adversely affected by the forthcoming change, Fours can feel deeply troubled, sometimes to the point of making special accommodations for this other person; this mirrors how Fours themselves would want to be treated. A Four can also feel distressed by having to choose between inflicting pain on an individual that he or she cares about and doing what is best for the organization.

Libby's personal sensitivity can be seen in the following example:

When Libby first received the consultant's feedback, she was reluctant to make any changes. However, after the consultant told Libby that the feedback on her overall leadership performance was excellent and that employees throughout the company respected her as an engineer and a leader, and also liked her as a person, Libby became emotional and told the consultant about a painful event that had occurred years earlier in another organization: during a 360° leadership feedback session, Libby's scores had been marginal, and she was deeply hurt and surprised to learn that several employees actively disliked her. For this reason, when she changed companies, Libby created a tightly knit group of engineers because they wanted it that way. She was reluctant to upset them, even though she had long realized that their exclusivity was not good for the organization. However, with the realization that she really was well thought of by everyone in the company, Libby was able to bypass her old fears and lead the change effort that she knew was important. She was nonetheless angry with herself for having let her feelings prevent her from doing what she had known all along was best for the organization.

Development Stretches for Fours

MAKE SUPPORTIVE STATEMENTS TO YOURSELF EVERY DAY Because Fours can be very hard on themselves, it is important for you to make positive statements to yourself on a daily basis, six times per day at a minimum. Statements such as "You did a very good job on that" and "How wonderful that you enjoy your children so much" are fine, as long as you actually believe what you say. When you do this many times a day for three months, you will find that your negative self-talk becomes less pervasive.

DEVELOP EFFECTIVE FILTERS FOR BOTH POSITIVE AND NEGATIVE INFORMATION ABOUT YOURSELF Fours tend to absorb negative information that they receive about themselves and have a limited ability to filter out what they believe is false. In addition, when Fours hear positive information about themselves, they often discard it without integrating any of it into their sense of self. It is important for you to develop well-functioning filters that allow you to absorb both positive and negative information *only after* you have decided that you agree with it. Each time someone tells you something about yourself, before you take it in or discard it, ask yourself this: *Do I really agree with this information?*

DEVELOP A WAY TO MANAGE YOUR FEELINGS THAT WORKS FOR YOU
Some Fours keep journals or write poetry. Others play musical instruments, sing, dance, or paint. Some Fours simply talk with friends and family. What is important is that you have an outlet for emotional expression and don't keep your feelings locked inside.

Enneagram Style Fives

Five leaders take charge of change by approaching it systematically—for example, conducting a thorough needs assessment, rigorously analyzing information, and benchmarking other organizations with similar issues. Once Fives have gathered all the relevant data, they map out a logical plan of action to ensure that the change process runs efficiently.

Enneagram Style
KNOWLEDGE

More than anything else, Five leaders need to understand how the entire change effort fits together before they commit to action.

Because Fives are fully aware of the ongoing business needs, they make sure that the change effort is not so demanding that the day-to-day business suffers. Thus, Fives do not normally embrace a change initiative without investigating the situation to answer the following questions:

1. Is the change really necessary?
2. Has the most effective and efficient solution been chosen?
3. Are there sufficient resources available to accomplish the change *and* meet ongoing business needs?
4. Do those in charge of the organization support the change?

When the answer to all these questions is yes, the Five leader will embrace the change. However, if the answer to question 1 is no, the Five leader will withhold her or his support. If the answer to the first question is yes, but the answer to one or more of the other questions is no, the Five will regroup and strategize in the hope of changing the situation. If this is not successful, the Five will usually wait until conditions are more favorable.

The following example shows the agile mind of the Five when taking charge of change:

> Charles, the CEO of a large aerospace company, had hired a consultant to help the company with a diversity initiative. When the consultant gave him a preliminary look at the data, he was impressed with the untapped potential within the organization, but was dismayed by the neutral attitude about diversity displayed by a few of his senior staff members.
>
> Pondering the data overnight, Charles decided that he was going to champion the initiative. During the senior staff data-feedback meeting the following day, the consultant shared the data with the entire senior team. Although several team members were clearly concerned by what they heard, others were not. One of the latter group said to the consultant, "Our information doesn't look so bad, especially if you compare it to other companies in our industry," whereupon Charles jumped into the conversation and said, "Yes, but do we want to be the best Neanderthal?"

Because Fives need to feel that the work they are responsible for is organized and under control, taking charge of complex change initiatives can be daunting to Five leaders who have not previously had this kind of responsibility. On the other hand, Fives with vast experience in leading change find leading such efforts intellectually stimulating.

Some Five leaders may pay insufficient attention to the human aspects of taking charge of change. They may, for example, neglect to fully address the resistance that can occur, believing that it can simply be countered with logic. In fact, resistance always has an emotional component because (1) people may feel strongly about their objections to the change; (2) resistance often masks deeper feelings of fear, anger, or sadness about the proposed new direction; or (3) people may have deep emotional responses to antici-pated shifts in the power structure.

In addition, Fives may underemphasize the need for a common and compelling vision for the change, thinking that the design of the future *is* the vision. Organizational designs, however, tend to be structural and operational, whereas a true vision of the change includes symbols, values, and far-reaching aspirations and thus helps motivate people to embrace the future.

Charles had not always been a change champion, even when he had led large change projects.

Charles had tried to lead his organization to refocus its work from defense to telecommunications, but had been unable to do so. Although this was partly the result of his having to deal with an entrenched organizational culture, it was also the result of the way in which Charles communicated the need for change. When he spoke about the need for change and how it would benefit the organization, he emphasized the logic, failing to recognize that most of the employees identified so closely with doing defense work that they had difficulty imagining themselves engaged in anything else. In retrospect, Charles realized that he had not communicated his passion for the change effort in a way that would have inspired others, using stories and symbols to ignite people's imaginations.

Development Stretches for Fives

SHARE STORIES   If people are feeling apprehensive, share a story about a situation in which people felt grave concern about a change, but experienced a positive outcome. If people are feeling angry, share a story about a situation that ignited people's positive and negative passions, with those passions then being transformed into energy for taking positive action. The stories do not need to be long, but they need to be compelling.

ALLOW FEELINGS TO BE SHARED, INCLUDING YOUR OWN   During any major change, people—yourself included—have a variety of different feelings that will change over time. Legitimize the expression of feelings by asking simple questions such as, "How do you feel about this?" Encourage others to share their feelings by selectively sharing your own reactions. If you are feeling optimistic about the change, share a real experience that elicited this feeling in you; if you are feeling concerned, share that as well. Just make sure that both your intention and the message are designed to help others accept their own feelings and move toward support of the change.

SHARE YOURSELF   Change can be hard on everyone, even when people support the new direction. Employees at all levels in the organization need you to be there for them. It is important that you share yourself by listening fully without distraction and then also speaking your truth. The latter means going several levels below your obvious reactions to find your deeper responses. For example, in explaining to a key manager why she was being passed over to lead a change initiative, a Five leader was prepared to tell the manager that the decision was made on the basis of her lack of experience. However, when reflecting on the decision, he realized that the deeper reason was that he thought the promotion would have placed the manager in a no-win situation, that he believed in her, and that he had another position in mind for her.

Enneagram Style Sixes

Six leaders experience a tremendous amount of satisfaction from taking a large, complex, and important organizational change from an uncertain beginning to a successful conclusion. Leading with clarity and dexterity, Sixes generally thrive on the ambiguity inherent in change efforts. At the same time, they rarely take credit for the success of a change, being far more likely

6 Enneagram Style
DOUBT

to say, "The team did it." While this statement may be true, because Sixes build cohesive, high-functioning teams, it also understates Six leaders' strength in being leaders that others want to follow.

Sixes usually conduct a thorough assessment of the current situation; their fertile yet practical minds are assets when designing the future scenario. They also are usually adept at creating a concrete transition plan with processes that involve the right people at the right time.

Here's an example of a Six leader, Megan, in action:

> Megan relished the idea of leading the planning group that had been authorized by top management to implement an entirely new billing process for accounts receivable. Because this involved five different functional areas, and because the company had been losing $10 million a year in uncollected billings, Megan likened the position to her race-car driving hobby, in which the risk and the speed thrilled her. Megan immersed herself in all aspects of the problem, brought together a variety of teams to achieve a solution, and developed a comprehensive plan for the managing the transition. Not only was the change extremely successful, but it was accomplished two months ahead of schedule.

Six leaders don't like surprises. They plan in an effort to stave off the unexpected, and they expect coworkers and employees to raise potential problems before they become crises. While this orientation is not negative, it may not be entirely realistic. Employees may have different perceptions of what could become a major problem, or they may believe that they can handle an issue, only to have it blow up unexpectedly into a crisis. When surprises occur—an inevitability in most change efforts—Sixes can become upset and take this as an affront, particularly if they believe that the problem could have been avoided.

Sixes want to trust others. However, when they believe that someone has violated that trust—for example, by not exposing a problem or by saying something unsupportive about the Six leader or another team member—Sixes may withdraw from that person or engage in projection, attributing highly negative motivations to the other person or anticipating far worse behavior and consequences than are likely to actually occur. Thus, it can be challenging for Sixes to sort out what is true and what they have imagined; it is also challenging for others, who may not understand what they have done.

The following story shows how Megan learned some hard lessons about taking charge of change:

> At an organization where she had previously worked, Megan was excited and anxious about being put in charge of the development and implementation of a customer service program. Although Megan was skilled at the planning aspects of this change effort, its complexity overwhelmed her. In addition, she experienced a great deal of difficulty dealing with the resistance that arose from both the customer service staff and her peers. Eventually, her boss expressed some doubts about how well the change was going, which greatly disturbed Megan. Ultimately, the customer service program worked adequately, but after it was complete, Megan spent a great deal of time gaining an understanding of what had made the process so difficult. Because she was insightful, Megan realized that this project had been larger in scope than she was ready to handle, and that she needed to work on her reactivity to resistance and treat it as a predictable response to change.

Development Stretches for Sixes

TAKE REASONABLE RISKS   Pay attention to your own feelings, making sure that you do not refuse to lead a change effort simply because you feel anxious about its likelihood of success. All change efforts involve uncertainty. At the same time, don't agree to lead a change initiative primarily on the basis of the thrill factor. If you do, you may end up in a situation in which it will be nearly impossible for you to be successful.

DEVELOP REALISTIC RELATIONSHIPS WITH YOUR BOSSES Many Sixes focus on their bosses, becoming highly concerned if their bosses appear to have a negative reaction to something that the Six does. Although it would be nice if all bosses were consistently supportive, this is not realistic. It is important that you give your boss the latitude to raise concerns without your reacting as though the relationship were in jeopardy.

LEARN TO PERCEIVE RESISTANCE AS SIMPLY ANOTHER PROBLEM TO BE SOLVED Resistance to change is normal, inevitable, and even desirable. You want people to disagree, preferably in a constructive way, because opposing ideas often generate better ways of doing things. In addition, resistance that is not dealt with directly during the change process usually surfaces again at a later date, sometimes in a more serious form. Treating resistance as a problem to be solved will help you reduce your emotional reactivity and increase your chances of a productive outcome.

Enneagram Style Sevens

Seven leaders view innovation and change as the most essential parts of their leadership jobs. Energized by creating ideas that they believe will take the organization to new heights, most Sevens are engaging storytellers and are adept at enlisting other people in the change that they are leading.

Enneagram Style
OPTIONS

Sevens identify issues in the current situation quickly, then move to a style of visionary leadership in which they paint vivid pictures of a desirable future. Often, Sevens are many steps ahead of other people in terms of their ability to quickly imagine what the change might look like and their mental processing of issues related to the change.

When they oversee the transition planning process, Sevens become most excited about developing a broad plan that includes key milestones and deliverables. Because Seven leaders are most stimulated by the bigger picture and also do not want to stifle the creativity of others, they prefer to do the master planning and have others manage the details, putting a great deal of faith in them to do so.

The following story about Randall shows the many facets of a Seven taking charge of change.

> When Randall took the position as director of research and development (R&D), he was told that the main part of his job would be to transform the 75-person unit from a stagnant department into a revitalized, customer-focused team. For the first six months, Randall met with employees, customers, and peers on a biweekly basis; established measurable perform-ance standards; and constantly communicated the need for R&D to deliver state-of-the-art research based on customers' current and future needs. During the next six months, Randall changed the reward system to match the performance stan-dards. After that, he installed a comprehensive leadership development program. At the end of two years, 20 percent of the staff had left voluntarily—all of them were people who lacked the necessary skills and education—and the revitalized work unit was perceived as one of the best in the company.

Because Sevens rely on others to carry out the detail work, they become extremely disappointed when others do not deliver what was expected of them, but they often fail to see what they them-selves have done to contribute to the problem. For example, Seven leaders tend to rely on people with whom they have intellectual rapport, but these employees may not have the skills or the forti-tude to carry out a large change project. In addition, Sevens may give people general guidance, but not provide enough detail to enable others to perform effectively.

While Sevens usually offer a multitude of ideas, some employees may have trouble differentiating between what was merely an idea and what was a call to action. With so many tasks to accomplish within a limited time frame and with limited resources, employees also may be confused about which activities are of high priority.

Finally, Seven leaders have a tendency to become so excited about ideas that they assume that others are equally enthused, and they may perceive a neutral or ambiguous reaction as a positive one. For example, if someone in the organization asks an interesting clarifying question about the change, the Seven may read this as support. Similarly, if someone doesn't voice a concern about the change, the Seven may wrongly assume that this person supports the effort.

Here's an example of a situation in which Randall was unsuccessful in leading a change initiative:

> Earlier in Randall's career, he was responsible for managing a small group of research scientists who needed to work collaboratively on projects but insisted on doing their work independently. Because Randall had many ideas about how to create a collaborative environment, he attempted to create a new team culture by experimenting with several different methods. Finally, after six months, the research scientists complained to senior management, asserting that they had no sense of direction, that their collaboration was even worse than it had been before Randall started, and that their time was being wasted in moving from one "flavor of the month" to another.

Development Stretches for Sevens

MAKE IT YOUR JOB TO KEEP EVERYONE FOCUSED ON THE THREE MOST IMPORTANT PRIORITIES You may think that your job is to continuously create innovative ideas and to encourage others to do the same. However, after the future direction has been decided upon, your job is to lead the change effort by helping others focus on the most essential priorities. If you intentionally limit yourself to the three most important priorities, your ability to focus will improve, and the initiative will be far more successful.

LEARN TO SAY NO TO NEW WAYS OF DOING THINGS As interesting and potentially useful as new ideas may be, the continuous accumulation of ideas may derail the change initiative. Once a plan and a process have been agreed to, make only minor adjustments. When you learn to say no, you are also saying yes to staying on course.

LEARN TO READ RESISTANCE ACCURATELY Unless you are absolutely sure that an individual or group supports the change effort, solicit more information. Make certain that you understand the issues and feelings involved, and also the intensity of the resistance or support. Gather a group of advisors—preferably people whose leadership style is different from yours—and ask them for their perceptions. When you do this over the course of several change projects that you lead, your ability to read both resistance and support accurately will grow. In addition, you are likely to realize that while resistance may not always appear rational, there is always some rationale behind it. This will help you respond to resistance in more effective ways.

Enneagram Style Eights

Enneagram Style
⑧ CHALLENGE

Above all, Eight leaders relish being responsible for taking charge of large change efforts and making the changes happen in the most expeditious way. Their minds go immediately to the big picture of what needs to happen and how to organize the systems and people in order to best execute the initiative. Eights thrive on this complexity and ambiguity, perceiving it as constructive chaos that they can use to form both a strategy and a working plan.

The bigger the potential positive impact of the change, the more Eights embrace their role. They take their responsibilities seriously and expect others to do the same. Eights trust those who keep their work agreements, but distrust those who don't live up to their commitments, produce inferior work products, or don't take responsibility for the areas they have been assigned.

Being politically astute, Eights are sensitive to both overt and covert organizational resistance, and they are usually skilled at developing effective strategies in response. Eight leaders gain the support of key stakeholders whenever possible by using their personal relationships and organizational credibility to enlist others or by involving and leveraging outside consultants and important influence leaders within the organization. Eights intuitively understand which domino needs to be pushed so that the remaining dominoes will also fall.

The following story shows the savvy ability of the Eight leader to take charge of change:

As the new vice president of human resources, Karen was designated to co-lead a steering committee that was in charge of a major change effort for the organization. Over a three-month period, it became obvious to Karen that Justin, her co-leader and a longtime manager, was incompetent and dishonest. Infuriated, she went to Justin with her concerns, although she was certain that he was not capable of changing and believed that he had to be removed from his position. Karen realized that she had to proceed cautiously because Justin was a close friend of the company president. When other members of the steering committee complained to Karen about Justin, Karen urged them to go directly to the company president. When the most knowledgeable and competent steering committee member told Karen that she was leaving the organization because of Justin's incompetence, Karen knew that it was time to go directly to the president herself. The president immediately removed Justin from the steering committee and moved him to another division. Although this decision did not appeal to Karen's sense of justice, she was pleased that Justin was no longer a problem for the committee and that her standing in the organization had not been damaged by challenging a long-term crony of the president. In addition, the president named a new co-leader for the steering committee—the committee member who had almost resigned over Justin's behavior.

Although Eight leaders enjoy being in charge of change, they prefer big projects with large impact. Low-impact projects hold little interest for them; when they are assigned such change efforts, Eights may simply not do the work involved or else do it half-heartedly, even when the consequences of doing so may be severe.

In addition, while Eights do lead change efforts from a vision, this vision is often intuitive and may not have been shared with those involved in the change. Some Eights think that everyone already knows, or should know, the vision. At other times, Eights don't fully understand the reason for their having to share the entire vision, as they believe that it is simply not necessary for others to know the vision in detail. They reason that people know what the objectives are and what work needs to be done, and that this is sufficient.

Finally, once they grasp what needs to be done, Eights are inclined to take action immediately. They may move too fast without having gained the support of others or educated them about the need or process for change. Such actions can derail a change effort.

Earlier in her career, Karen had learned some hard lessons about leading change:

At another company where she had worked, Karen had been responsible for developing a performance management system for the organization. Although Karen had anticipated that she and her planning committee would be in charge of designing the entire system, her boss was adamant that an original DVD that demonstrated how to give effective performance feedback be included in the performance management package.

While Karen did not overtly object to her boss's idea, she did not think that the DVD would be very useful. In addition, she was already overwhelmed with work and did not have the time to oversee the DVD's production. Instead of delegating that task to someone else, Karen went ahead and made the initial arrangements for the actors, script, and camera crew, but she never followed through on the details of execution. When everyone arrived at the arranged time to shoot the DVD, Karen was not there. Via cell phone, she instructed those involved to proceed with the taping. Although the DVD was part of the final package, Karen's boss was horrified that she had simply absented herself from the work.

Development Stretches for Eights

FORMULATE AND ARTICULATE YOUR VISION Don't assume that others know what you are thinking, what to do, and why they should do it. Formulate your vision in sufficient detail that all the essential ideas are clear, then share your vision widely and solicit reactions. You can test your vision in advance by writing it down, showing it to others, and gaining their reactions before you disseminate it to a wider audience. You can also express your vision verbally to a small focus group, solicit members' feedback, and make adjustments before you share the vision more broadly.

LEARN THE ART OF TIMING Remember that not everything has to happen immediately. It is important that you pace a change initiative so that people have time to adjust to and integrate the changes. It is also essential that you avoid trying to get so much done so quickly that everyone, including you, becomes exhausted. When this occurs, many benefits of the change may not be fully realized. Finally, some changes will be accepted more readily if you wait for the best opportunity to introduce them. Be patient and observant so that you can develop and act from an artful sense of optimal timing.

REMEMBER THAT SMALL THINGS CAN PRODUCE BIG RESULTS   There are many instances where a big impact results from a small change. For example, one company was able to retain more of its high-ranking female employees by changing its customary meeting time from 8:00 a.m. to 9:00 a.m. A manufacturing organization saved $10 million in a one-hour impromptu meeting by getting all the managers and key engineers in the same room to identify the three areas in the manufacturing process that were causing product defects. Pay attention to the small changes that produce large impacts.

Enneagram Style Nines

⑨ Enneagram Style
HARMONY

Nine leaders enjoy the complexity and rigor involved in leading change. They take charge in a low-key, inclusive manner by (1) getting people involved, (2) soliciting input, (3) developing approaches that will enlist the support of others, and (4) creating a careful, methodical transition plan and process for moving the organization from where it is currently to where it needs to be. Nines also make sure that they fully understand the current situation by taking the time to assess both the facts and the perceptions involved. This helps them develop a more reliable sense of what direction to take and allows them to proceed with a greater sense of certainty.

The relational, easygoing style of Nine leaders tends to make others feel comfortable with their leadership and to instill confidence that everything is going to run smoothly. Nines typically take a systematic, well-planned approach to the entire change effort, and they seldom make abrupt shifts in direction or take other people by surprise. Paying attention to detail and even more attention to process, Nines keep their own bosses well informed. They usually raise difficult issues in a nonthreatening way, and their desire to hear multiple points of view and to encourage others to have a voice in the process enables them to prevent some resistance from occurring and to deescalate conflict once it emerges.

The following story illustrates how a Nine leader takes charge of change:

> Evan was elected managing partner of the law firm, and he felt humbled by the honor. Although Evan had been a partner in the firm for over 20 years, was well respected for his expertise, knew all the partners and associates, and got along very well with the firm's administrative staff, he had never had ambitions to play such a key role in the firm. However, the other partners convinced Evan that because he related to everyone so well and had served on the law firm's governing council, he was the perfect choice to take on the managing partner's role and to change the firm from a political and volatile organization to a stable and inclusive one.
>
> Flattered by the opportunity and committed to the excellence of the firm, he accepted the position. After five years as the managing partner, Evan was considered to have been one of the best in the firm's history. His command of the administrative details, his ability to relate well to others but not play politics, and his focus on business development all contributed to his success.

Although it seems as if nothing upsets Nines very much, they are actually very sensitive, particularly to negativity and personal attacks. When Nines encounter relentless pessimism or faultfinding—which is not uncommon among certain individuals and groups at certain phases of change efforts—they become disturbed and angry. The continuous dissension creates a discordant environment that they feel unable to correct. Similarly, Nines feel especially unsettled and anxious when negativity is aimed at them, particularly if it takes the form of either a direct or an indirect personal attack. These critiques hurt their feelings deeply and also create physical distress, including sleep disturbances.

Nine leaders can also become overwhelmed by the magnitude of what is involved when they take charge of change, especially if unexpected work is added to their area of responsibility. Nines' tendency to procrastinate by engaging in secondary tasks instead of addressing more significant agenda items becomes intensified when they feel overworked, overcommitted, or angry about unexpected work demands. Their tendency to become overworked is aggravated by their orientation toward delegating less and doing more of the actual work themselves.

When Nines feel overwhelmed, they can become highly resistant to doing the work that is in front of them. When they feel pressured to do the required work, Nines may become entrenched and stubborn in their refusal to do it, or they may become more overtly angry, sometimes saying things that they later regret. While usually moderate in temperament, Nines have a strong, negative visceral reaction to being told what to do.

Here's an example of Evan's reaction to negativity:

Before Evan became the law firm's managing partner, he took the leadership role in a team that was reviewing the firm's current vendors. The team's task was to eliminate those vendors whose services, products, or billing practices did not match the firm's expectations. Evan led the review committee well, assessing the current situation, establishing criteria for future vendor selection, and developing a plan and process for eliminating inferior vendors and securing new ones.

Evan agreed to contact the vendors whose services were no longer wanted. One vendor became so furious that she called Evan on three different occasions to yell at him. On the last call, the vendor said, "How dare you do this!" and began using extreme profanity. Evan had met this woman only once, and he knew that her words were simply those of an angry, out-of-control person. However, his last conversation with her disturbed Evan so deeply that for three months he would wake up in the middle of the night, replaying her comments in his mind.

Development Stretches for Nines

LEARN TO EXPRESS YOUR THOUGHTS, NEEDS, AND FEELINGS TO OTHER PEOPLE   The more you practice expressing yourself to others, the more comfortable you will feel doing this. It also will improve your rapport with others, because they'll know more about who you really are. Expressing your thoughts and feelings may feel awkward at first, but if you experiment with doing this with people you know well and let them know that this behavior is new for you, they are likely to be far more receptive than you might expect.

LET YOUR ANGER EMERGE IN ITS EARLIER STAGES   Nines are referred to as having "anger that went to sleep." Although anger is a normal emotion, Nines do not usually allow themselves to bring their angry feelings to the surface for fear of upsetting themselves and others and creating discord. However, unexpressed anger does not usually go away. It lies below the surface, where it festers until it finally explodes. When you learn to read the early signs that you are upset—for example, a certain sensation in your stomach or a particular recycling of thoughts in you mind—and acknowledge to yourself and others that something is wrong, you will be able to discuss your anger in a less emotionally charged and more reasoned way.

BE DIRECT WHEN YOU ENLIST THE HELP OF OTHER PEOPLE   You really can count on many people being willing to help you if you ask for assistance directly. Not everyone will respond affirmatively, but many people will be delighted to support you because you support them. Ask for help directly and delegate work. If you ask indirectly—for example, by saying that you are fatigued or by asking someone how to do something—others may not understand that you are actually asking them to do something concrete for you.

Development Stretches for Everyone

- Assess the extent to which you are regarded as a champion of change in your organization by asking your boss, your peers (select three peers if you have them), and three subordinates the following question: *On a five-point scale, with 1 being low and 5 being high, to what extent do you perceive me as a champion of change?* Write down all the answers that you receive. After each person has answered this question, ask two follow-up questions: *What factors caused you to give that answer? What would you recommend that I do more of and less of to become even more of a change champion?* Analyze all the responses to determine what you can do to increase your capability as a champion of change.

- At the top of separate pieces of paper, write down the organizational changes you have led over the last five years. Underneath each change, write down the change strategy formula, $D \times V \times P > R = C$. Assess each change that you have led, assigning numbers from 0 to 5 (where $0 = $ low and $5 = $ high) to the first four elements of the formula. Multiply your assigned numbers for $D \times V \times P$ to assess whether or not the product of these numbers is greater than R. Review each equation to gain insight into why the change effort was successful, and/or how it could have been more effective.

- Educate yourself further by reading one of the recommended books under "Take Charge of Change" in the Resources section at the back of this book.

Chapter 9

Stretch Your Leadership Paradigms

$\mathcal{T}$he purpose of this book has been to show you how to use the Enneagram system to help you grow both as a leader and as a person by developing your core leadership competencies. If you make a commitment to practice the development stretches designed for your Enneagram style, you will make great strides in your ability to contribute to your company and to become an excellent role model for others in the organization.

There are additional ways to use the Enneagram to work on your development as a leader. The first is to truly know who you are by understanding and accepting both your strengths and the areas where you need development. For leaders with each Enneagram style described in the preceding chapters, in addition to the strengths, there are special gifts that come naturally to individuals with that Enneagram style (see Figure 9.1). It is important to know what these are and to use them wisely.

At the same time, it is essential that you do not overuse your gift, as an overused strength can derail your leadership and throw you off the path to leadership excellence. For example, inclusion and consensus (the Nine's gift), while useful in many contexts, can

FIGURE 9.1 **Special Leadership Gifts of Each Enneagram Style**

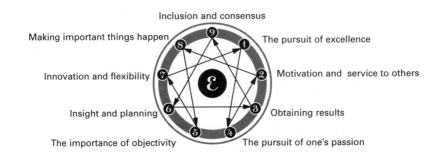

become a derailer when decisions must be made quickly or when a consensually made decision may not be the wisest one. Similarly, the Five's gift for objectivity may serve the organization well when systematic planning is required, but it can become a derailer when an organization requires risk taking in a context of uncertainty.

Most leaders work on their derailers only after they have received feedback indicating that they need to change, usually as a result of a boss's concern about how the business unit is being run or of complaints from customers, peers, or subordinates about interpersonal style. Either situation creates a sense of urgency for doing self-development work. However, working on derailers only after they have become obvious issues means that the individual must engage in self-development while he or she is already under stress. By using the information in this book to work on your potential leadership derailers *before* they become impediments to your success, you can enhance your leadership capability without pressure and also prepare yourself for the future.

There is a third way to engage in self-development that is quite extraordinary in the sense that it is both low-stress and high-impact. This technique involves expanding your existing leadership paradigm to include additional paradigms of leadership. Our leadership paradigms—our implicit belief systems concerning the role of leadership—influence what we pay attention to and what we ignore. While we tend to develop skills and strengths in areas that we deem important, skills that do not fit our view of leadership tend to be underdeveloped.

The nine leadership paradigms common to the nine Enneagram styles discussed in Chapters 1 and 4 are repeated here for easy reference.

Ones: Leaders set clear goals and inspire others to achieve the highest quality.

Twos: Leaders assess the strengths and weaknesses of team members and motivate and facilitate people toward the achievement of organizational goals.

Threes: Leaders create environments that achieve results because people understand the organization's goals and structure.

Fours: Leaders create organizations that give people meaning and purpose so that they are inspired to do excellent work.

Fives: Leaders develop effective organizations through research, deliberation, and planning so that all systems fit together and people are working on a common mission.

Sixes: Leaders solve organizational problems by developing a creative problem-solving environment in which each person feels that he or she is part of the solution.

Sevens: Leaders get people excited and create innovative ventures so that organizations can take advantage of important business opportunities.

Eights: Leaders move organizations forward by leading decisively, getting capable and reliable people in the right jobs, and empowering competent people to take action.

Nines: Leaders help achieve the collective mission by creating a clearly structured and harmonious work environment.

You can expand your current leadership repertoire by incorporating one or more additional leadership paradigms into your existing one. The most effective way to do this is to add one paradigm at a time—preferably a paradigm from one of your wing styles (the Enneagram numbers on either side of your own style) or from your stress or security point (the Enneagram numbers that are connected to your style by an arrow)—and to integrate it fully with your current leadership paradigm before adding another paradigm.

The rationale for incorporating a wing style or stress or security leadership paradigm into your current leadership paradigm is that you are likely to be more familiar with these styles and will therefore find them easier to assimilate. Once you add a new paradigm to your existing one, you will begin to pay attention to more aspects of your organization, and your behavior and skills will improve and expand accordingly.

Figure 9.2 shows the wing styles and stress and security points for each Enneagram style.

To select the best leadership paradigm to add to your current one, consider these questions:

- *Which leadership paradigm would add the greatest value for my employees?*

FIGURE 9.2 **Wings and Stress-Security Points**

Wings 9 **1** 2 4 7 Stress and Security	Wings 1 **2** 3 8 4 Stress and Security	Wings 2 **3** 4 9 6 Stress and Security
Wings 3 **4** 5 2 1 Stress and Security	Wings 4 **5** 6 7 8 Stress and Security	Wings 5 **6** 7 3 9 Stress and Security
Wings 6 **7** 8 1 5 Stress and Security	Wings 7 **8** 9 5 2 Stress and Security	Wings 8 **9** 1 6 3 Stress and Security

- *Which leadership paradigm would add the greatest value for the organization?*
- *Which leadership paradigm would make me feel both more effective and less stressed?*

Looking at Figure 9.2, for example, an Eight could chose from among styles Seven, Nine, Five, and Two. An Eight leader who wants to develop a less intense interpersonal style might add either the Two paradigm, thus adding more warmth when listening to others, or the Nine paradigm, which would support growth in the direction of creating a more consensual orientation and listening more fully to different points of view. If the focus of the Eight's growth is on becoming less intense by becoming more playful and lighthearted, the Eight leader might choose the Seven paradigm. Finally, the Five leadership paradigm might be useful as a way for the Eight leader to become more objective and self-contained when interacting with others, thus making the Eight less prone to intense interchanges.

Every one of us has the capacity to grow and develop. Choosing to take the path of accelerated growth is critical for both current and future leaders who want to achieve leadership excellence. A student from an MBA program where I teach addressed this issue in the following e-mail:

> I was hoping you could help me find a term that I'm looking for as part of a paper I'm writing for a leadership class.
>
> I'm looking for a word to describe someone who's extremely perceptive and in touch with the environment and the people around him or her—a word that describes someone who can walk into a meeting and immediately pick up on the type of energy in the room. This is the sort of person who can see beauty where others overlook it—for instance, if a group were hiking through the mountains, this person would be the first to stop the group to admire the view from a lookout.

It's someone who, on picking up an object, notices not only the object's function, but also its design, texture, and quality of construction; the time and craftsmanship that went into its manufacture; and so on—someone whose senses are more open and acute than the average person's.

Words I've come up with so far include *perceptive, self-aware, emotionally intelligent*, and *spiritual*. However, none of these really encapsulates everything I'm trying to describe about this quality.

Any other terms you would suggest?

Baron

My response to Baron was a single word: *conscious*. Organizations need conscious leaders.

Becoming an excellent leader, not just a good one, means being conscious of many factors: (1) who you are and the assets you bring to the organization, (2) the impact your behavior has on others, (3) the areas in which you need to develop, and (4) the ways in which you handle your power and authority. Being conscious also means demonstrating integrity in dealing with the ethical challenges that leaders face on a daily basis and being a role model for future leaders. In today's business climate of competing demands and constant change, conscious leadership is not optional; it is essential.

Resources

Drive for Results

Bossidy, Larry, and Ram Charan, *Execution: The Discipline of Getting Things Done* (New York: Crown Business, 2002).

Collins, Jim, *Good to Great: Why Some Companies Make the Leap . . . and Others Don't* (New York: HarperBusiness, 2001).

Drucker, Peter F., *Managing for Results: Economic Tasks and Risk-Taking Decisions* (New York: Harper & Row, 1993).

Galbraith, Jay R., *Designing the Customer-Centric Organization: A Guide to Strategy, Structure, and Process* (San Francisco: Jossey-Bass Publishers, 2005).

Lawler, Edward E., and Christopher Worely, *Built to Change: How to Achieve Sustained Organizational Effectiveness* (San Francisco: Jossey-Bass Publishers, 2006).

Strive for Self-Mastery

Arbinger Institute, *Leadership and Self-Deception: Getting Out of the Box* (San Francisco: Berrett-Koehler Publishers, 2002).

Bennis, Warren G., *On Becoming a Leader* (Cambridge, Mass.: Perseus Publishing, 2003).

Dotlich, David L., and Peter C. Cairo, *Why CEOs Fail: The 11 Behaviors That Can Derail Your Climb to the Top* (San Francisco: Jossey-Bass Publishers, 2003).

Goleman, Daniel P., *Emotional Intelligence* (New York: Bantam Books, 2005).

Kouzes, James M., and Barry Z. Posner, *Credibility: How Leaders Gain It and Lose It, Why People Demand It* (San Francisco: Jossey-Bass Publishers, 2003).

Know the Business: Think and Act Strategically

Kaplan, Robert S., and David P. Norton, *Strategy Maps: Converting Intangible Assets into Tangible Outcomes* (Boston: Harvard Business School Press, 2004).

Mintzberg, Henry, *The Rise and Fall of Strategic Planning: Reconceiving Roles for Planning, Plans, Planners* (New York: The Free Press, 2000).

Porter, Michael E., *Competitive Strategy: Techniques for Analyzing Industries and Competitors* (New York: The Free Press, 1998).

Van der Heijden, Kees, *Scenarios: The Art of Strategic Conversation* (West Sussex, England: John Wiley & Sons Ltd., 2005).

Become an Excellent Communicator

Bradford, David L., and Allan R. Cohen, *Power Up: Transforming Organizations through Shared Leadership* (New York: John Wiley & Sons, 1998).

Clarke, Boyd, and Ron Crossland, *The Leader's Voice: How Communication Can Inspire Action and Get Results!* (New York: SelectBooks, 2002).

Conger, Jay Alden, *Winning 'Em Over* (New York: Simon & Schuster, 2001).

Patterson, Kerry, Joseph Grenny, Ron McMillan, and Al Switzler, *Crucial Confrontations* (New York: McGraw-Hill, 2004).

Patterson, Kerry, Joseph Grenny, Ron McMillan, Al Switzler, and Stephen R. Covey, *Crucial Conversations: Tools for Talking When Stakes Are High* (New York: McGraw-Hill, 2002).

Trompenaars, Alfons, *Riding the Waves of Culture: Understanding Cultural Diversity in Global Business* (New York: McGraw-Hill, 1998).

Lead High-Performing Teams

Hackman, J. Richard, ed., *Groups That Work (and Those That Don't): Creating Conditions for Effective Teamwork* (San Francisco: Jossey-Bass Publishers, 1990).

Katzenbach, Jon R., and Douglas K. Smith, *The Wisdom of Teams: Creating the High-Performance Organization* (New York: HarperCollins Essentials, 2003).

Mohrman, Susan Albers, Susan G. Cohen, and Allan M. Mohrman, *Designing Team-Based Organizations: New Forms for Knowledge Work* (San Francisco: Jossey-Bass Publishers, 1997).

Nadler, David A., Janet L. Spencer, and Associates, *Executive Teams* (San Francisco: Jossey-Bass Publishers, 1998).

Smith, Kenwyn K., and David N. Berg, *Paradoxes of Group Life: Understanding Conflict, Paralysis, and Movement in Group Dynamics* (San Francisco: Jossey-Bass Publishers, 1997).

Make Optimal Decisions

Gunther, Robert E., Stephen J. Hoch, and Howard C. Kunreuther, eds., *Wharton on Making Decisions* (New York: John Wiley & Sons, 2004).

Klein, Gary A., *Intuition at Work: Why Developing Your Gut Instincts Will Make You Better at What You Do* (New York: Doubleday Publishing, 2004).

Pfeffer, Jeffrey, *Managing with Power: Politics and Influence in Organizations* (Boston: Harvard Business School Press, 1994).

Russo, J. Edward, Paul J. H. Shoemaker, and Margo Hittleman, *Winning Decisions: Getting It Right the First Time* (New York: Currency, 2002).

Schein, Edgar H., *Organizational Culture and Leadership* (San Francisco: Jossey-Bass Publishers, 2004).

Take Charge of Change

Beckhard, Richard, and Wendy Pritchard, *Changing the Essence: The Art of Creating and Leading Fundamental Change in Organizations* (San Francisco: Jossey-Bass Publishers, 1992).

Gladwell, Malcom, *The Tipping Point: How Little Things Can Make a Big Difference* (Boston: Back Bay Books, 2002).

Kotter, John P., *Leading Change* (Boston: Harvard Business School Press, 1996).

Lawler, Edward E., and Christopher Worely, *Built to Change: How to Achieve Sustained Organizational Effectiveness* (San Francisco: Jossey-Bass Publishers, 2006).

Nadler, David A., Robert B. Shaw, Elise Walton, and Associates, *Discontinuous Change: Leading Organizational Transformation* (San Francisco: Jossey-Bass Publishers, 1995).

Senge, Peter M., et al., *The Fifth Discipline Fieldbook: Strategies and Tools for Building a Learning Organization* (New York: Currency, 1994).

Stretch Your Leadership Paradigms

Friedman, Thomas L., *The World Is Flat: A Brief History of the Twenty-First Century* (New York: Farrar, Straus and Giroux, 2006).

Levine, Rick, et al., *The Cluetrain Manifesto: The End of Business as Usual* (Cambridge, Mass.: Perseus Publishing, 2001).

Pascale, Richard Tanner, Mark Millemann, and Linda Gioja, *Surfing the Edge of Chaos: The Laws of Nature and the New Laws of Business* (New York: Crown Publishers, 2000).

Zander, Rosamund Stone, and Benjamin Zander, *The Art of Possibility* (New York: Penguin Books, 2000).

General Leadership

Goleman, Daniel, Richard Boyatzis, and Annie McKee, *Primal Leadership: Realizing the Power of Emotional Intelligence* (Boston: Harvard Business School Press, 2004).

Kouzes, James M., and Barry Z. Posner, *The Leadership Challenge* (San Francisco: Jossey-Bass Publishers, 2003).

Maister, David H., *Managing the Professional Service Firm* (New York: Free Press Paperbacks, 1997).

McCall, Morgan W., and George P. Hollenbeck, *Developing Global Executives* (Boston: Harvard Business School Press, 2002).

Morrell, Margot, Stephanie Capparell, and Alexandra Shackleton, *Shackleton's Way: Leadership Lessons from the Great Antarctic Explorer* (New York: Penguin Group, 2002).

The Enneagram

Daniels, David N., and Virginia A. Price, *The Essential Enneagram: The Definitive Personality Test and Self-Discovery Guide* (San Francisco: HarperSanFrancisco, 2000).

Goldberg, Michael J., *The 9 Ways of Working* (New York: Marlowe & Company, 1999).

Lapid-Bogda, Ginger, *Bringing Out the Best in Yourself at Work: How to Use the Enneagram System for Success* (New York: McGraw-Hill, 2004).

Naranjo, Claudio, *Ennea-type Structure: Self-Analysis for the Seeker* (Nevada City, Calif.: Gateway Books & Tapes, 1990).

Palmer, Helen, *The Enneagram in Love and Work: Understanding Your Intimate and Business Relationships* (New York: HarperCollins, 1996).

Riso, Don Richard, and Russ Hudson, *The Wisdom of the Enneagram: The Complete Guide to Psychological and Spiritual Growth for the Nine Personality Types* (New York: Bantam Books, 1999).

www.internationalenneagram.org

Index

Achiever, 8. *See also* Enneagram
    style Three
Aesthete, 10. *See also*
    Enneagram style Four
Anger
    body center styles, 25
    Eights, 287
    Ones, 75
Appreciative One, 81
Artist, 10. *See also* Enneagram
    style Four
Astute insight, 221
    Eights, 246
    Fives, 236
    Fours, 233
    Nines, 250
    Ones, 224
    Sevens, 243
    Sixes, 240
    Threes, 230
    Twos, 227
Attention to detail, 209

Authentic relating, 221
    Eights, 247
    Fives, 236
    Fours, 233
    Nines, 250
    Ones, 224
    Sevens, 243
    Sixes, 240
    Threes, 230
    Twos, 227

"Being," 80
Believer, 78–79
Bibliography, 295–300
Body (gut) center
    Eights, 247
    Fives, 237
    Fours, 233
    Nines, 250
    Ones, 225
    Sevens, 243
    Sixes, 240

Body (gut) center *(continued)*
Threes, 230
Twos, 227–228
Books to read, 295–300
Boss, 19. *See also* Enneagram style Eight
Bringing Out the Best in Yourself at Work: How to Use the Enneagram System for Success (Lapid-Bogda), 34, 64, 135, 182, 214
Bully, 93

Calculator, 79–80
Caretaker, 5. *See also* Enneagram style Two
Centers of Intelligence, 24–26
Challenge, 19. *See also* Enneagram style Eight
Challenger, 19. *See also* Enneagram style Eight
Champion of change, 256
Change strategy formula, 254–255
Change vision, 257
Changes. *See* Take Charge of Change
Communication, 137–182
communicating clearly, 138–139
conflict management, 140
e-mail. *See* E-mail
Eights, 172–176
feedback, 139
Fives, 159–164
Fours, 155–159
influencing others, 140
listening, 139
Nines, 177–181
Ones, 141–144
relationships, 138–139

Sevens, 168–172
Sixes, 164–168
Threes, 151–155
Twos, 144–151
Compassion, 221
Eights, 247
Fives, 237
Fours, 233
Nines, 250
Ones, 225
Sevens, 243
Sixes, 240
Threes, 230
Twos, 227
Conflict management, 140
Eights, 173–174
Fives, 161
Fours, 158–159
Nines, 178
Ones, 142–143
Sevens, 170
Sixes, 166
Threes, 153
Twos, 146
Connector, 21. *See also* Enneagram style Nine
Connoisseur, 17. *See also* Enneagram style Seven
Conscious, 294
Context, 217
Courageous One, 86
Coward, 87
Crusader, 3. *See also* Enneagram style One

Decision making, 215–251
body (gut) center, 220, 221–222
context, 217
development stretches for everyone, 250–251

Eights, 244–247
Fives, 234–237
Fours, 231–233
head center, 220, 221
heart center, 220, 221
honor decision-making
    authority structure, 217
instincts, 218–219
integrate head, heart, gut, 219
listening, 218
Nines, 247–250
Ones, 222–225
organizational culture, 216
rational decisions, 218
Sevens, 240–243
Sixes, 237–240
Threes, 228–230
Twos, 225–228
Defective One, 82
Derailer, 289–290
Devil's advocate, 14. *See also*
    Enneagram style Six
Diligence, 3. *See also*
    Enneagram style One
Discouraged, 198
Doubt, 14. *See also* Enneagram
    style Six
Drive for Results, 35–64
    development stretches for
        everyone, 63–64
    Eights, 58–61
    evaluating results, 38
    Fives, 49–51
    Fours, 46–49
    goal-setting, 36
    high performance, 37
    Nines, 61–63
    Ones, 38–41
    Sevens, 55–57
    Sixes, 52–54
    stewardship, 38
    task assignment, 37
    Threes, 43–46
    Twos, 41–43
    workable plans, 37

E-mail
    Eights, 174–176
    Fives, 162–164
    Fours, 158–159
    Ones, 143–144
    Sevens, 170–172
    Sixes, 166–168
    suggestions/pointers, 181–182
    Threes, 154–155
    Twos, 146–151
Eights. *See* Enneagram style
    Eight
Emotional center styles, 25
Emotional intelligence (EQ), 65.
    See also Strive for
    Self–Mastery
Emotional maturity, 68, 72
Empathy, 221
    Eights, 247
    Fives, 236
    Fours, 233
    Nines, 250
    Ones, 224
    Sevens, 243
    Sixes, 240
    Threes, 230
    Twos, 227
Enabler, 5. *See also* Enneagram
    style Two
Enneagram, 1
Enneagram stress/security
    points, 28–33
Enneagram style Eight, 19–21
    are you an Eight?, 21
    attention to detail, 209
    body center style, 25

Enneagram style Eight
(continued)
body (gut) center, 247
change, 280–284
communication, 172–176
conflict management,
173–174
decision making, 244–247
dependency vs. autonomy,
210
e-mail, 174–176
empower others, 60
excessive action, 221
feedback, 173
flexibility, 130–131
four additional styles, 33
fun, 60–61
head center, 246
heart center, 247
humor, 130
impulsiveness, 93–94
influencing others, 174
know the business, 128–131
leadership paradigm, 20
listening, 173
patience, 131
relationship with coworkers,
60
relationships, 172
results, 58–61
self-mastery, 91–94
share feelings of vulnerability,
94
small things/big results, 284
special leadership gift, 290
strategic thinking/action,
128–131
stress/security points, 32
take care of yourself
physically, 93
teams, 207–210

timing, 283–284
vision, 283
wings, 28
Enneagram style Five, 12–14
allow yourself to need others,
85
are you a Five?, 14
ask big questions, 51
body (gut) center, 237
body language, 200, 201
change, 271–274
collective vision, 122
communicate continuously,
51
decision making, 234–237
engage, don't withdraw, 86
express your feelings, 85
feelings, 200
four additional styles, 33
gut reactions, 121–122
head center, 236
head center style, 24
heart center, 236–237
know the business, 119–122
leadership paradigm, 13
overanalyzing, 221
results, 49–51
self-mastery, 83–86
share feelings, 274
share stories, 274
share yourself, 274
special leadership gift, 290
strategic thinking/action,
119–122
stress/security points, 32
take time to consider your
reactions, 201
taking action, 51
teams, 198–201
use your feelings, 121–122
wings, 28

Enneagram style Four, 10–12
    appreciate others' qualities,
        83
    appreciate the ordinary, 82
    body (gut), 233
    change, 267–271
    communication, 118–119,
        155–159
    conflict management,
        158–159
    decision making, 231–233
    discouraged, 198
    do uninteresting tasks, 119
    e-mail, 158–159
    feedback, 157
    feelings, 271
    filters re information about
        yourself, 270
    follow your mind, 48
    four additional styles, 33
    give people what they need,
        48–49
    head center, 233
    heart center, 233
    heart center style, 25
    influencing others, 159
    know the business, 117–119
    lay out plans in detail, 49
    leadership paradigm, 11
    listening, 156–157
    oversensitivity, 221
    playfulness, 198
    relationships, 155–156
    results, 46–49
    self-mastery, 81–83
    self-referencing behavior, 83
    special leadership gift, 290
    strategic thinking/action,
        117–119
    stress/security points, 32
    supportive statements to
        yourself, 270
    teams, 196–198
    wings, 27
Enneagram style Nine, 21–23
    anger, 287
    are you a Nine?, 23
    be strategic, 133
    body center style, 25
    body (gut) center, 250
    change, 284–288
    clarity, 212
    communication, 177–181
    conflict management, 178
    decision making, 247–250
    e-mail, 179–181
    express thoughts/feelings, 287
    express your needs directly,
        96
    feedback, 178
    focus on big picture, 63
    Four additional styles, 34
    getting help, 287–288
    head center, 250
    heart center, 250
    influencing others, 178–179
    keep work moving, 63
    know the business, 131–134
    leadership paradigm, 22
    listening, 177
    make mission, strategy
        explicit, 133
    passivity, 222
    priorities, 96, 134
    relationships, 177
    results, 61–63
    self-assessment, 63
    self-mastery, 94–96
    special leadership gift, 290
    strategic thinking/action,
        131–134
    stress/security points, 232

Enneagram style Nine
  (continued)
  take a position, 96
  teams, 210–213
  wings, 28
Enneagram style One, 3–5
  anger, 75
  are you a One?, 5
  big picture, 110
  body center style, 25
  body (gut) center, 225
  change, 259–261
  communication, 141–144
  conflict management,
    142–143
  decision making, 222–225
  e-mail, 143–144
  feedback, 142
  focus on successes, 41
  four additional styles, 333
  get help, 261
  head center, 224
  heart center, 224–225
  influencing others, 143
  know the business, 108–111
  lead from highest level of
    strategy, 111
  lead from vision, 110–111
  leadership paradigm, 4
  listening, 142
  pay attention to people, 41
  positive reactions, 76
  reactivity, 222
  relationships, 141
  relax-enjoy yourself, 190
  relinquish tactical work, 189
  resentment, 75
  results, 38–41
  right/wrong thinking, 75
  self-mastery, 73–76
  special leadership gift, 290

  stress/security points, 31
  teams, 187–190
  unintended consequences of
    your behavior, 190
  vision, 40
  wings, 27
Enneagram style Seven, 17–19
  are you a Seven?, 18–19
  body (gut) center, 243
  change, 277–280
  communication, 168–172
  conflict management, 170
  decision making, 240–243
  e-mail, 170–172
  emotional repertoire, 91
  feedback, 169–170
  focus on priorities, 57,
    279–280
  four additional styles, 33
  get things done in advance,
    57
  go for depth, 127
  head center, 243
  head center style, 24
  heart center, 243
  influencing others, 170
  inner focusing, 91
  know the business, 125–128
  know when to stop, 207
  lead from clearly defined
    leadership role, 206
  leadership paradigm, 18
  listening, 90–91, 169
  overplanning, 221
  relationships, 168–169
  resistance to change, 280
  results, 55–57
  saying "no" to new ways of
    doing things, 280
  self-mastery, 89–91
  slow down, 128

special leadership gift, 290

stay the course, 127–128

strategic thinking/action, 125–128

stress/security points, 32

teams, 204–207

wings, 28

work plan, 57

Enneagram style Six, 14–16

are you a Six?, 16

authority, 203–204

body (gut) center, 240

change, 274–277

communication, 164–168

conflict management, 166

decision making, 237–240

e-mail, 166–168

feedback, 165–166

four additional styles, 33

get positive feedback from others, 204

half-empty/half-full, 88

head center, 239–240

head center style, 24

heart center, 240

influencing others, 166

insight vs. projection, 88

know the business, 122–125

lead from vision and strategy, 124–125

leadership paradigm, 15

listening, 165

positive self-talk, 204

power, 203–204

projection, 221

projects/jobs, 124

relationship with boss, 277

relationships, 164

remain calm, 54

resistance to change, 277

respond in positive way, 125

self-advice, 88

self-mastery, 86–88

special leadership gift, 290

strategic thinking/action, 122–125

stress/security points, 32

teams, 201–204

wings, 28

worst-case scenario/best-case scenario, 54

Enneagram style Three, 8–10

are you a Three?, 9–10

ask yourself how you feel, 46

"being," 80

body (gut) center, 230

change, 264–267

communicate with others, 116

communication, 151–155

conflict management, 153

decision making, 228–230

directions/instructions, 45

e-mail, 154–155

feedback, 152–153

four additional styles, 33

head center, 230

heart center, 230

heart center style, 25

human capital vs. work structures, 195

identifying with work, 80

influencing others, 153

know the business, 114–116

leadership paradigm, 9

listening, 152

playing roles, 221

relationship with coworkers, 45–46

relationships, 151

Enneagram style Three
  (continued)
  results, 43–46
  self-mastery, 78–81
  special leadership gift, 290
  strategic thinking/action,
    114–116
  stress, 267
  stress/security points, 32
  teams, 193–196
  weaknesses, 80–81
  wings, 27
Enneagram style Two, 5–7
  are you a Two?, 7
  balanced approach to difficult
    issues, 264
  become expert in business,
    113
  body (gut) center, 227–228
  change, 261–264
  communication, 144–151
  conflict management, 146
  decision making, 225–228
  deliver tough news, 43
  e-mail, 146–151
  emotional manipulation, 221
  energy level, 264
  feedback, 145–146
  finances, 113–114
  focus on work objectives, 43
  four additional styles, 33
  giving in order to get, 78
  head center, 227
  heart center, 227
  heart center style, 25
  influencing others, 146
  know the business, 111–114
  leadership paradigm, 7
  listening, 145
  make strategic process
    explicit, 114

overextending yourself, 43
  relationship, 144
  results, 41–43
  self-mastery, 76–78
  solo activities, 77
  special leadership gift, 290
  strategic thinking/action,
    111–114
  stress level, 264
  stress/security points, 31
  teams, 190–193
  visible leadership, 192–193
  wings, 27
  your needs, 78
Enneagram style wings, 26–28
Enneagram symbol, 1
Epicure, 17. See also Enneagram
    style Seven
EQ, 65. See also Strive for
    Self–Mastery
Excessive action, 221

Fear, 24. See also Head center
    styles
Fearful Strategist, 85
Feedback, 139
  Eights, 173
  Fives, 161
  Fours, 157
  Nines, 178
  Ones, 142
  respond to, 67, 71
  Sevens, 169–170
  Sixes, 165–166
  Threes, 152–153
  Twos, 145–146
Fives. See Enneagram style Five
Focused Inspirer, 89
Fours. See Enneagram style Four
Frenetic Escape Artist, 90
Friend, 76–77

Fully Conscious One, 94–95
Fun, 60–61
Further information (resources), 295–300

Generalist, 17. *See also* Enneagram style Seven
Giving, 5. *See also* Enneagram style Two
Goal-setting, 36
Goals, 105, 107
Gut center, 25. *See* Body (gut) center
Gut knowing, 222
 Eights, 247
 Fives, 237
 Fours, 233
 Nines, 250
 Ones, 225
 Sevens, 243
 Sixes, 240
 Threes, 230
 Twos, 228

Harmonizer
 Enneagram style Nine, 21
 self-mastery, 95
Harmony, 21. *See also* Enneagram style Nine
Head center
 Eights, 246
 Fives, 236
 Fours, 233
 Nines, 250
 Ones, 224
 Sevens, 243
 Sixes, 239–240
 Threes, 230
 Twos, 227
Heart center
 Eights, 247

Fives, 236–237
Fours, 233
Nines, 250
Ones, 224–225
Sevens, 243
Sixes, 240
Threes, 230
Twos, 227
Helper, 5. *See also* Enneagram style Two
Hexad, 30, 31
High performance, 37
Hudson, Russ, 70n
Humble One, 76
Humor, 130

Image, 25. *See also* Heart center styles
Immovable Rock, 92–93
Impulsiveness, 93–94
Individualist, 10. *See also* Enneagram style Four
Influencing others, 140
 Eights, 174
 Fives, 161–162
 Fours, 159
 Nines, 178–179
 Ones, 143
 Sevens, 170
 Sixes, 166
 Threes, 153
 Twos, 146
Initiator, 8. *See also* Enneagram style Three
Inner triangle, 30
Instincts, 218–219
Instinctual center, 25
Integrated Wizard, 84
Integrity, 68–69, 72
Investigator, 12. *See also* Enneagram style Five

Judge, 75

Know the business, strategic
    thinking/action, 99–135
  development stretches for
    everyone, 134–135
  Eights, 128–131
  Fives, 119–122
  Fours, 117–119
  goals, 105, 107
  know the customers, 102
  know the finances, 103
  know the industry, 101
  know the marketplace,
    101–102
  know the products and
    technology, 103
  know the structure and
    people, 102
  mission, 104, 106
  Nines, 131–134
  Ones, 108–111
  Sevens, 125–128
  Sixes, 122–125
  strategy, 104, 106
  tactics, 105, 107
  Threes, 114–116
  Twos, 111–114
  vision, 103–104, 106
Knowledge, 12. *See also*
    Enneagram style Five

Lead High-Performing Teams,
    183–214
  developmental stretches for
    everyone, 213
  Eights, 207–210
  Fives, 198–201
  Fours, 196–198
  Nines, 210–213
  Ones, 187–190

quality products/services, 187
  Sevens, 204–207
  Sixes, 201–204
  team architecture, 186
  team culture, 186–187
  team leadership, 184–185
  team processes, 186
  team talent, 185
  team vision, 185
  Threes, 193–196
  Two, 190–193
Leader, 19. *See also* Enneagram
    style Eight
Leadership derailers, 289–290
Lifelong learning, 69, 72
Listening, 139, 218
  Eights, 173
  Fives, 160
  Fours, 156–157
  Nines, 177
  Ones, 142
  Sevens, 169
  Sixes, 165
  Threes, 152
  Twos, 145
Loyalist, 14. *See also* Enneagram
    style Six, 86–87

Manipulator, 77
Mediator, 21. *See also*
    Enneagram style Nine
Mission, 104, 106
Mood, 10. *See also* Enneagram
    style Four
Moralist, 3. *See also* Enneagram
    style One

Nines. *See* Enneagram style Nine

Objective analysis, 221
  Eights, 246

Fives, 236
Fours, 233
Nines, 250
Ones, 224
Sevens, 243
Sixes, 239
Threes, 230
Twos, 227
Observer, 12. *See also*
      Enneagram style Five
Ones. *See* Enneagram style One
Options, 17. *See also* Enneagram
      style Seven
Organizational culture, 216
Overanalyzing, 221
Overplanning, 221
Oversensitivity, 221

Passivity, 222
Peacemaker, 21. *See also*
      Enneagram style Nine
Perfectionist, 3. *See also*
      Enneagram style One
Perform, 8. *See also* Enneagram
      style Three
Personal vision, 68–69, 72. *See
      also* Vision
Personality integration, 69
Personality Types
      (Riso/Hudson), 70n
Playfulness, 198
Positive self-talk, 204
Productive planning, 221
   Eights, 246
   Fives, 236
   Fours, 233
   Nines, 250
   Ones, 224
   Sevens, 243
   Sixes, 240
   Threes, 230

Twos, 227
Projection, 221
Protector, 19. *See also*
      Enneagram style Eight

Quality products/services, 187
Questioner, 14. *See also*
      Enneagram style Six

Recluse, 12. *See also* Enneagram
      style Five
Reference books, 295–300
Reformer, 3. *See also* Enneagram
      style One
Relationships, 138–139
   Eights, 172
   Fives, 159–160
   Fours, 155–156
   Nines, 177
   Ones, 141
   Sevens, 168–169
   Sixes, 164
   Threes, 151
   Twos, 144
Relaxation, 30
Remote Expert, 84
Resistance to change, 258
Resources, 295–300
Respond to feedback, 67, 71
Results. *See* Drive for Results
Risk taking, 276–277
Riso, Don Richard, 70n

Security points, 28–33
Self-advice, 88
Self-assessment, 63
Self-awareness, 67, 71
Self-development, 290–291
Self-management, 68, 72
Self-Mastery. *See* Strive for Self-
      Mastery

Self-motivation, 67–68, 71
Self-responsibility, 67–68, 71
Serene Acceptor, 74
Sevens. *See* Enneagram style
     Seven
Sixes. *See* Enneagram style Six
Skeptic, 14. *See also* Enneagram
     style Six
Sleeper, 95–96
Special leadership gift, 290
Star, 79
Steadfastness, 222
     Eights, 247
     Fives, 237
     Fours, 233
     Nines, 250
     Ones, 225
     Sevens, 243
     Sixes, 240
     Threes, 230
     Twos, 228
Stewardship, 38
Stimulator, 89–90
Strategic action. *See* Know the
     business, strategic
     thinking/action
Strategy, 104, 106
Stress, 267
Stress and security points,
     28–33
Strive for Self-Mastery, 65–97
     development stretches for
          everyone, 97
     Eights, 91–94
     emotional maturity, 68, 72
     Fives, 83–86
     Fours, 81–83
     general behavior, 71
     integrity, 68–69, 72
     lifelong learning, 69, 72
     Nines, 94–96

Ones, 73–76
     personal vision, 68–69, 72
     personality integration, 69
     respond to feedback, 67, 71
     self-awareness, 67, 71
     self-management, 68, 72
     self-mastery, 71–72
     self-motivation, 67–68, 71
     self-responsibility, 67–68, 71
     Sevens, 89–91
     Sixes, 86–88
     Threes, 78–81
     Twos, 76–78
Succeeder, 8. *See also*
          Enneagram style Three

Tactics, 105, 107
Take Charge of Change, 253–288
     anchoring the change, 258
     champion of change, 256
     change strategy, 254
     change strategy formula,
          254–255
     change vision, 257
     developing desire/demand for
          change, 256–257
     developing/implementing the
          plan, 257
     development stretches for
          everyone, 288
     Eights, 280–284
     Fives, 271–274
     Fours, 267–271
     managing change, 253
     Nines, 284–288
     Ones, 259–261
     resistance to change, 258
     Sevens, 277–280
     Sixes, 274–277
     Threes, 264–267
     Twos, 261–264

Taking effective action, 221
    Eights, 247
    Fives, 237
    Fours, 233
    Nines, 250
    Ones, 225
    Sevens, 243
    Sixes, 240
    Threes, 230
    Twos, 227
Task assignment, 37
Teacher, 74
Teams. *See* Lead High-
    Performing Teams
Thinker, 12. *See also* Enneagram
    style Five
Threes. *See* Enneagram style
    Three
Tragic-romantic, 10. *See also*
    Enneagram style Four

Truth Seeker, 92
Twos. *See* Enneagram style Two

Unique One, 81–82

Vision
    change, 257
    Eights, 283
    Fives, 122
    Ones, 40
    self-mastery, 68–69, 72
    team, 185
    think and act strategically,
        103–104, 106
Visionary, 17. *See also*
        Enneagram style Seven

Wisdom of the Enneagram
        (Riso/Hudson), 70n
Workable plans, 37

About the Author

Ginger Lapid-Bogda, Ph.D., is an organization development consult-ant with more than 30 years of con-sulting experience. Dr. Lapid-Bogda has worked with companies such as Apple Computer, Kaiser-Perma-nente, Whirlpool, Genentech, The Clorox Company, Hewlett-Packard, TRW, Sun Microsystems, and Time Warner, as well as with service organizations, nonprofits, and law firms. She is the past president of  the International Enneagram Association (IEA) and a member of the Organization Development Network (ODN) and National Training Labs (NTL).

Through her consulting firm, Bogda & Associates (Santa Monica, California), Dr. Lapid-Bogda provides organization develop-ment (OD) consulting, executive coaching, and training services that integrate the Enneagram with the theory and practice of OD. In addition, she offers training materials, leadership and team assessments, and train-the-trainers programs based on the con-cepts of both this book and her first book, *Bringing Out the Best in Yourself at Work: How to Use the Enneagram System for Success* (McGraw-Hill, 2004).

Dr. Lapid-Bogda teaches at colleges and universities, and her writing has appeared in numerous publications. She has been the recipient of speaking awards from the American Management Asso-ciation and of writing awards from the *National Business Employ-ment Weekly*.

Her previous book, *Bringing Out the Best in Yourself at Work: How to Use the Enneagram System for Success*, has been translated into six languages.

For more information, go to www.TheEnneagramInBusiness .com or contact Dr. Lapid-Bogda directly at (310) 829-3309 or ginger@bogda.com.